Who Should Read This Book?

"**R**ead" may be the wrong word. "Engage" would be better, because this is not so much a book as it is a classic text, and Jewish classics are not read so much as they are engaged. Included here are a classic text of Jewish prayer, spanning 2,000 years of Jewish experience with the world and with God; and ten thoughtful commentaries on that text, each one reaching back in a different way, again through 2,000 years of time. The question ought to be "Who should engage this book in personal dialogue?"

If you like to pray, or find prayer services baffling: Whether you are Orthodox, Conservative, Reconstructionist, or Reform, you will find that *My People's Prayer Book* tells you what you need to know to pray.

- The Hebrew text here is the most authentic one we have, and the variations among the Jewish movements are described and explained. They are all treated as equally authentic.

- The translation is honest, altogether unique, and outfitted with notes comparing it to others' translations.

- Of special interest is a full description of the Halakhah (the "how-to") of prayer and the philosophy behind it.

If you are a spiritual seeker or Jewishly curious: If you have wondered what Judaism is all about, the prayer book is the place to begin. It is the one and only book that Jews read each and every day. The commentaries explain how the prayers were born and synopsize insights of founding Rabbis, medieval authorities, Chasidic masters, and modern theologians. The layout replicates the look of Jewish classics: a text surrounded by many marginal commentaries, allowing you to skip back and forth across centuries of insight.

If you are a teacher or student: This is a perfect book for adult studies, or for youth groups, teenagers, and camps. Any single page provides comparative insight from the length and breadth of Jewish tradition, about the texts that have mattered most in the daily life of the Jewish people.

If you are a scholar: Though written in friendly prose, this book is composed by scholars: professors of Bible, Rabbinics, Medieval Studies, Liturgy, Theology, Linguistics, Jewish Law, Mysticism, and Modern Jewish Thought. No other work summarizes current wisdom on Jewish prayer, drawn from so many disciplines.

If you are not Jewish: You need not be Jewish to understand this book. It provides access for everyone to the Jewish wisdom tradition. It chronicles the ongoing Jewish-Christian dialogue and the roots of Christian prayer in Christianity's Jewish origins.

The *My People's Prayer Book: Traditional Prayers, Modern Commentaries* series

Volume 1—The *Sh'ma* and Its Blessings
      168 pp, ISBN 1-879045-79-6

Volume 2—The *Amidah*
      240 pp, ISBN 1-879045-80-X

Volume 3—*P'sukei D'zimrah* (Morning Psalms)
      240 pp, ISBN 1-879045-81-8

Volume 4—*Seder K'riat Hatorah* (The Torah Service)
      264 pp, ISBN 1-879045-82-6

Volume 5—*Birkhot Hashachar* (Morning Blessings)
      240 pp, ISBN 1-879045-83-4

Volume 6—*Tachanun* and Concluding Prayers
      240 pp, ISBN 1-879045-84-2

Volume 7—Shabbat at Home
      240 pp, ISBN 1-879045-85-0

Volume 8—*Kabbalat Shabbat* (Welcoming Shabbat in the Synagogue)
      240 pp, ISBN 1-58023-121-7

Volume 9—Experiencing Nightfall: *Minchah* and *Ma'ariv* for Shabbat and Weekdays
      240 pp (est.), ISBN 1-58023-262-0, Projected September 2005

My People's Prayer Book

TRADITIONAL PRAYERS, MODERN COMMENTARIES

Vol. 8—*Kabbalat Shabbat* (Welcoming Shabbat in the Synagogue)

EDITED BY RABBI LAWRENCE A. HOFFMAN

CONTRIBUTORS

MARC BRETTLER

ELLIOT N. DORFF

DAVID ELLENSON

ELLEN FRANKEL

ALYSSA GRAY

JOEL M. HOFFMAN

LAWRENCE A. HOFFMAN

REUVEN KIMELMAN

SHARON KOREN

LAWRENCE KUSHNER

DANIEL LANDES

NEHEMIA POLEN

WENDY I. ZIERLER

Jewish Lights Publishing
Woodstock, Vermont

My People's Prayer Book: Traditional Prayers, Modern Commentaries
Vol. 8—*Kabbalat Shabbat* (Welcoming Shabbat in the Synagogue)

2005 First Printing
© 2005 by Lawrence A. Hoffman

Comments to Psalms 92, 93, and 95–99 are adapted, by permission of Oxford University Press, from Marc Brettler's commentary to *The Jewish Study Bible,* ed. Adele Berlin and Marc Zvi Brettler (New York: Oxford University Press, 2004).
The diagram on p. 146 is adapted from Reuven Kimelman, *The Mystical Meaning of "Lekhah Dodi" and "Kabbalat Shabbat"* (Jerusalem: The Hebrew University Magnes Press; Los Angeles: Cherub Press, 2003). Used by permission.

The excerpt on p.127 is reprinted from *Seyder Thkines,* © 2004, by Devra Kay, published by The Jewish Publication Society, with the permission of the publisher.

The excerpt on p. 152 is reprinted from *The Book of Jewish Women's Prayers,* © 1995, by Norman Taylor, published by Jason Aronson, with the permission of the publisher.

Library of Congress Cataloging-in-Publication Data
My people's prayer book : traditional prayers, modern commentaries / edited and with introductions by Lawrence A. Hoffman.
p.   cm.
Includes the traditional text of the siddur, English translation, and commentaries.
Contents: vol. 8. *Kabbalat Shabbat* (Welcoming Shabbat in the Synagogue).
ISBN 1-58023-121-7 (hc)
1. Siddur. 2. Siddurim—Texts. 3. Judaism—Liturgy—Texts.
I. Hoffman, Lawrence A., 1942– . II. Siddur. English & Hebrew.
BM674.39.M96 1997
296.4'5—dc21   97-26836
                                       CIP

First Edition

10 9 8 7 6 5 4 3 2 1

Manufactured in the United States of America

Published by Jewish Lights Publishing
A Division of LongHill Partners, Inc.
Sunset Farm Offices, Route 4, P.O. Box 237
Woodstock, VT 05091
Tel: (802) 457-4000   Fax: (802) 457-4004
www.jewishlights.com

Contents

Contributors

Marc Brettler . . . . *Our Biblical Heritage*

Elliot N. Dorff . . . . *Theological Reflections*

David Ellenson . . . . *How the Modern Prayer Book Evolved*

Ellen Frankel . . . . *A Woman's Voice*

Alyssa Gray . . . . *Our Talmudic Heritage*

Joel M. Hoffman . . . . *What the Prayers Really Say*

Lawrence A. Hoffman . . . . *History of the Liturgy*

Reuven Kimelman . . . . *Kabbalah*

Sharon Koren . . . . *The Context of Kabbalah*

Lawrence Kushner and Nehemia Polen . . *Chasidic and Mystical Perspectives*

Daniel Landes . . . . *The Halakhah of Prayer*

Wendy I. Zierler . . . . *Jewish Feminism*

About My People's Prayer Book

My People's Prayer Book is designed to look like a traditional Jewish book. Ever since the dawn of modern printing, Jews have arranged their books so that instead of reading in a linear fashion from the first line of the first page to the last line of the last one, readers were encouraged to linger on a single page and to consult commentaries across the gamut of Jewish thought, all at one and the same time. Every page thus contained a cross-cut of the totality of Jewish tradition.

That intellectual leap across many minds and through the centuries was accomplished by printing a text in the middle of the page and surrounding it with commentaries. Readers could scan the first line or two of the various commentaries and then choose to continue the ones that interested them most, by turning the page— more or less the way newspaper readers get a sense of everything happening on a single day by glancing at all the headlines on page one, then following select stories as they are continued on separate pages further on.

Each new rubric (or liturgical section) is, therefore, introduced in traditional style: the Hebrew prayer with translation in the middle of the page, and the beginning lines of all the commentaries in the margins. Commentaries are continued on the next page or a few pages later (the page number is provided). Readers may dwell for a while on all the comments, deciding which ones to pursue at any given sitting. They may want to compare comments, reading first one and then another. Or having decided, after a while, that a particular commentator is of special interest, they may instinctively search out the opening lines of that commentator's work, as they appear in each introductory page, and then read them through to arrive at a summary understanding of what that particular person has to say.

Introduction to the Liturgy of Kabbalat Shabbat

Politics, Piety, and Poetry

Lawrence A. Hoffman

Kabbalat Shabbat is a liturgy without parallel in Jewish tradition. Its relatively few pages reflect Jewish history all the way from our biblical origins to the great age of Safed mysticism in the sixteenth and seventeenth centuries. Designed specifically for Shabbat, it omits plaintive petitions and mournful elegies—thought to be out of place on this most magic of Jewish days. But otherwise it contains everything a worshiper might desire: psalms of antiquity, material for study, a hidden acrostic, *L'khah Dodi* (arguably the Jewish People's favorite hymn), and a mystical secret to boot. Gilbert and Sullivan's *H.M.S. Pinafore* features Little Buttercup, a wise old woman who alone knows the secret of the operetta, and who divulges it only after singing, "Things are seldom what they seem; skim milk masquerades as cream." As it has come down to us, *Kabbalat Shabbat* is cream masquerading as milk: it looks like ordinary words and sentences, but it is much richer than that. Here, too, "Things are seldom what they seem." *Kabbalat Shabbat* is "Little Buttercup theology."

It is also a late example of "stand-alone" liturgy; that is, it can be appreciated solely in terms of what it is, without regard for a larger structural whole that lends it its glory. Liturgical services are rarely like that. They tend to be compounds of many different units that revolve around a central core, or spiritual fulcrum. The morning service, for example (our subject throughout Volumes 1 to 6 in this series), has at its center the *Sh'ma* (see Volume 1), the *Amidah* (see Volume 2), and the public reading of Torah (see Volume 4). None of these three units is "stand-alone," because Jewish prayer requires all three for its completeness: talking about God *(Sh'ma)*, talking with God (the *Amidah*), and studying God's word (reading Torah). They fit together in a nicely orchestrated sequence, with other liturgical compositions framing them here and there.

Kabbalat Shabbat was originally intended as an introduction to a similarly orchestrated whole, the evening service *(Ma'ariv)* of Friday night. But it eventually surpassed that secondary role, to take on a stand-alone life of its own—not in theory, of course (it was meant only to introduce what follows), nor even in practice (Jews who come for *Kabbalat Shabbat* stay for the rest of the service), but in the way it is experienced and, therefore, generally thought about. It speaks a message that has come to overshadow the *Ma'ariv* service that it once just introduced. It attracted its own melodies, even its own distinctive *nusach*, or cantorial sound, which changes the minute we get to *Ma'ariv* proper. It usually lasts longer than *Ma'ariv* does, too. It has become a liturgical tail that wags a liturgical dog.

As usual, in examining liturgy, it helps to list the order of prayers first, and only afterward to try to understand them. Medical students wade through courses on anatomy before they are able to appreciate the miracle of the human body. The order of prayers is like liturgical anatomy: not the most interesting of subjects, but the topic most necessary at the outset.

Sefardi Jews follow a somewhat different order (see below, Landes, p. 62) but here are the constituents of the *Kabbalat Shabbat* service as most Ashkenazi Jews have it.

1. Six psalms (Psalms 95–99, 29)
2. A poem, *Ana B'kho'ach*
3. A poem, *L'khah Dodi*
4. Two psalms (Psalms 92/93)
   (*Kaddish* as semicolon)
5. A "study" selection from Mishnah Shabbat, Chapter 2, *Bameh Madlikin* (rules of kindling Shabbat lights)
   (*Kaddish* as period)

The two recitations of the *Kaddish* (pronounced kah-DEESH, or, popularly, KAH-dish) are unnumbered and in parentheses because they are not part of the essential structure of the service. Though the *Kaddish* began as a prayer in its own right, a messianic cry of hope (see L. Hoffman, Volume 6, *Tachanun and Concluding Prayers*, pp. 158–160), it came, in time, to function differently. Sometimes it is outfitted with a separate paragraph seeking blessing for students of Torah, in which case it follows a passage of study and is called *Kaddish D'rabbanan* (pronounced kah-DEESH d'-rah-bah-NAHN), "The *Kaddish* of the Rabbis." Sometimes a *Kaddish* is reserved for mourners to say—it is a *Kaddish Yatom* (pronounced kah-DEESH yah-TOHM), a "mourners' *Kaddish*"). But frequently—since worshipers had no prayer books before the printing press was invented—it came to be used as oral punctuation. A "whole *Kaddish*" is a liturgical "period"; a "half *Kaddish*" is a "semicolon."

We would expect a period-like *Kaddish* to separate *Kabbalat Shabbat* from *Ma'ariv*, the service that follows. In this case, it is a *Kaddish D'rabbanan* as well, since it follows the study section from the Mishnah (No. 5, above). But why the other *Kaddish*, the half *Kaddish* following Psalms 92/93 (No. 4)? The answer, as we shall see in greater detail below, is that Psalms 92/93 (No. 4) constituted the Palestinian *Kabbalat Shabbat* ("Palestine" was the medieval name for the Land of Israel), while the Mishnah reading (No. 5) was added to the liturgy in Babylonia (contemporary Iraq). As separate entities, developing independently from each other, they probably both ended with a *Kaddish*, and when some unknown editor combined them, he left both *Kaddishes* in place. There are, then, at least two independent constituents to our *Kabbalat Shabbat,* one Palestinian (Psalms 92/93) and one Babylonian (Mishnah Shabbat 2:1). There is also a third building block: all the prayers that precede Psalms 92/93, from Psalm 95 to *L'khah Dodi* (Nos. 1–3).

We can now revisit the order of prayers that we looked at above, this time omitting the *Kaddish* punctuation marks and labeling each of the three components according to the place and approximate time when it came into being.

1. Six psalms (Psalms 95–99, 29)
2. A poem, *Ana B'kho'ach* .... (fifteenth century, Palestine)
3. A poem, *L'khah Dodi*

4. Two psalms (Psalms 92/93) .... (by fifth century, Palestine)

5. Mishnah Shabbat, Chapter 2,   (by eighth to ninth century,
   Bameh Madlikin ....   Babylonia)

Each of these three parts of the service has its own story. The stories are especially fascinating because they raise the question of how our prayers get written in the first place. Is prayer an exercise in politics, piety, or poetry?

WHO WROTE OUR PRAYERS?

Who wrote our prayers and why? The "who" is relatively straightforward. Most of the prayer book was composed by anonymous authors, whose names are probably lost to us forever. In many cases, however, prayers change style in the middle; and sometimes they show structural anomalies, as when a prayer starts out in one of the typical forms known to us but then diverges and does not end the way it should. Then we have reason to suspect that more than one author has been at work, and that sometime afterward, an equally anonymous editor combined both efforts.

By the fifth or sixth century, however, we find poetry (*piyyutim,* pronounced pee-yoo-TEEM; sing. *piyyut,* pronounced pee-YOOT) that can be ascribed to individual authors whose names we know. They exist in manuscript form with their authors' names already associated with them; the authors sometimes made sure their names would remain attached, by including them in alphabetic acrostics within the poems themselves. That form of poetry continued well into the Middle Ages, as we will see later when we get to *L'khah Dodi,* the most familiar prayer in the *Kabbalat Shabbat* liturgy. It will forever be associated with Solomon Alkabetz, a sixteenth-century kabbalist who began each verse with a different letter so as to spell out "Shlomo Halevi," the Hebrew name by which he was known.

But just as most ancient art is anonymous, so too are the bulk of our earliest and even our medieval prayers. People tended to conceal their authorship, since only things from antiquity were presumed to have value. From late antiquity, for example, we have inherited many books like those in our Bible (but excluded from it) purporting to have been composed by Ezra, or by Jeremiah's disciple, Baruch. Another instance, from the end of the thirteenth century, is the *Zohar,* written mostly by a Spanish Jew, Moses de Leon—who, however, called it a long-lost work from the third century, even faking the language to make it look ancient.

By contrast, contemporary authors insist on supplying their names; citing their works without giving them credit is called plagiarism. So the closer we get to modernity, the more likely it is that authors' names are retained other than acrostically. Loyal disciples record the words of their revered masters; printers include the names of authors alongside their work. Many reform-minded authors of nineteenth-century prayer books attached their names to their books. By the twentieth century, when prayer books were being composed by committees, the names of individual writers are recorded in minutes to the meetings, accompanying appendices, or separate reference volumes. Sometimes their names appear right in the prayer book itself, not just to credit them for their creativity but to lend weight to the words because of the fame of the writer. Knowing that a meditation on the nature of the universe is by Albert Einstein makes us sit up and take notice.

So much for the "who." The "why" is much more complicated, and, by and large, the answers boil down to politics, piety, and poetry.

PRAYER AS POLITICS?

Ever since talmudic days, it has been common to explain the genesis of prayers through politics, albeit politics rooted in piety. Behind this explanation was the underlying question "How can a religion given entirely by God at Sinai constantly be changing?" Rabbinic theology answered that question by positing an oral law that allows the written law to be understood differently through history. But that rationale could sometimes seem deficient. A famous instance is a letter composed in 987 C.E. by Sherira Gaon (the leading authority in Babylonia) to the Jews of Kairuan (now Algeria) explaining the growth of the oral law itself. The first canonical instance of recording that law in writing is the Mishnah, authored about 200 C.E. by Judah Hanasi, the patriarch and leading rabbi of Roman Palestine. But a parallel compilation of rabbinic opinion, the Tosefta (meaning "Additions"), had apparently been written shortly thereafter by Rabbi Chiyya, a younger contemporary of Judah. If Judah's Mishnah was the perfect crystallization of the oral law—as theology would dictate—why did Rabbi Chiyya have to add to it? To put it another way, if Rabbi Chiyya's Tosefta was truly authentic, why did Judah Hanasi omit its teachings from the Mishnah just a few years earlier?

Sherira provides what had become by then the standard political answer. In general, he claimed that Judah did indeed include all that was necessary for his time, but the political instability then was so great that people forgot what Judah assumed they would know. Rabbi Chiyya had, therefore, to provide the background knowledge that Judah took for granted. That is to say, "The times were hard; persecution was rampant; the Jews forgot what they used to know; so leaders arose to correct the situation by taking emergency action."

The Talmud had already used such political reasoning to explain the parallel attribution of the *Amidah* both to Rabban Gamaliel II (about 90 C.E.) and the Men of the Great Assembly (presumed to have lived from the fifth to the second century B.C.E.). How could two authoritative voices living several centuries apart have done the same thing? The answer had to be that in the interim the war with Rome had occurred, disrupting the natural transmission of tradition enough for people to have forgotten their prayers; after the war, Gamaliel had to restate what otherwise would have been obvious. Similarly, the Rabbis of the Babylonian Talmud wondered how a prayer called the Eighteen Benedictions (the *Sh'moneh Esreh*) could have nineteen, not eighteen, units. Again, the answer was political: One of the benedictions is really a malediction against heretics. After Gamaliel restated the Eighteen Benedictions that people had forgotten, he observed the rise in heresy and commissioned someone to add a nineteenth benediction.

By the Middle Ages, this mode of reasoning was being applied to all sorts of liturgical anomalies. The *Sh'ma,* for example, is mandated twice a day: "when you rise up and when you lie down" (morning and evening). But its first line occurs elsewhere in the liturgy: while removing the Torah from the ark, in the early morning service *(Birkhot Hashachar),* and in the middle of the *Amidah* for *Musaf* (the additional service of Shabbat and holidays). In explanation, an eighth-century source says:

> An edict of persecution was issued against the inhabitants of the Land of Israel forbidding the recitation of the *Sh'ma* and saying the *Amidah.* They were, however, allowed to gather on Shabbat mornings to say liturgical poetry. So they inserted a *Sh'ma* and a *K'dushah* in the Shabbat morning liturgy [where it normally would not be found]. They did these things only because they had to, but now that God has put an end to the Roman Kingdom annulling their edicts, and now that the Muslims have once again permitted us to read Torah, recite the *Sh'ma,* and say the *Amidah,* it is forbidden to say anything except in its proper place, according to the rules of our sages.

The author, a Babylonian known as Ben Baboi, is writing to convince people to reinstate the practice that held prior to the persecutions, and perhaps some of them obeyed. But perhaps others continued to retain echoes of the practice that had become common during the persecutions, and perhaps on other occasions similar retentions of emergency regulations were preserved out of a respect for what had by then become customary.

That, at least, is the argument of a very great scholar, Jacob Mann, who accepted such medieval reports explaining away oddities in the liturgy, and wrote about them in a famous essay from 1927, entitled "Changes in the Divine Service of the Synagogue Due to Religious Persecution." The report of Ben Baboi was typical of others, many of which Mann cited as proof for his contention that much of liturgy is determined by politics. If he is right, we ought to see prayer not simply as "the service of the heart" (as the Talmud puts it), but as a political statement—in this case, a response to persecution.

But should we trust the medieval reports? Ben Baboi, who lived at least two hundred years after the persecution that Mann thinks he is talking about, had precious little historical sophistication. We do not know whether he had records that he consulted or whether he made the whole thing up as a likely explanation for what was otherwise unexplainable to him. Very much is at stake here: not just an explanation of a stray *Sh'ma* here and there, but the very nature of prayer. Is prayer always, usually, or even sometimes a result of political calculation? When we read the "extra" *Sh'ma* that Mann reads back to Ben Baboi's letter, are we really reading a political manifesto that should remind us of a persecution once upon a time, and, perhaps, by extension, make us think about similar situations of Jews in other times and places, and consider all the while not the literal message of the *Sh'ma* but the blessing of freedom that we now enjoy instead?

What should make us suspect the veracity of these medieval accounts is precisely the fact that similar explanations occur everywhere, and not just for an oddly redundant liturgical line like the *Sh'ma* but also for the liturgical *piyyutim* I mentioned above. *Piyyutim* are poetic insertions into the standardized prayers for holidays. They began with liturgical poets in the Land of Israel around the fifth century and culminated a hundred years later in the work of a poetic genius, Eliezer Kalir. Other schools of poetry arose later, in medieval Spain and Germany, for example. But Kalir's masterpieces are so brilliantly complex that many authorities throughout Jewish history have objected to their inclusion on the grounds (among other things) that no one can understand them. We should not be surprised, then, to find medieval authorities explaining them away as secondary to the *real* prayers because they originated in some far-away time of persecution.

In this case, the main testimony comes from two twelfth-century authors, Judah ben Barzillai al-Bargeloni and Samau'al b. Yahya al-Magribi. Judah explains:

> The enemies decreed that Israel must not occupy themselves with the Torah. Therefore the sages among them ordained for them, in the midst of the prayers, to mention, and to warn the ignorant about, the rules of Sukkot on Sukkot, and the [rules] of other festivals and the rules of Shabbat and the minutiae of the commandments by way of praises and thanksgivings and rhymes and *piyyutim*.

Samau'al, a Jewish convert to Islam, describes a similar process from his own perspective:

> The Persians forbade them [the Jews] from the practice of circumcision and likewise prayer, because they knew that most of the prayers of that community were invocations of God against the nations—that He destroy them and make the world desolate, except their own fatherland which is the Land of Canaan. But when the Jews saw that the Persians were serious about the prohibition of the worship service, they composed [new] prayers.... They called those prayers *al-hizana*.... The remarkable thing about this is that when Islam permitted the Jews the practice of their religion, and when the obligatory prayer was permitted to them again, the *hizanat* had become for the Jews a meritorious religious exercise on festivals and holy

days. They made them a substitute for the obligatory prayer. (Translation of this and prior passage by Jakob J. Petuchowski, in Joseph Heinemann with Jakob J. Petuchowski, *Literature of the Synagogue* [New York: Behrman House, 1975], pp. 206–7.)

The reports are inconsistent in detail, but they talk about the same thing: *piyyutim* (in Hebrew), *al-hizana* (in Arabic). And despite the contradictions in detail, and some information that is patently wrong (Samau'al's charge that Jews pray for the destruction of all but their own Land of Israel), we get the same explanation here for poetry that we saw above regarding the extra *Sh'ma* and *K'dushah*. So the question remains: do we believe this "persecution" theory of prayer or not? Are prayers really political in origin?

Fortunately, there is an alternative explanation, and it is provided by none other than master-poet Kalir himself. He begins one of his most famous poems, a prayer for dew, by saying: "With God's permission, I will utter riddles to give Israel pleasure." Does this sound like a poet motivated by persecution? Besides, the classical poets of whom Kalir is the finest example created hundreds, if not thousands, of poems over the course of more than a century. Politics might explain one poem—even several—but not an entire corpus, once recited weekly and even daily. It is far more likely that Jews turned to poetry for the same reason anyone else does: the innate human search for aesthetics.

Jacob Mann was an extraordinary scholar. So too were any number of early writers about prayer. Louis Finkelstein, for example, perhaps the most influential chancellor of the Conservative Movement's Jewish Theological Seminary of America, also characterized prayer as a political statement. He explained the earliest strata of the Passover Haggadah as an expression of the years after Alexander the Great, when Jews in Eretz Yisrael had to prove their loyalty to the Ptolemies who ruled Egypt, and therefore had to mute the theme of Israel's servitude to Pharaoh. Why would scholars of this magnitude have believed that the true explanation of prayer is politics?

In part, political explanations were simply acceptable scholarly rhetoric. It had been taken for granted by the nineteenth-century pioneers of Jewish studies, whose books were read and widely admired. They too had seen politics behind cultural expression. But they had been influenced by German romanticism, which considered politics spiritual. The notion of politics as spirit reached fruition in the philosophy of Hegel (1770–1831), who believed that all of history was the playing out of *Geist*, "spirit," by which he meant universal reason. Though historical events in and of themselves might sometimes seem random or even bizarre, history on the macrocosmic level obeyed a strictly reasonable evolutionary plan, moving inexorably toward its ultimate end. Saying that prayers were a response to history did not necessarily debase the prayers, since historical events and culture were intertwined in the larger whole of the human spirit.

By the time American Jewish historians like Mann and Finkelstein wrote, however, the Hegelian spiritualization of history had been lost. Finkelstein, for instance, was a Marxist. He thought the Rabbis were late antiquity's equivalent of the urban proletariat, breaking free from the old-guard landed bourgeoisie represented by the Temple priests. Scholars of his generation thus approached prayer with the Hegelian rhetoric of historical cause and effect, but without the Hegelian spirituality that once lay behind it. Out came theories not just of prayer as politics, but prayer as politics *alone,* politics in the worst sense, politics *instead of* piety. And that theory found a ready acceptance in lesser minds and readers, for whom prayer had virtually ceased being anything spiritual anyway.

I am referring to huge numbers of eastern European Jews who came to these shores after the oppressive Czarist laws handed down in 1881. They were part of a larger migration from eastern and southern Europe that virtually inundated America until the 1920s, when congressional law put a stop to their arrival. We sometimes romanticize the religious vitality of those immigrants. Most of them had either already dropped their medieval orthodoxy by the time they came, or did so after their arrival. Some were out-and-out socialists, who had abandoned religion on ideological grounds, believing it to be a negative influence on the coming class struggle. Others just found old-country piety a nuisance, given the life they were trying to build here.

Many immigrants attended services anyway, for any number of reasons other than halakhic duty. Some prayed out of habit or the desire to retain a connection with tradition. Others gave up communal prayer altogether but saw their children move out of the first-generation areas of settlement on their route to middle-class status, where they attended services because Americans then, as now, expected people to be at least nominally religious. Of these second-generation Jews, some joined Reform temples and others took up Orthodoxy, but the majority became Conservative, the movement that burgeoned most among eastern Europeans. A certain proportion attended services to enjoy the schmoozing and socializing that went on there.

Schmoozing was itself reason enough to go, as anyone familiar with *davening,* even today, can attest. Sociologist Samuel Heilman, who studied the phenomenon, explains that even though it is technically a breach of synagogue ethics, talking during services is really an unofficial and more than acceptable part of what goes on.

> [While the Torah is being read], many people talk with one another. The *gabbais* [officials in charge of assigning Torah honors] are trying to *shush* them, but small cliques and klatches defy this *shushing* and keep on talking. Indeed, in one or two cases, the people being quieted engage the *gabbai* in conversation. They succeed in making listening deviant and talking acceptable. (*Synagogue Life* [Chicago: University of Chicago Press, 1973], p. 148)

For any one of these reasons, then, second- or even first-generation Jews from eastern Europe might pray with a community. But they were not likely to believe in prayer as a way of connecting with a personal God, nor did they find rational significance in what the prayers were saying, most of which they found troublesome. There were endless pages of seemingly unnecessary praise, and God didn't seem to listen all that well to the petitions. For these worshipers, political interpretations explained the liturgy in a way that made sense. Even intellectual rubbish could be important as an expression of Jewish history. That was especially the case because medieval explanations emphasized persecution, which was the very experience that the eastern European immigrants knew best. They took it for granted that the standard state of the Jewish condition was what historian Salo Baron later castigated as "the lachrymose theory of Jewish history." Reciting the liturgy was tantamount to identifying oneself personally with the tribulations Jews had faced through time.

For these Jews, liturgy was a form of ethnic piety. If Jews in years past were sometimes killed for the traditional words of prayer, still saying them became a religious act of solidarity. We would not call this spiritual in today's idiom, but it was not on that account impious. Even the schmoozing was an exercise in building Jewish community and identifying with other Jews worldwide.

Moreover, even if the political interpretation of prayer formation sometime strains credulity, it is not altogether wrong. Sometimes liturgy really is a political response of its time. Such is the case for the very last part of the *Kabbalat Shabbat* service, the section from the Mishnah called *Bameh Madlikin:* "With what do we light [Shabbat lights]?"

TRULY POLITICS—*BAMEH MADLIKIN:* THE CONTRIBUTION OF MEDIEVAL BABYLONIA

Traditionally, refusing to kindle light on Shabbat is a sign of piety. But insofar as they pit one set of pietists against another, even acts of piety become embroiled in politics. In this case, the political flurry revolved about the interpretation of Exodus 35:3, "You shall kindle no fire throughout your habitations on the Sabbath day." At the very beginning of the rabbinic period, equally well-intentioned Jews fought over the meaning of this passage. Does God want us to douse all fires before Shabbat arrives— in which case, we must spend Friday night of Shabbat in darkness? Or does God want us just to avoid kindling *new* lights on Shabbat—in which case we can light up our home before it gets dark, and enjoy the light and heat until the candles go out and the fire in the fireplace crackles to its end.

The two earliest rival interpretive camps of the rabbinic period, known as Pharisees and Sadducees, differed on this very important point. Sadducees read the Torah literally: The Torah had been given on Mt. Sinai; every word of it is true; if it says to begin Shabbat in darkness, that is what it must mean. The Pharisees agreed that the Torah hailed from Sinai and that its every word is true, but they believed also that the "written" law had been given alongside the "oral" one. Attending only to the written word would lead people astray. The only way to understand God's written instructions was to supplement it with an oral understanding, which might or might not accord with the literal Hebrew wording. The Rabbis saw themselves as heirs to the Pharisees.

And ever since, we have read Torah only with the wealth of interpretive understanding that oral tradition demands.

Among other things, the Rabbis believed that God demanded joy *(oneg)* on Shabbat. Hadn't Isaiah himself written (Isaiah 58:13), "You shall call the Sabbath 'joy' *(oneg)*"? How could a Jew celebrate Shabbat with requisite *oneg* without lights to enjoy Shabbat dinner by? God could hardly have meant us to sit in the dark. Exodus 35:3 must mean only that we must kindle all necessary Shabbat light before Shabbat arrives.

The Rabbis went so far as to transform the permission to kindle lights and leave them lit into an obligation to do so, and to this day, we light candles just before Shabbat arrives. (For details, see L. Hoffman, Volume 7, *Shabbat at Home*, pp. 43, 53–56.)

The Mishnah is the definitive compendium of Jewish law that was promulgated about the year 200 C.E. It is divided into six lengthy books, each one called a *seder*, or "order." *Seder Mo'ed*, for instance, is the order dealing with sacred time. Each *seder* is subdivided into tractates (each one a *massekhet* [pronounced mah-SEH-khet]). *Massekhet Shabbat* is the tractate in *Seder Mo'ed* that details the regulations for Shabbat. Each *massekhet* is then broken down into chapters (each one a *perek*, pronounced PEH-rehk), and each *perek* is broken down further into paragraphs. The word *mishnah* can refer to the entire compendium or just to any one of the paragraphs that make it up.

Chapter *(perek)* two of tractate *(massekhet)* Shabbat discusses the complex ins and outs of properly kindling Shabbat light. It explains how to kindle the requisite light without inadvertently breaking God's law at the same time—like using wicks that burn unevenly, so that they sputter and cause at least tiny amounts of their flame to spread and light miniscule new fires within and around the already existent flame. Though an important part of Shabbat law, the Rabbis who composed it never imagined it would some day be read as part of a service that later generations would call *Kabbalat Shabbat*.

By the eighth century, most Jews lived under Muslim rule. In the middle of that century, the Islamic caliphate moved from Damascus to Baghdad. As money and power flowed away from the vicinity of Eretz Yisrael and toward Baghdad, the worldwide center of rabbinic gravity slowly moved there also, leading the rabbinic leaders of Babylonian Jewry (called Geonim, pronounced g'-oh-NEEM) to claim the sole right of interpreting what the oral law had to say to Jews of their time.

Not everyone agreed with this Babylonian claim. Among the holdouts were rabbis in Palestine, who had lived with their own rabbinic traditions for centuries and resented the Babylonian attempt to stand in judgment over them. More thoroughgoing was an attack on rabbinic Judaism everywhere, by the Karaites (from the word *k'ra*, meaning "Scripture"), who denounced the very idea of the oral law as a fraud. In effect, the ancient claim of the Sadducees was revived. "Read your Bible," instructed Anan ben David, the man regarded as the sect's founder.

In effect, this was an earlier Jewish version of the Protestant Reformation that split apart European Christianity in the sixteenth century. Martin Luther too attacked the official interpreters of Scripture, in his case by denying their theory that reserved authentic understanding of the Bible to the Catholic Church of Rome. The Christian instance was successful, and for some time it appeared as if the Karaite challenge would be also. Looking back now, we can see that the Karaites eventually dwindled to almost nothing. But that is retrospect. From the eighth to the eleventh centuries, they posed a serious challenge to rabbinic Judaism, attacking especially the Babylonian authorities who claimed the right to represent rabbinic Judaism worldwide.

Especially symbolic of the Karaite position was their insistence once again on reading Exodus 35:3 literally. Under attack by Karaites, the Geonim responded in two ways. First, they elevated Shabbat candles to the level of a *mitzvah,* complete with a blessing, which we all take for granted now but which was especially revolutionary in its time (see L. Hoffman and Landes, Volume 7, *Shabbat at Home,* pp. 43, 48–55). Second, they added the Mishnah's chapter on candle lighting to the liturgy—an especially significant warning to worshipers who might be contemplating a switch to Karaism, because its sixth paragraph threatened death in childbirth to women who failed to light candles according to rabbinic demand. (See Zierler, "Shedding Feminist Light on Sabbath Candles," pp. 27–32.)

All of this happened in the ninth century. Our first instance of *Kabbalat Shabbat* liturgy is an instance of politics.

TRULY PIETY—PSALMS 92 AND 93: THE CONTRIBUTION OF PALESTINE

Jews had occupied the Land of Israel since the days of Joshua. The Babylonian exile of 587 B.C.E. affected a small number of leaders, but the population as a whole remained there, and half a century later, even some of the Babylonian captives began returning. In time, the Temple was rebuilt and the third Jewish commonwealth was established. Rabbinic Judaism had its roots there, too, and even after the Second Temple fell, Palestinian Jews saw themselves as the spiritual center for all of Judaism.

The wars with Rome, however, had spurred migration elsewhere, including Babylonia. In the third century (the traditional date is 219 C.E.), a rabbi we call Rav made his way there, bringing the Mishnah with him, and shortly thereafter (226 C.E.), with a new dynasty, the Sasanians, in power, the specifically Babylonian variety of rabbinic Judaism began to flower. It culminated in the Babylonian Talmud.

From about 550 C.E. (the traditional date given for the codification of the Talmud) until about 750 C.E. (fully two hundred years), we know little of Jewish life in Babylonia or in Palestine. In 632 C.E., however, Islam began its rapid spread outward from the Arabian peninsula and conquered both. The institution called the Gaonate may have emerged around that time, although the first Geonim of whom we have any significant knowledge began functioning only in the middle of the eighth century, when (as we saw) the Islamic caliphate relocated from Damascus to Baghdad, carrying the center of commercial and political gravity with it.

A cultural struggle quickly broke out between Jews in the ancient homeland of Eretz Yisrael (we can call it by its English medieval name, Palestine, from now on) and what the Palestinian Jews considered the fresh Babylonian upstarts. The Babylonians won. Jews worldwide have adopted the Babylonian Talmud as decisive and the Babylonian prayer book as normative. But the victory came only after centuries, abetted by another set of wars, this time the Crusades. In 1099 Crusaders reached Palestine, and for almost a hundred years they ruled it in the form of several feuding fiefdoms, the most famous being the Latin Kingdom of Jerusalem, ruled by Godfrey de Bouillon until the Muslim reconquest under Saladin. Throughout the century of Crusader rule, Jews fled to neighboring countries, but by the time they returned, they had adopted Babylonian customs and abandoned their own native Palestinian forms of piety. Since the end of the nineteenth century, we have been piecing together that culture, largely from evidence that we call the Genizah fragments. (See L. Hoffman, "How the *Amidah* Began," pp. 26–29, and J. Hoffman, "The Genizah Fragments: How Our Ancestors Prayed in the Ancient Land of Israel," Volume 2, *The Amidah,* pp. 37–42.)

Vestiges of Palestinian custom remained in the writings of medieval rabbis who preserved reports handed down to them, so even before the Genizah discovery we knew already that Palestinian Jews had their own distinctive manner of prayer. But we had no idea how unique it was. It was, of course, not altogether unlike prayer in Babylonia (since they both went back to the Mishnah, the formative volume of rabbinic practice that the communities shared). But unlike Babylonian Jews, the Palestinians had refrained from codifying their liturgy in a single normative prayer book, and they retained a special interest in liturgical poetry—not just medieval poetry (the *piyyutim*) but the ancient poetry of the Bible, the Psalms, including Psalms 92 and 93.

Psalm 92 is already listed in the Bible as "A Psalm for the Sabbath Day." In Second Temple times, it became one of the daily psalms that the Levites sang. For reasons that are not clear, Psalm 93 became another one, Psalm 92 for Shabbat and Psalm 93 for Fridays. When the Temple fell, the daily psalm ceased, although centuries later it was reintroduced to the service, this time in the synagogue. So in our service, Psalms 93 and 92 are said independently at the end of the morning service, on Friday and on Saturday, respectively.

Meanwhile, psalms were finding their way in droves into the prayer book. The Bible is cited everywhere in our prayers, but psalms far more than anything else. In today's standard traditional liturgy, psalms constitute about 50 percent of all biblical citations, not just in the parts of the service that are self-consciously built on psalmody (like the *P'sukei D'zimrah* [Volume 3], 74 percent) but everywhere. In the *Amidah* (Volume 2), they are 40 percent, and in the Torah service (Volume 4), 52 percent. These are counts for our own prayer book, based on the Babylonian prototype. And in the rival Palestinian tradition, psalms were even more central. It was in Palestine that Psalms 92 and 93 entered the liturgy as *Kabbalat Shabbat.*

Palestinian Jews reserved specific psalms for all kinds of days: Psalm 135 for the first day of Passover, 136 for the last day, 47 for Rosh Hashanah, 103 for Yom Kippur, 29 for Shavuot, 98 for Rosh Chodesh, 7 for Chanukah, 22 for Purim, 99 and 137 for Tisha B'av—and others for special Torah portions like *Hachodesh* (Exodus 12:1–20, read on the first Shabbat of Nisan, announcing the beginning of the biblical year).

As time went on, holiday psalms were further outfitted with other psalms to introduce them. Psalm 93 was usually used for that purpose, and when holidays fell on Shabbat, Psalm 92 ("A psalm for the Sabbath day") preceded that. But then it was felt that the Sabbath psalm (92) deserves its own preliminary psalm, so Psalm 121 was appended as an apt introduction, giving us four psalms in a row: 121 (to introduce Psalm 92), 92 (the psalm for the Sabbath), 93 (to introduce the holiday psalm), and the psalm for whatever holiday it was. Psalm 92 eventually became associated with Psalm 93, the psalm that followed it on festivals, so the average Sabbath now featured three psalms: 121 (to introduce the Sabbath psalm), 92 (the Sabbath psalm), and 93 (to introduce the festival psalm, even though there was none to introduce). Ezra Fleischer, the Israeli scholar to whom we owe this information, says that all this must have happened by the fifth century because by then, synagogue poetry written for Shabbat was based on Psalm 92 and included citations from Psalm 93 as well. Apparently, Psalm 121 dropped out, but 92 and 93 remained, partly perhaps because they had once been the two psalms for Friday and Saturday anyway, and the liturgy in question was right in the middle—Friday night.

Originally, in fact, Palestinian Jews introduced their psalms with a blessing as well.

> Blessed are You, Adonai our God, ruler of the universe, who chose David his servant, and who took pleasure in his praise and sacred songs, to extol, praise, and glorify Him for his many acts of greatness throughout all time. Blessed are You, Adonai, who causes full and imminent deliverance to spring up for his People and builds up Jerusalem.

The blessing fell out of circulation, however, and we no longer say it.

From medieval Palestine, then, the *Kabbalat Shabbat* service inherited Psalms 92 and 93. As far as we know, their selection had nothing to do with politics. This second stratum of *Kabbalat Shabbat* liturgy, the uniquely Palestinian contribution, predating by several centuries the Babylonian adoption of the Mishnah's chapter on candle lighting, is a consequence of piety.

TRULY POETRY—*L'KHAH DODI*: THE CONTRIBUTION OF MEDIEVAL KABBALAH

What gives *Kabbalat Shabbat* its final glory, however, is neither *Bameh Madlikin* nor Psalms 92 and 93. Most services have "warm-ups" of some sort, but nowhere other than here has the warm-up become more popular than the main service it introduces, and by themselves, neither *Bameh Madlikin* nor Psalms 92 and 93—nor even both together—can account for that. The genius of *Kabbalat Shabbat* has been the third and most recent part of our service: the kabbalistic introduction of six psalms ending with *L'khah Dodi*. Without the kabbalistic prayers, would the service even have its own name? I doubt it. The term comes originally from a talmudic account (Shab. 119a): "R. Chanina would wrap himself in his cloak and stand at sunset of Sabbath eve, proclaiming, 'Come, let us go forth to welcome Queen Shabbat!' R. Yannai put on his Sabbath cloak on Sabbath eve and exclaimed: 'Come forth, O Bride, Come forth, O Bride!'" But no one much discusses that account before sixteenth-century poet Shlomo Halevi Alkebetz decided to build his brilliant poem *L'khah Dodi* around it. Without *L'khah Dodi,* Rabbi Yannai's dictum would likely have remained submerged in the sea of Talmud along with most of the other cryptic stories about Rabbis that rarely get cited except among specialists. *L'khah Dodi* is the actualization of Rabbi Yannai's dream: the ritualized means for whole communities to greet Shabbat. Rarely has a single liturgical creation seized the imagination of an entire people so quickly, so thoroughly, and so lastingly as *L'khah Dodi* has.

The details of this remarkable liturgy are the subject of comment by almost everyone throughout this book. Its backdrop is the sixteenth-century community of mystics gathered in Safed and surveyed here by Sharon Koren ("The Mystical Spirituality of Safed," pp. 33–42). She draws our attention to the hidden meanings that the kabbalists took for granted and that still mesmerize those who recognize the "Little Buttercup theology" that underlies its surface appearance. Reuven Kimelman (pp. 118, 128–132) deals extensively with the details of that theology as its set of double entendres unfolds line by line in *L'khah Dodi*.

At its heart is the bold reconceptualization of the coexistence of God and God's world. Imagine the creation of the world in terms of Einstein's time-space continuum. At some primeval time, when there is nothing at all except God, God fills all space and time as well. There is, as it were, just a single point in space/time—no more, because without creation, there is neither extension nor duration yet. Imagine, moreover, that the God who is that primeval point (there being nothing else, remember) is best likened to a point of light, like a minuscule candle flame. Creation is the expansion of that flame to bring into being both time and space as it projects beyond itself.

But imagine further that the metaphoric flame that is God cools as it extends beyond its source, the way gas cools into liquid and then hardens into solids: steam to water to ice, for example. In just that fashion, the solidity of a universe was born. Theoretically, we can array the process two-dimensionally (see diagram 1): the single point of fire at the beginning of the process, and the created universe at its end.

At various points along the way, we theoretically arrest the light's expansion by making a cross-cut in it, watching each cross-cut get larger and larger but also duller and duller, just the way a real candle's flame would appear if we were to measure its intensity and size as it expands outward from a candle placed in the center of a room

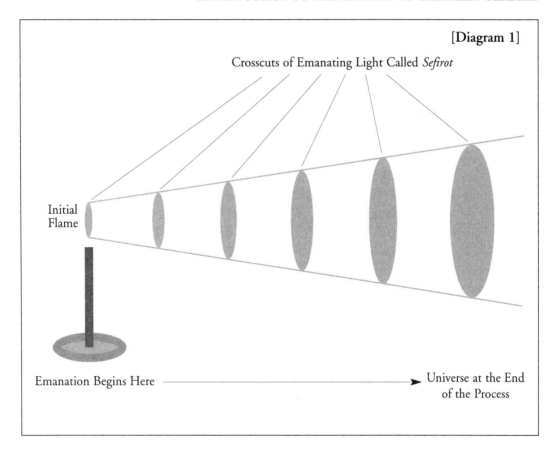

[Diagram 1]

Crosscuts of Emanating Light Called *Sefirot*

Initial
Flame

Emanation Begins Here → Universe at the End
of the Process

to the room's four corners. The light, it would appear, has mixed with darkness. In kabbalistic imagery, each cross-cut is a *sefirah* (pronounced s'fee-RAH; plural: *sefirot*, pronounced s'fee-ROHT). Just so, in the kabbalistic myth of creation, God's pure light was polluted by evil until, at the end of the sefirotic flow, the universe we inhabit congealed, but with evil intertwined.

Look again at diagram 1. From the perspective of the final point in time (looking from right to left, that is), we have a picture of the universe, its various stages of creation appearing in reverse order, going (that is) from the final "largest" *sefirah* (which is on the right) backward in time to the candle at the far left end of the line, where the whole process began. But looking at the same thing from the perspective of God—that is, from left to right—we see a picture of God's own process of self-emanation, building progressively through time until God became the universe. The same diagram is really both: it is the universe but also God. They are the same.

Theologically, we get a doctrine of God that Baruch [Benedict] Spinoza (1632–1677) adopted and for which he was excommunicated. But Spinoza was just expressing philosophically what Jewish kabbalists had put in mythical terms. Kabbalists too were excommunicated on occasion by more literally minded traditionalists. But their mythic tale of creation has proved lasting. To be sure, it has points in common with the theory of the big bang, but its impact on Judaism has nothing to do with any parallels it may by chance turn out to have with whatever science teaches at any given time. If we view Kabbalah as a scientific or even a philosophic explanation of the universe, we miss its point. Kabbalah is unashamedly a myth, a picturesque way of putting into perspective the grand themes of history and humanity: such things as the proper awe we ought to have for the very fact that there is a universe altogether—that there is "something" rather than "nothing"; our human role in the unfolding of time and circumstances; and the existence of unspeakable evil alongside human responsibility to do something about it. Kabbalah's everlasting contribution is a mythic set of metaphors with which to talk about these things. It is compelling not for its correspondence to fact but for its imagery.

It is no different from poetry on love, another reality uncapturable by science. Imagine that some day scientists isolate the love gene, explaining at long last why we love and why we love being loved. We will still need poems like this:

> How do I love thee? Let me count the ways.
> I love thee to the depth and breadth and height
> My soul can reach, when feeling out of sight
> For the ends of Being and ideal Grace.
> I love thee to the level of every day's
> Most quiet need, by sun and candle light.
> I love thee freely, as men strive for Right;
> I love thee purely, as they turn from Praise.
> I love thee with a passion put to use
> In my old griefs, and with my childhood's faith.
> I love thee with a love I seemed to lose
> With my lost saints—I love thee with the breath
> Smiles, tears, of all my life!—and, if God choose,
> I shall but love thee better after death.

I love Elizabeth Barret Browning's poem. Though science explains cause and effect, reducing most phenomena to a set of equations set down on paper, black on white, life is led in Technicolor. It is passion, rage, love, faith, commitment, purpose, and destiny. Life is not a science but an art. It is the artistic appeal of kabbalistic imagery, then, that has proved so lasting.

The imagery has almost holographic consequences that leap out at anyone who takes it seriously. Since God and the universe are the same, what happens to us must happen simultaneously to God. Affairs on earth are mirrored by parallel activity within the divine *sefirot*. Take just the concept of exile, which has so characterized the Jewish story of centuries. The story of Adam and Eve expelled from the Garden of Eden is our first mythic struggle with the incomparable feeling of alienation, loneliness, and powerlessness that an exile faces as a stranger in a strange land. Kabbalah is no different in kind, but much richer in depth.

The kabbalistic myth describes the inner workings of the *sefirot* that correspond to Jewish exile. If exile is utter loneliness, then God too must experience loneliness and a yearning for wholeness in its place. Every human act on earth affects the harmony of the divine *sefirotic* realm: our sins that drive the *sefirot* farther apart, and our acts of good, most specifically (for Jews) the *mitzvot,* which bring them back together.

A favored metaphor here is the experience of two lovers lost from each other's presence. Wholeness is the moment of sexual union when they finally meet and become one. God too must experience that sexual longing. Hence God must be both male and female, sometimes coming together in perfect union. Exile is not just a geographic accident of this historical event or that; it is a metaphysical necessity, the permanent state of being as long as history has a say. It ends only at the end of time, when both God and we will know the perfect wholeness of messianic peace. In the interim, we persist, doing our duty to bring that time about, rescuing sparks of God from their entanglement with evil (another kabbalistic image). And we manage because, in part, we get a glimpse of perfect unity on Shabbat, the day the Rabbis called a foretaste of the world to come.

The kabbalistic liturgy begins with a set of six psalms (95–99 and 29), chosen because they highlight God as king. I choose the masculine word with care. If the liturgy is a sacred drama, what we have here is a two-act play with only two characters, both of whom are God. God as king makes his appearance in the introductory psalms, which simultaneously stand for the six days of the week. This first act ends with God quite obviously enthroned, as the second to last verse in the final psalm announces: "Adonai sits enthroned, king forever!"

The female side of God makes her appearance only at the end, but what an appearance, what an ending! Of the ten *sefirot,* the final seven represent the seven days of creation. The last one, *Malkhut* (also known as *Shekhinah*), and the feminine aspect of God, must therefore be the seventh day, Shabbat. *L'khah Dodi* heralds the appearance of Shabbat as God's queen and bride. Her arrival at the end of *L'khah Dodi* is presaged by *Ana B'kho'ach,* a short poem written in kabbalistic code and not included in all prayer books. It reads like a rambling petition for God's mercy and guidance, but it might equally have said anything else, since its manifest message is just the excuse to include an acrostic. The poem has seven lines of six words each, making forty-two words in all. The initial letters of the words combine to spell God's forty-two-letter name, held by the kabbalists to be particularly effective in working wonders. Not that anyone knows how to pronounce it or even uses it—but theoretically, if we could and did, who knows what we might manage to pull off? Unable to say it, we can at least allude to it, pronouncing the forty-two relatively arbitrary words that the letters begin.

It ends with *Barukh shem k'vod malkhuto l'olam va'ed,* a line with syntax garbled enough to defy certain translation: literally, word for word, it reads, "Blessed name glory his kingdom forever." Our rendering is "Blessed is the One the glory of whose kingdom is renowned forever," but however we understand it, it is what is called a liturgical doxology, a cry of undiluted praise of God, in this case, God as king (see Volume 1, *The Sh'ma and Its Blessings,* pp. 83, 93). We are well used to this line: it appears as a quiet congregational response to hearing the *Sh'ma.* But it began in the

Temple as part of the sacrifices offered on Yom Kippur. There the people shouted it aloud after hearing the ineffable name spoken by the high priest. No wonder it is appended to *Ana B'kho'ach*. There too, it follows God's name, in this case, the forty-two-letter one.

This is high drama. The coronation of God the king, the expression of God's magical name and the traditional response going back to Temple times, and the arrival of Queen Shabbat for a truly divine wedding ceremony. In the sefirotic realm, the masculine principle *(Tiferet)* marries his feminine parallel *(Shekhinah);* here on earth, we discover the wholeness and peace that Shabbat alone can offer.

How can we see all of this as anything other than piety? But appreciating it as the drama that it is allows us to reopen the question with which we began. How did our prayers get written? Politics or piety?

The answer, we now see, is both. The scholars I mentioned earlier went too far in imagining political machinations when there were none, and passing blithely over genuine Jewish piety through the centuries. But we dare not remove politics altogether from the equation. We don't always know the whole story, but we can be reasonably sure that any critical prayer had its supporters and detractors. Piety is the yearning to express our deepest religious beliefs and experience. Politics enters in because we live in a world where we often have to fight for our beliefs against those of others. Poetry is an art that goes a long way toward guaranteeing that our expression will prove lasting. We need a final word, then, on poetry.

THE POETRY OF PRAYER

We began by asking who writes our prayers and why. We close by asking what makes prayers lasting. Anyone who has spent any time with the prayer book faces that question, usually in the form of amazement: "Why in the world do we still say that?" Why do some prayers never even get printed, while others seem to last forever?

There is no single answer to this conundrum. We regularly dig up manuscripts of prayers that seem to be better written than what we have. The Genizah fragments show us that some Palestinian Jews did not say *Ahavah rabbah* or *Ahavat olam,* the two blessings we now say prior to the morning and evening *Sh'ma.* Instead, they had this alternative:

God brought forth a vine from Egypt...	גֶּפֶן מִמִּצְרַיִם הֶעֱלָה אֱלֹהֵינוּ.
expelled the [Canaanite] nations	וַיְגָרֶשׁ גּוֹיִם
And planted it	וַיִּטָּעֶהָ
Nurturing it with Sinai's waters	מַיִם מִסִּינַי הִשְׁקָה אוֹתָם
With flowing streams from Horeb.	וְנוֹזְלִים מֵחוֹרֵב.

Why didn't this prayer succeed? It makes the same point that *Ahavah rabbah* and *Ahavat olam* do: God's love for Israel. But literarily, anyway, it is far better. It is filled with biblical allusions, written poetically, and memorable for its extended metaphor that plays on the word "land" *(eretz)* from "Land of Israel" (Eretz Yisrael). As in English, "land" can mean earth, not just nation. The *land* of Canaan, therefore, is not just a country but richly fertile real estate. The image here is God as loving gardener. The Land of Israel is God's own garden. God plucks a tiny shoot from Egypt, takes it lovingly through the desert, and then transplants it there. The weeds that have sprung up (Canaanite tribes) are removed, and Israel is newly planted in their place, then watered with Torah, without which it dies. Why didn't this prayer make it?

The answer in this case seems to be "pure accident." I suspect every poet, artist, and song writer has similar creations that probably ought to have lasted but somehow never did. Chaim Stern, *z"l,* the editor for the Reform Movement's *Gates* liturgies, often told me, "Some of my best stuff didn't get past the committee." So the first reason for a prayer making it into the prayer book and staying there is just dumb luck.

We saw also, however, that prayers often get there for political reasons. The Genizah prayer was composed in an era when there was no central authority to determine what prayers belonged and what prayers didn't. By contrast, by the time *Bameh Madlikin* was added, it was already part of Judaism's legal canon, and the Geonim who chose it for liturgical expression had enough political clout to make their decision stick. Some Jews find it sufficiently traditional to give it the right to remain, even today. Tradition is its own argument, especially once it gets codified as Halakhah, the chief determinative factor for many. But many other Jews nowadays omit that "prayer." The politics that animated its admission to the service have long disappeared, and it lacks other qualities that might make everyone keep it. As liturgy, it is relatively recent. It is unpoetic—indeed, not even worshipful.

So we now have other criteria for prayers that last. They may be poetic, worshipful, traditional, or even halakhically mandated. What counts as any of these things varies, of course. What is Halakhah for some is not for others. Jews have different "traditions," some of which we despise. "Worshipful" is in the eye of the beholder, and what counts as poetry varies from age to age. (The *piyyutim* by Kalir, remember, were perfectly poetic in their day but were dismissed by many later rabbis—and not just liberal nineteenth-century ones, because the poetry was lost on them.)

And we have not exhausted the list of what matters. Politics raises a more sophisticated issue: theology, which is to say piety in philosophical guise. The early morning service features *Yigdal* (see Volume 5, *Birkhot Hashachar: Morning Blessings,* p. 99), a medieval poem composed to express Maimonides' Thirteen Principles of Faith. In the volume you are reading, *L'khah Dodi* is a prime example of mystical theology, for which people either loved it and included it (Chasidic Jews), or hated it and rejected it (nineteenth-century rationalists). Or, take Zionism. For over a hundred years, Reform

Judaism systematically expunged Zionistic references from prayers; now it equally systematically includes them.

Other concerns come to mind also, like more dumb luck: what happened to be around when printing was invented. Kabbalah got lucky here, since its spread from Safed coincided with the establishment of the first Jewish printing presses. Politics, then, merges not only with piety but also with technology (printing press), power (the Geonim had it), aesthetics (what counts as poetry), and a whole lot else to determine a prayer's lasting power.

One more criterion must be mentioned: music. The art of prayer is, in the end, the art of worship. For Jews, at least, worship is an oral thing, whether or not we use a prayer book. Sometimes what may otherwise seem stupid, offensive, irrelevant, and downright poorly written persists because of its melody, as any cantor who has tried to introduce new music can attest. *Kol Nidre* itself is a prime illustration. When nineteenth-century German Jews translated its Aramaic, they were appalled to discover that they had been asking God to pardon them for vows they did not keep. To be sure, there were lots of ways to explain away the embarrassment, but it remained an embarrassment anyway, especially since Jews were trying to gain civil rights at the time, and the last thing they wanted to imply was that they were not trustworthy. So almost every modern Jewish authority—from Samson Raphael Hirsch, the founder of modern Orthodoxy, to the many rabbinic leaders of Reform—omitted it from their prayer books. But Ashkenazi Jews loved the melody. It stuck. In America too, Reform rabbis fought it, and lost again.

All the more potent are prayers that we sing as a congregation. Our prayer book is filled with materials that may have other redeeming qualities (or may not) but that stay mostly because we sing them. *Adon Olam* is really a very nice poem, sophisticated theologically as well, but sung as a common closing hymn because people keep writing catchy tunes for it. *Ein Keloheinu* (see forthcoming volume on *Musaf* for Shabbat) is not offensive in its message, but it is banal, and we keep it because we like the traditional song that goes with it (a German drinking song in its origin). *Y'did Nefesh* was never a synagogue favorite until a prizewinning melody composed for the Israeli Chasidic Folk Festival migrated here and became everyone's favorite (see Volume 7, *Shabbat at Home*, pp. 135–146).

Kabbalat Shabbat has captured our imagination for many reasons these days, politics least of all, since the politics are largely irrelevant today. Piety ranks higher in importance, since *Kabbalat Shabbat* is filled with piety, and its mystical message of Shabbat appeals especially to our time of spiritual search. Most of all, it is our most poetic service, filled with psalms and highlighted with *L'khah Dodi*. Because of its poetry and its piety, it is richly provided with music. All told, *Kabbalat Shabbat* is a brilliant work of art.

Kabbalat Shabbat

A Liturgy from Psalms

Marc Zvi Brettler

Kabbalat Shabbat is a Bible scholar's dream. This short service is almost entirely composed of selections from the Book of Psalms, and the nine psalms incorporated in *Kabbalat Shabbat* represent about 5 percent of Psalms. It is thus impossible to understand this service without understanding the structure and function of the biblical Book of Psalms.

WHAT ARE THE PSALMS?

The word "psalms" comes from the Greek *psalmoi,* a translation of Hebrew *mizmor;* both likely mean a song sung to the accompaniment of a stringed instrument, the best reflection of which is the final psalm (150): "Praise Him with blasts of the horn; praise Him with harp and lyre. Praise Him with timbrel and dance; praise Him with lute and pipe. Praise Him with resounding cymbals; praise Him with loud-clashing cymbals."

Our Book of Psalms (sometimes called the Psalter) is best understood as a collection of collections of different genres of ancient Israelite poetic prayers, many of which may have been used by worshipers in the First and Second Temples. It is divided into 150 chapters, most of which constitute single, stand-alone prayers. (There are some likely exceptions—Psalms 9–10 constitute a single work, as indicated by the content of the chapters and their sharing an alphabetic acrostic, while several chapters, such as 19 or 137, likely contain more than one composition.)

The Book of Psalms does not contain all the psalms that existed in ancient Israel. Other poetic prayers are preserved elsewhere in the Bible, such as Hannah's prayer in 1 Samuel 2, Jonah's prayer from the belly of the fish (Jonah 2), and Habakkuk 3. Many more must have been lost. The psalms it does preserve are extremely varied. The majority are Judean, though some likely come from the Northern Kingdom (e.g., Ps. 80:3, "Ephraim, Benjamin, and Manasseh"), which broke away after the death of

Solomon (ca. 922 B.C.E.). Many, but certainly not all, psalms begin with the superscription *mizmor l'david* or *l'david mizmor,* "a psalm of David." The meaning of this is uncertain—it might suggest that the author believed that the particular psalm was written by David, or that it follows the style of psalms written by David. In any case, analysis of the language of these psalms suggests that they were not written by David, even though some Rabbis attribute the entire Psalter to him. Some psalms come from the monarchic period (ca. 1000–586 B.C.E.), while others—like Psalm 137:1, "By the rivers of Babylon"—reflect the Babylonian or later periods. They encompass many different genres. Most are laments (sometimes called petitions, because after complaining, the person praying typically offers a request or petition) and hymns of praise; both varieties (petition and praise) appear in both singular and plural, indicating that some were composed for recitation by individuals, and others by the community.

Exactly when and where psalms were recited is unclear. Psalm 118:27b, "bind the festal offering to the horns of the altar with cords," suggests that psalms could be recited while offering a sacrifice. Other psalms do not contain such explicit clues, so scholars look for other suggestions internal to the psalm's content that hint at their setting. For example, many scholars suggest that Psalm 15, which asks, "Adonai—who may sojourn in your tent, who may dwell on your holy mountain?" is an entrance liturgy, recited as an individual approached the Temple precincts. (Psalm 24:3, "Who may ascend the mountain of Adonai? Who may stand in his holy place?" may have played a similar role.) The original setting of most psalms, however, remains obscure.

Given that the psalms are of different types and come from different time periods and locations, it is not surprising that the order of Psalms seems quite haphazard. Indeed, it is often difficult to know why any two particular psalms are adjacent. There is, however, a macro-structure to the book as a whole. It moves from laments, which predominate at the beginning, to hymns, which predominate at the end. In addition, Psalms 41, 72, 89, and 106 end with statements of praise that are remarkably similar. We call them doxologies, from the Greek *doxa,* meaning "glory."

- Psalm 41:14: Blessed is Adonai, God of Israel from eternity to eternity. Amen and amen.
- Psalm 72:18–19: Blessed is Adonai, God, God of Israel, who alone does wondrous things. Blessed is his glorious name forever. His glory fills the whole world. Amen and amen.
- Psalm 89:53: Blessed is Adonai forever. Amen and amen.
- Psalm 106:40: Blessed is Adonai, God of Israel, from eternity to eternity. Let all the people say Amen, Halleluyah.

In addition, Psalm 150, the conclusion of the Psalter, may be understood as one long doxology; it begins "Halleluyah! Praise God in his sanctuary. Praise him in his heaven of power." And it concludes "Let every breath praise God! Halleluyah!"

These psalms suggest that the Psalter has deliberately been divided into five sections, each one ending with a doxology. If so, the book we call "Psalms" has been subdivided into five separate books (Pss. 1–41, 42–72, 73–89, 90–106, 107–150) to parallel the Torah. Psalm 1 serves as an introduction to an entire collection: "Happy is the man who has not followed the counsel of the wicked…. Rather the Torah of Adonai is his delight." In this context, Torah may not only refer to the Five Books of Moses but to the five-part Book of Psalms that follows.

There are additional structures also within Psalms. Groups of psalms may be connected through title or through content. For example:

- Psalms 120–134 are all "songs of ascent" (though we are not sure just what that means).
- Psalms 73–83 (and 50) are a collection attributed to the levitical court singer Asaph.
- Psalms 48–83 are often called the Elohistic Psalter, since they predominantly use "Elohim" rather than "Adonai" for God's name (compare especially the parallel Psalms 14 and 53).
- Psalms 93–99, often called enthronement or kingship psalms, depict God as king and often (Pss. 93:1, 96:10, 97:10, 99:1) contain the phrase *Adonai malakh,* "Adonai is [or has become] king." Significantly, as we will see, Psalms 95–99, the bulk of this collection, are used to introduce *Kabbalat Shabbat.*

THE KINGSHIP PSALMS

Since the enthronement, or kingship, psalms (as we will call them) are so central to the liturgy featured here, we should stop to ask why these psalms were composed in the first place. We do not know for sure, of course, but some scholars think they reflect a ritual (maybe an annual event) from Temple times through which God was (re-)enthroned, and his kingship celebrated. The enthronement could have been celebrated as part of the Rosh Hashanah–Sukkot complex of festivals. Perhaps a remnant of this ancient ritual is the *malkuyot* or kingship theme, so prevalent in the Rosh Hashanah service. (A centerpiece of its *Musaf Amidah* is called *malkuyot*). In addition, it is possible that the ancient Palestinian custom of reciting Psalm 29, which deals with God's kingship, on Sukkot preserves a memory of enthronement psalms being connected to the fall holidays. No such enthronement-of-God ritual is actually explicit in the Bible, but some scholars have tried to reconstruct what the ancient enthronement ritual would have been, including which psalms were recited during the festival, and which rituals accompanied them.

Psalms 95 and 98 lack the formula *Adonai malakh,* but they highlight God's kingship using different formulae (95:3, "a greater king than all other gods"; 98:6, "the king, Adonai"). Psalm 94 lacks any of these formulae, but it shares with the other kingship psalms of the collection the idea of God as a just and great judge. In addition, two psalms from elsewhere, 29 and 47, share this kingship motif. Psalm 29 is included in *Kabbalat Shabbat,* and Psalm 47 is recited as the shofar is sounded on Rosh Hashanah.

However they were used, these psalms all celebrate aspects of God's kingship—a major biblical theme found elsewhere as well, as in Exodus 15:18, one of the earliest passages in the Bible: "Adonai will reign for ever and ever." They all depict God as an idealization of the human, Davidic king. God will be enthroned forever (Ps. 29:10) and has been enthroned forever (Ps. 93:2). He is superlative, greater than all other kings (Ps. 95:3; cf. Pss. 96:4, 97:9). Kings engaged in human building projects, but Adonai "built" the whole world (Pss. 95:4, 96:5). Kings judged their people, and so does God, but God is the fair judge (Pss. 96:13, 98:9, 99:4), more equitable than any human king might be. Most evidently, kings led their armies in battle, and Adonai does so as well (note the expression "Adonai of hosts"), but Adonai is so powerful in this role that even nature fears his power (Ps. 97:5). Elements from the coronation ceremony are projected onto God, as people and even nature rejoice noisily at God's kingship, just as there was great joy and noise during the coronation of Saul, Solomon, and their successors (see, e.g., 1 Sam. 10:24; 1 Kings 1:40, 45). These various elements, such as God as judge, builder, leader of armies, or being joyously acclaimed, may be called entailments of the image of God as king.

It is difficult to date the collection of kingship psalms from Psalm 93 to Psalm 99. In contrast, the psalm that follows them in *Kabbalat Shabbat,* Psalm 29, is probably among the earliest psalms of the Psalter. It was most likely an adaptation of a poem celebrating the victory of the high god of the Canaanites, Baal, over his enemies. This explains several of its features: (1) Unlike Psalms 93–95, its main image is of Adonai as God of the thunderstorm, one of the traits of Baal. (2) It uses the noun *kol,* thunder, seven times in nine verses. (3) It highlights the Lebanon mountain range (v. 5), outside of the Land of Israel. Indeed, the kingship of Baal is a major theme of a set of Canaanite myths called the Baal cycle. An early Israelite poet transformed a composition concerning Baal by replacing every mention of Baal with Adonai, and suddenly a poem commemorating the kingship of Baal became a poem commemorating the kingship of Adonai, who "reigned during the flood and will reign supreme forever" (v. 10).

KINGSHIP PSALMS BECOME *KABBALAT SHABBAT*

The selection of psalms for *Kabbalat Shabbat* is far from haphazard and has a complicated history (see L. Hoffman, "Politics, Piety, and Poetry," p. 1–20). One might have expected the seven kingship psalms, 93–99, to have been chosen (seven psalms for the seven-day week), but that is not the case. Instead, the sequence begins only with Psalm 95 because of its opening verse, "Let us sing to Adonai," a natural introduction for the entire service. Psalm 29 was chosen as the sixth psalm because it describes the end of creation prior to Shabbat, when God finally "sat enthroned at the Flood ... King forever" (v. 10), after which, properly enough, we get (as the seventh psalm) Psalm 92, the "Psalm for the Sabbath Day." But to end on the theme of kingship, yet one more psalm (Ps. 93) follows, replete with the formula, "Adonai is king." God has finally become universal king, but better than human rulers, because (v. 5) God's laws "endure forever." As the beginning of the Sabbath, Friday night becomes the ideal time to reflect on that kingship by reciting psalms that clarify how God became king.

The addition of Psalms 92 and 93 to "cap" this collection is brilliant. Psalm 92 begins with the obvious implication of God's kingship, which undergirds the recitation of these psalms: "It is good to praise Adonai." Psalm 93, thematically related to it, concludes with a major theme of post-biblical Judaism: "Your decrees endure forever."

Thus, Psalms, itself a collection of collections, is reworked as various psalms are chosen, reused, and reorganized to create a new collection. The contextualization of these psalms as part of the Friday night liturgy, and the combination of kingship psalms and a Shabbat psalm, give the psalms in the new collection an equally new meaning that they lacked in their original, biblical context. But this should be no surprise. The greatness and power of biblical psalms is that even though they might have originated in a particular context, they are open to constant recontextualization, always gaining new meaning and power.

Shedding Feminist Light on the Sabbath Candles

Wendy I. Zierler

Most of us have entirely positive associations with the *mitzvah* of lighting Shabbat candles. Embedded in this *mitzvah* are images of tradition and home; of Friday night family dinners; of quiet Shabbat serenity; and of our mother, circling her hands and covering her eyes before saying *lehadlik ner shel shabbat,* the words that magically transform ordinary time *(chol)* into the sacred *(kodesh).* Shabbat commemorates God's day of rest after six days of creation. There is always something of Eden in Shabbat, some spark of that original seventh day in the garden, in the glow of Shabbat candles.

It feels like being cast out of the garden when we encounter some of the negative rabbinic pronouncements about the origin and rationale of this women's commandment. First and foremost, perhaps, is the statement from Mishnah Shabbat 2:6, which is included in the liturgy every Friday night: "There are three transgressions on account of which women die in childbirth: for not being careful about the laws of menstruation [*niddah,* pronounced nee-DAH, or, popularly, NEE-dah], of *challah* [pronounced chah-LAH, or, popularly, CHAH-lah, a portion of dough that is ritually removed from the bread before baking], and of lighting the Sabbath candle." With this teaching, the lighting of candles—or the failure to do so properly—suddenly becomes associated with every woman's nightmare of death in childbirth, a kind of anti-blessing. Perhaps the Mishnah's admonition to women was the rabbinic way of giving women a sense of control as they confronted the terrifying dangers of bearing children. If only you do these things right, the Mishnah implies, you'll be okay. This recuperative reading notwithstanding, the Mishnah does violence to our otherwise pristine view of the experience of candle lighting. Suddenly we find death lurking in the shadow of the candles.

Notions of punishment and death and their relationship to candle lighting are even more apparent in the statements of Rabbi Joshua as recorded in Genesis Rabbah (Vilna Edition) 17. Here the rationale for candle lighting is explicitly connected to Eden, or rather, our expulsion therefrom:

> Why was she [woman] given the precept of menstruation [*niddah*]? Because she spilled the blood of the first man [Adam], the precept of *niddah* was given to her. And why was she given the precept of *challah*? Because she corrupted Adam who

was the *challah* of the world, she was given the precept of *challah*. And why was she given the precept of Sabbath lights? Because she extinguished the soul of the first man, she was assigned the precept of kindling Sabbath lights.

If we thought candle lighting was a positive, life-giving, and rest-giving ritual, Rabbi Joshua construes it, together with the other women's *mitzvot,* in purely punitive terms. Eve sinned and caused Adam to sin, and, in so doing, corrupted him, spilled his blood, and extinguished his soul. Because of Eve's transgressions, all women are condemned eternally to carry out these compensatory rituals. Could there be any formulation of the meaning of candle lighting more alien to our sense of this *mitzvah?* Thankfully, the Babylonian Talmud (Shab. 31b–32a) offers a positive view of these three women's *mitzvot.* We are grateful to "a certain [unnamed] Galilean," who interprets as follows:

> I have put into you a portion of blood: therefore I have given you a commandment having to do with blood. I have called you "firstling"; therefore I have given you a commandment having to do with the first [dough]. The soul which I have given you is called candle; therefore I have given you a commandment having to do with candles. If you keep them, well and good, but if not I will take away your soul." [translation from Daniel Boyarin, *Carnal Israel*]

To be sure, the death threat persists even in this interpretation. What is different, of course, is that the women's *mitzvot* do not originate with death and punishment. Instead, they commemorate women's honored status as firstlings, as honored vessels of human blood and soul.

But just when we are beginning to find our way toward an appreciation of women and their role in performing women's *mitzvot* in general, and Shabbat candle lighting in particular, we confront another talmudic source that undermines the first one. Rav Huna states that "*he* who habitually practices [*haragil*] the lighting of candles will have many sons learned in the Torah" (Shab. 23b). If the Mishnah promised a death sentence to women who failed to perform this *mitzvah* properly, this Gemara promises reward to a habitual candle lighter who is a man. This reward comes as part of a list of benefits promised to men for the performance of such traditionally male *mitzvot* as *tallit* and *Kiddush,* indicating a male desire to take credit for what otherwise seems to be the spiritual province of women. As if to curtail female ownership of this *mitzvah* on the grounds that it is a time-bound commandment, the Gemara tells a story about R. Joseph's wife who habitually lit candles too late. R. Joseph tries to encourage her to light them on time, whereupon she gets in the habit of lighting them too early and needs to be encouraged to light neither too early nor too late. Women's domestic role may place them in a position of special responsibility with regard to this home-related *mitzvah.* Even so, this Gemara suggests that women cannot really be trusted to get it right. Because women's domestic roles make them incapable of managing time and time-bound rituals, men must preside over and regulate their performance of this *mitzvah.* Maimonides (Laws of Shabbat, 5:3) could not be clearer about the limitations of women:

Women are given this mandate even more than men because they are present in the home and are involved in the business of housework. Even so, men are required to admonish them and check up on them. On Sabbath eve, before it gets dark they should announce *Hadliku et haner!* [pronounced, hahd-LEE-koo et hah-NAYR], "light the candles!"

And so, with each one of these sources, our beautiful, glowing, edenic sense of women's role in the performance of this *mitzvah* is at best challenged and at worst shattered. Some sources cast the pall of death over the light of the candles and see this *mitzvah* as punitive. Others seem to value, and even envy, women's control of this *mitzvah* but attempt to claim it for men. Cast out of ritual Eden, what do women do with our newfound knowledge? Disabused of our prior notions, how do we find our way back to an appreciation of this *mitzvah* and its origins?

Jewish literary tradition did not give the final word on candle lighting to the Rabbis. Later writings, particularly by Jewish women, provide important counter-visions that endow earlier readings with positive, recuperative meaning.

One such source comes from the literature we call *tkhines* (pronounced t'KHI-nis), a body of prayers composed by or for women, from the seventeenth to the nineteenth century. One of them is *T'khinah Sh'loyshe Sh'orim* ("The *T'khinah* of the Three Gates"), an eighteenth-century Yiddish prayer for the three women's *mitzvot* of menstruation, *challah,* and kindling Shabbat lights. It was composed by the renowned Sarah bas Tovim, a Ukrainian rabbi's daughter who wrote several important *t'khin's* and became something of a folk hero in the Yiddish literary world (so much so that she appears as a fairy godmother figure in a Cinderella story by Y. L. Peretz entitled "The Match"). In several different places in this *t'khinah,* Sarah bas Tovim recalls rabbinic statements about women and candle lighting and yet makes certain crucial changes.

Sarah bas Tovim's treatment of the women's *mitzvah* of candle lighting includes an instructional and a liturgical section. In the instructional section, Sarah paraphrases rabbinic literature to recollect the custom of lighting two candles, one to symbolize the commandment to "remember" the Sabbath *(zakhor)* and one to symbolize the commandment to "observe" the Sabbath *(shamor).* In *gematria,* the Hebrew word *ner* ("candle") equals 250. The numerological value of two candles, therefore, is 500, which she equates with the value assigned by tradition to the total number of human anatomical parts. "By virtue of this," says Sarah, "*hashem yisborekh* [God, may He be praised] will heal the bodies of man and woman." In contrast to the rabbinic sources that relate the lighting of candles to the wrong Eve did to Adam, and the necessary gender antagonism that ensued, Sarah bas Tovim sees in candle lighting a restorative means of ritual healing that brings men and women together.

The instructional section further promises women that if they "light candles with serious intent … *hashem yisborekh* will illumine the eyes of your children so that they will understand the holy *toyre* [pronounced TOY-r']." This statement recalls Rav Huna's assertion in Shabbat 23b, promising this same reward to "*he* who habitually practices [*haragil*] the lighting of candles," but here, the reward is assigned specifically to the mother. The *t'khinah* also promises that "if you keep these three *mitsves* faithfully, you will give birth quickly, that is your lying-in will be quick and without pain … *Hashem yisborekh* will protect you from death and disaster, that you may see happiness and joy." Here Sarah bas Tovim adeptly revises the teaching from Shabbat 2:6. In contrast to the threat of dying in childbirth as a punishment for not performing the three women's *mitzvot* faithfully, Sarah bas Tovim promises an easy delivery to those who do perform it right. Writing from a knowledgeable perspective, Sarah bas Tovim is able to recast traditional imagery in positive terms.

In the liturgical section of the *t'khinah,* Sarah bas Tovim takes even bolder interpretive steps. First, she includes a prayer in which the reciter asks, "May I perform this *mitsve* properly and may it be valued as equivalent to all the 613 *mitsves* of all of *yisro'el.*" The rabbis often likened the importance of isolated *mitzvot*—the learning of Torah, for example—to all of the other *mitzvot* put together, but nowhere does the tradition prior to Sarah bas Tovim elevate candle lighting to this level of importance.

Even more astonishing is the following liturgical section, where Sarah bas Tovim bravely likens the candle lighting by women to the ancient lighting of the Temple menorah by the high priest:

> *Riboyne shel oylem* [pronounced ree-BOY-n' shel OY-l'm, Yiddish for the Hebrew *ribono shel olam*—"Master of the Universe"] may the *mitsve* [pronounced MITS-v', Yiddish for the Hebrew *mitzvah* "commandment"] of my lighting candles be accepted as equivalent to the *mitsve* of the *koyen godl* [pronounced KOY-'n GU-d'l, Yiddish for the Hebrew *kohen gadol,* "high priest"]when he lit the candles in the precious *beys hamikdesh* [pronounced BAYS ha-MIK-d'sh, Yiddish for *bet hamikdash,* "Temple"]. As his observance was accepted, so may mine be accepted…. I also ask at this time that this *mitsve* of lighting candles be accepted as equivalent to the olive oil, which burned in the *beys hamikdesh* and was never extinguished.(Adapted from Tracy Guren Klirs, *The Merit of Our Mothers* [New York: HUC Press, 1992].)

To be sure, this invocation of the high priest subtly reinforces the gendered separation of spheres: it renders the female candle lighter "a high priestess in the sanctuary of her own home"—a term borrowed from a letter written by Jewish Theological Seminary chancellor Louis Finkelstein to a young woman named Gladys Citrin, rejecting the idea of a woman rabbi on the grounds that "a woman should be a high priestess in the sanctuary of her own home" (see Pamela Nadell, *Women Who Would Be Rabbis: A History of Women's Ordination 1899–1985* [Boston: Beacon Press, 1998], p. 18). At the same time, it represents an imaginative liturgical leap into a sacred space traditionally off-limits to women. Sarah then moves on to counter the punitive statements of Genesis Rabbah: "May the merit of the beloved *shabes* [pronounced SHAH-b's, Yiddish for Shabbat, "the Sabbath"] lights protect me, just as the beloved *shabes* protected *odem horishn* [pronounced UH-d'm hah-RIH-sh'n, Yiddish for *adam harishon,* "the first man," that is, Adam] and kept him from premature death." Here Sarah bas Tovim chooses a midrash from *Pirkei D'rabbi Eliezer* 19, in which Shabbat, personified as a woman, pleads with God not to kill Adam and Eve: "Master of the Universe, in the first six days of creation, no death was created. Why should the first death [Adam and Eve] start with me [Shabbat]"? Sarah thus echoes the rabbinic discussion of candle lighting within the context of Eve's "sin" against Adam. For the Rabbis, the message of the midrash had been Eve's role as "creatrix" of death; Sarah revises the tale to emphasize the merits of Shabbat, personified as a woman.

A similar revision of rabbinic pronouncements on candle lighting comes from the celebrated Hebrew poet Zelda Schneerson Mishkovsky (1914–1984). A descendant of prominent Chasidic rabbis, Zelda (as she is known) immigrated with her family from Russia to Palestine in 1925 and began writing poetry in the 1940s. Her first collection of poetry *(Pnai)* appeared in 1967. Zelda's poetry, which often treats religious subjects, has been embraced by both secular and religious readers, including some of the most avant-garde poets of her day.

In "Sabbath Candle," which I have translated here, Zelda evokes the horrors of eastern European life, against the backdrop of Sarah bas Tovim's imagery of Shabbat candles said now to be kindled "in the gloom of pain."

> My heart asked the evening,
> My gracious, deep friend:
> How do golden wings
> Grow from fire?
> And the many-charmed darkness flies.
> What is its secret?
>
> A lone flower answered the heart
> Love is the source of the fire.
> The sea wind
> Answered my thoughts:
> Lily of all freedom in the universe
> Is this fire, wondrous in its splendor.
>
> My blood listens—
> And cries and cries.
> Oy, a flame—is also an auto-da-fe.
> Still it is said—
> Astonishingly the fire scorned the dust.
>
> Does it befit a tender-
> Hearted mortal
> To wander and walk, and roam
> In a garden of fire?
> How does one probe
> The confusion of smoke to discern
> The spark of peace,
> That spark from which Sarah bas Tovim
> Would light her Sabbath candle
> In the gloom of pain.
>
> Within the nightmare walls
> It will flicker, it will slowly burn

In the house of ruin, the pit.
Across—the grieving one in the depths
Closed her eyes
To worry, to mourning, to shame, and to the profane.

The gleam of the candle—temples,
And inside the temples
Mothers singing to the skies
Until the end of time.
And she wanders among them
Toward God, with a barefoot baby
And with the murdered.
Hurrah!
The tender-hearted one goes out dancing
In the golden sanctuary, in a spark.

Zelda's poem begins by exploring the holiness and magic of candle lighting: How does the flame "fly" magically to heaven? Surely the two candles represent love and freedom, two ideas that are new to our discussion of candle lighting. In the third and sixth stanzas, however, she contrasts these positive images with two negative ones: the auto-da-fe of the Inquisition, and the burnt houses of the pogroms, the pits of the *Sho'ah*. No less than the Rabbis, Zelda draws on images of death and destruction, but in a gender-neutral sense: not the sins of woman, but the tragedies of the Jewish people. Against the background of these opposing images, Zelda recollects Sarah bas Tovim, an exemplary woman scholar and poet, who overcame life's hardships in Lithuania and managed to live a life so spiritual that she could discern a heavenly spark in Shabbat candles. In the last stanza Zelda pays tribute to Sarah bas Tovim's iconoclastic comparison of candle lighting to the kindling of the Temple menorah, by likening "the gleam of the candle" to temples. She thus links her own meditation on the lighting of Shabbat candles to the work of Sarah bas Tovim, and to the more general tradition of women's spirituality, through her reference to "Mothers singing to the skies / Until the end of time."

Rabbinic tradition, then, saw the women's *mitzvah* of kindling Shabbat candles negatively. Eve herself had brought death into the world by extinguishing the light of Adam's soul, and women who rejected their punitive *mitzvah* of having to light candles ever after were sure to die in childbirth. But Judaism has a countervailing understanding by women who were fully aware of the rabbinic tradition and responded to it. Taken together, Sarah bas Tovim's *t'khinah* and Zelda's poem present a creative counter-tradition that restores the spark, the magic, the love, and the light of this transformative ritual.

The Mystical Spirituality of Safed

Sharon Koren

According to the Talmud, Rabbis would change into their finest clothing before sundown Friday night and exhort one another to greet the Sabbath Queen. More than a thousand years later, Jewish mystics in Safed enlarged upon this tradition to create the *Kabbalat Shabbat* service. The beauty and spirit of this ceremony can best be understood in its historical context.

SAFED IN HISTORY

Between 1530 and 1590, Safed (pronounced *tsfaht*), a small city nestled in the hills of the northern Galilee, became the center of Jewish mysticism. That it would attain such stature seems highly unlikely at first. It goes unmentioned in the Bible and appears only once in talmudic literature. But in the twelfth century, European crusaders realized the strategic importance of the hilltop town and built a fortress there. When the Mamluk dynasty of Egypt took over the area in the mid-thirteenth century, they made Safed a regional capital. By 1400, Safed had a Jewish community, and a hundred years later, it was home to several important Rabbis, with a prominence that surpassed even Jerusalem.

For Jews, Safed rapidly emerged as the center of economic growth and of spiritual development. Appreciating its strategic importance, both the Mamluks and the Ottomans (the Turkish rulers who followed) kept the city well protected. Economic growth flowed from its protected status, leading Safed to become a center of textile manufacture. Jews flocked there to take advantage of business opportunities.

But Safed's geography fostered spirituality, too. When the Temple was destroyed, Jewish activity had moved from Jerusalem to the Galilee. The Mishnah itself was edited in Tsippori (Sephoris) in the second century C.E., and the Palestinian Talmud emerged from nearby Tiberias. Prominent rabbinic figures like Shimon bar Yochai were buried throughout the Galilean countryside, and their graves were believed to have magical qualities. According to one talmudic opinion, even the messiah would hail from the Galilee. These religious factors made Safed a magnet for the many sixteenth-century Jews who were seeking meaning in their lives.

THE SPIRITUAL QUEST: THE EXPULSION FROM SPAIN AND ITS AFTERMATH

The Ottoman Turks were Muslims from a small state in Asia Minor. After capturing Constantinople in 1453, thereby defeating the Byzantine Empire, they went on to extend their rule throughout southeastern Europe, portions of the Balkans, Greece, and the Middle East. The Ottomans welcomed Jewish émigrés forced to leave Spain in 1492, since they depended on minorities to enrich the economy, and the Jewish exiles numbered many intellectuals, artisans, tradesmen, and physicians. Indeed, Ottoman Sultan Bayezid II purportedly said, "You call Ferdinand [of Aragon and Castile, now Spain] a wise king? In expelling the Jews he has impoverished his country and enriched mine." The many Iberian refugees who settled in the Ottoman Empire soon dominated the existing Jewish population. Their culture and experience became the backdrop for Jewish life in the most powerful political empire of the sixteenth century.

Jews throughout the world had been traumatized by the expulsion. We should compare it to the American experience after 9/11. New Yorkers were not the only ones stunned by the destruction of the twin towers; the catastrophe was felt by all Americans. Just as Americans began to look inward, question our values, and seek more spiritual lifestyles, so too did sixteenth-century Jews seek to imbue their lives with meaning. Where Americans found their answers in patriotism, family, or new age spirituality, sixteenth-century Jews looked to God and Jewish mysticism. This spiritual awakening of sixteenth-century Jewry was spearheaded, however, by the Jews most immediately touched by the trauma: the Iberian exiles themselves.

THE EMERGENCE OF KABBALAH

The particular form of medieval Jewish mysticism known as Kabbalah (meaning "tradition") emerged in Provence in the 1180s. But cultural ties were strong between southern France and northern Iberia, and schools of Kabbalah soon emerged in the northern Iberian province of Catalonia. Thirteenth-century Castile saw the flowering of kabbalistic symbolism and the production of the *Zohar*, a mystical commentary on the Torah said to have been composed by the second-century rabbi Shimon bar Yochai but actually written by a man named Moses de Leon and his circle. Various schools of kabbalistic studies thrived among the initiated throughout fourteenth-century Iberia.

After the expulsion, Sefardi mystics shared their ideas with kabbalists in other countries. The experience of the expulsion, however, changed their perspective. Feeling pain, loss, and guilt, many refugees sought ultimate answers in Kabbalah, with the result that mysticism became a part of everyday life rather than an esoteric object of study reserved for a privileged few.

The democratization of Kabbalah was a major breakthrough. Already in the time of the Mishnah, mysticism was being treated as an arcane object of study that should be transmitted only within a small circle of the theologically elite.

> The subject of forbidden sexual relations (Leviticus 18) may not be expounded before three persons, the works of creation (Genesis 1–3) before two, or the works of the chariot (Ezekiel 1) before one, unless he is a sage and understands his own knowledge.
>
> Whoever speculates upon four things would have been better off if he had not been born. What is above, what is beneath, what before, what after. And whoever takes no thought for the honor of his maker would have been better off if he had not been born (Chag. 2:1).

Jewish mystics took these warnings very seriously. By the tenth century, Jewish mystics assumed that the "work of the chariot" was recorded in *Hekhalot* literature, the earliest written expression of Jewish mysticism. *Hekhalot* literature, named after the *hekhal,* the vestibule that stood before the Holy of Holies in the Jerusalem Temple, describes two major mystical goals: (1) to ascend to the realm of the angels and join them in singing God's praise and (2) to call down a heavenly angel who would divulge the secrets of Torah. Only the worthy could learn the divine names and the ascetic rituals that would facilitate their mystical quest. In the twelfth century, German pietists inherited the esoteric lore and, in keeping with the Mishnah, transmitted their interpretations of it just to the initiated few. When Kabbalah emerged in the twelfth century, the mystical circle widened, but only a little. Heeding the Mishnaic warning, kabbalists considered the divine secrets too dangerous for popular consumption.

KABBALISTIC THEOLOGY

Kabbalistic theology emerges as a traditional response to the challenge of Maimonides and medieval Aristotelianism. Aristotle defined God as an unmoved mover, completely unchangeable, pure being contemplating itself. The notion of such a cosmic force is awe-inspiring but hardly comforting. An unmoved mover cannot interact with humanity; it cannot worry about the persecution of the Jewish people, nor hear a mother's prayers when her child is ill. Caring would make God change with the result that God would no longer be the unmoved mover. As the view advanced by Maimonides, this Aristotelian perspective of a completely transcendent God influenced Jewish thought. Kabbalistic theology provided an answer to the challenge of a God who, by definition, cannot possibly be involved in human affairs.

Indeed, Kabbalah emerged in Provence in southern France, the epicenter of the Maimonidean controversy, and later moved to Catalonia in northern Spain, between the Pyrenees and Barcelona. This early school of Spanish kabbalists included Ezra and Azriel of Gerona, Nachmanides (1194–1270) in Barcelona, and Abraham Abulafia (b. 1240), who fused Maimonidean philosophy with language mysticism to pioneer ecstatic Kabbalah.

In the late thirteenth century, kabbalistic symbolism flourished in the area of Iberia known as Castile, lying west and south of Catalonia. Mystics from all over Europe flocked to Castile to be part of its intense kabbalistic activity. Moses de Leon and several of his colleagues joined forces to compose the *Zohar,* a mystical commentary on the Pentateuch based on earlier kabbalistic traditions, and the crowning achievement of medieval Kabbalah, which achieved semicanonical status shortly after it was completed.

According to the *Zohar,* there is an infinite aspect of God that lies beyond the realm of human cognition known as the *Ein Sof* (pronounced ayn-SOHF), literally "without end." The *Ein Sof* is unapproachable, completely hidden from us—like the unmoved mover. But other aspects of God are manifest and within human reach. These attributes correspond to descriptions of God in the Bible and rabbinic literature. They are the ten *sefirot,* which emanate from the *Ein Sof:*

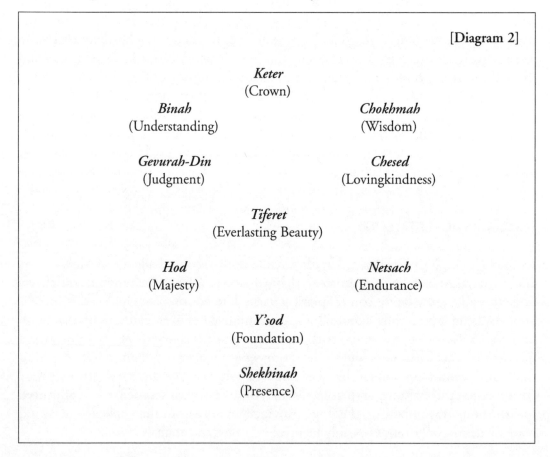

[Diagram 2]

Keter
(Crown)

Binah
(Understanding)

Chokhmah
(Wisdom)

Gevurah-Din
(Judgment)

Chesed
(Lovingkindness)

Tiferet
(Everlasting Beauty)

Hod
(Majesty)

Netsach
(Endurance)

Y'sod
(Foundation)

Shekhinah
(Presence)

The sefirotic realm exists in perfect balance and harmony. Six *sefirot* exist side by side, as in a scale. Those in the center, *Tiferet, Y'sod,* and *Shekhinah,* balance each other, but in a different way. *Tiferet* (the uppermost one) is described as a king. Through the agency of *Y'sod* (the middle one), *Tiferet* joins in union with *Shekhinah* (the lowermost one), who is the feminine aspect of the male God, *Tiferet's* queen. Balance is necessary for maintaining the homeostasis of the divine realm. And harmony above fosters harmony below because the *Shekhinah* metes out positive divine energy from the divine realm to the material world.

According to Kabbalah, however, not only can God influence us; we can influence God! Any human action on earth has the power to affect the Divine. Performing the commandments correctly promotes divine union; sinning causes divine separation. Moreover, according to the *Zohar,* the messiah will arrive only if one community acts piously and is completely repentant. Safed, near the grave of the purported author of the *Zohar,* and in the Galilee—traditionally thought to be the messiah's birthplace—was the obvious community to carry through this redemptive plan.

SAFEDIAN SPIRITUALITY

Convinced that communal activism would bring about messianic deliverance, Safedian kabbalists made the quest for redemption the cornerstone of their lives. Many Safedian Rabbis, such as Shlomo [Solomon] Alkabetz and Eliyahu [Elijah] de Vidas, wrote ethical treatises to popularize Kabbalah. Men, women, and children were taught to imbue every ritual act with cosmic import. Some engaged in extreme ascetic behavior such as fasting, abstention from certain types of food, self-flagellation, donning sackcloth and ashes, ritual immersions, and heightened concern for sexual propriety. Some created spiritual brotherhoods, like fraternities, to strengthen the fortitude of those trying to hasten redemption. The tenets of Kabbalah were transformed into innovative communal rituals. Many of these activities such as midnight prayer vigils and *tikkun leil shavuot* (pronounced tee-KOON layl shah-voo-OHT: staying up all night on Shavuot to learn Torah) were nocturnal—introduced and popularized, at least in part, because they coincided with the introduction of coffee into the Ottoman empire.

Other kabbalistic rituals focused on reenactments of divine processes that made the kabbalistic myth come alive. For example, although the Spanish émigrés in Eretz Yisrael were (Zionistically speaking) finally "home," many saw themselves as if they were in exile from the Iberian peninsula. They made sense of their plight by recognizing it as a reflection of a cosmic drama: they were like the *Shekhinah,* the divine presence forced into exile from the Holy Land until the messianic age. Moses Cordovero and Solomon Alkabetz wandered the hills of Safed barefoot to imitate the suffering and peregrinations of the exiled *Shekhinah.* Sometimes the practice resulted in a mystical experience.

In a similar vein, Isaac Luria attempted to relive the narrative portions of the *Zohar.* Kabbalists believed that the *Zohar* was written by the second-century sage Shimon bar Yochai—the *Zohar* even reads as if it were the ongoing adventures of Rabbi Shimon bar Yochai and his students. Not content just to read about their exploits, Luria saw fit to act them out. Luria's personal fascination with Shimon bar Yochai becomes even more understandable when we consider that he believed he had been Shimon bar Yochai in a previous life!

The practice of "possession," *yichud* (pronounced yee-KHOOD; plural, y*ichudim,* pronounced yee-khoo-DEEM) was another innovation by which the Safedian kabbalists tried to relive the past. They would lie on a sage's grave to unite their soul with his. If this was successful, the mystic would spontaneously become possessed by the soul of the sage, who would teach kabbalistic mysteries through the agency of the kabbalist's body.

Now we understand *Kabbalat Shabbat;* it was yet another ceremony of ritual reenactment. Where the Rabbis of the Talmud merely spoke about welcoming the Sabbath Queen in general, Solomon Alkabetz and others designed a liturgical welcome through psalms and a hymn: *L'khah Dodi.* Isaac Luria initiated the practice of physically welcoming the *Shekhinah:* he and his students would leave the city for the surrounding fields just before sundown on Friday night and exclaim, "Come my beloved [*Tiferet,* the masculine aspect of God], let us greet the bride [the feminine aspect, the *Shekhinah*]."

Kabbalat Shabbat was not the only way these Safedian kabbalists reenacted the cosmic Sabbath drama. Indeed, the most important aspect of the ritual lay not in the synagogue or in the field but in the privacy of the home. The Talmud had taught that it was especially meritorious to engage in conjugal relations on Shabbat. Medieval kabbalists provided the mystical justification for this idea. They believed that the Sabbath Queen, the *Shekhinah,* united with her husband, *Tiferet,* on Friday night, thereby fostering unity and harmony in the cosmos. Sexual relation between a mystic and his wife not only reenacts the ceremony of divine marriage; it brings about divine sexual union. But the sexual act advances the mystic's own spiritual path as well. Just as *Tiferet* unites with his bride, *Shekhinah,* so the kabbalist unites with his own wife, who thereupon becomes a vessel for the *Shekhinah.* Physical union with a terrestrial woman allows the mystic to achieve divine union with the feminine aspect of God.

WOMEN IN SAFED

The popularity of *Kabbalat Shabbat* may reflect a change in women's status in Safed. Indeed, although the importance of conjugal relations on Friday night was an established part of mystical practice in early Kabbalah, the first text to laud a woman's participation hails from Safed in the sixteenth century. Until then, women were not allowed to participate in Jewish mysticism. We know the names of no female kabbalists.

Kabbalistic works like the *Zohar* go out of their way to provide rationalizations for the exclusion of women. In Safed, by contrast, there is evidence of women engaging in types of spiritual activities (albeit not kabbalistic study) that were respected by the male leadership. Indeed, Isaac Luria's most famous disciple, Chaim Vital, describes the prophecies of several women. Moreover, although Lurianic Kabbalah by no means espouses the gender equality, the Lurianic myth (which we will look at below) contains many positive female symbols.

There are several possible explanations for this attitude shift. Spanish Kabbalah was the province of an elite few, but in Safed it was the *raison d'être* of the entire community. All Safedians—women as well as men—were expected to act in accordance with the tenets of Kabbalah in order to bring about redemption. In addition, in the sixteenth century, spirit possession was a common cultural phenomenon, not just among Jews but among Christians and Muslims as well, and women were believed to be especially susceptible to spiritual possession. The women's experiences described by Chaim Vital are strikingly similar to those found in Christian and Muslim sources also. That is not to say that Christian or Muslim culture influenced Jews and Judaism, but rather that there was a universal trend toward belief in the occult.

FAMOUS KABBALISTS OF SAFED

Kabbalists descended on Safed from everywhere. One of the greatest Jewish jurists of all time, Joseph Caro, fled Portugal for Salonika. Frustrated by the many different legal opinions that proliferated because of the availability of printing, he embarked at age thirty-four on a project to create a definitive halakhah. He traced the entire corpus of Jewish law until his day, attempting to resolve the rulings of the three major codifiers (Isaac Alfasi, Moses Maimonides, and Asher ben Yechiel [the RoSH]), on the principle of "majority rules." He completed this legal digest, known as the *Bet Yosef* ("House of Joseph"), over the course of twenty years and then abridged it as the *Shulchan Arukh,* "The Set Table"—still the definitive halakhic guide for modern Orthodox Jews.

In addition to being a great halakhist, Caro was an outstanding mystic. Many people hold the mistaken notion that mysticism and Jewish legal thought are at odds. Yet, Jewish mysticism is not antinomian. In fact, quite the contrary, as we have seen: sixteenth-century mystics believed that every correctly performed ritual act had the power to create divine union. Caro's life is a case in point. While writing the *Bet Yosef* he began to receive visitations from a *maggid,* a heavenly teacher, who would impart kabbalistic mysteries to him. This *maggid,* whom he identified as both the *Shekhinah* and the Mishnah personified, would not just appear to him as a vision but would possess him (benevolently), speaking words of Torah through his mouth (like the modern phenomenon of "channeling"). Caro was conscious during these episodes of automated speech and recorded his mystical visitations in a book entitled *Maggid*

Mesharim, "The *Maggid* of Righteousness." His *maggid* instructed him to leave Salonika for the most spiritual city of the age: Safed.

In 1536, Caro arrived in Safed with his close friend, Shlomo Alkabetz, and soon became the most prominent rabbi in the city. His students included some of the greatest Safedian kabbalists, most notably Moses Cordovero, who combined knowledge of the *Zohar* with Abulafian ecstatic Kabbalah and ancient magical notions popularized during the Renaissance in a systematic compendium of Kabbalah that he called *Pardes Rimmonim,* "The Orchard of Pomegranates" (a name derived from the Song of Songs). Cordovero composed the book not just as a scholarly treatise but because he believed that systematizing kabbalistic ideas could restore order to the exile.

His *Pardes Rimmonim* was immediately printed and became a Bible of sorts to the kabbalists—a means of teaching the masses Kabbalah, because participation by the entire community was essential to achieve redemption. When Cordovero died in 1570, the Safedian community was left with no obvious leader, but his old age and death coincided with the arrival of the most famous kabbalist of Safed, Isaac Luria (1534–1572). Luria is popularly known as the *Ari* (literally, "the lion," but also an acronym for Ha*Elohi R*abbi *I*saac, "the divine Rabbi Isaac"). Those who do not believe in his divine powers use the acronym to signify Ha*Ashkenazi R*abbi *I*saac.

Born to an Ashkenazi family in Jerusalem in 1534, Luria moved to Cairo with his mother after his father's death. In his youth, he studied with David ibn Zimra, a renowned Egyptian kabbalist and halakhist. He eventually married and became a spice dealer. At a certain point, Luria had a spiritual epiphany and became a recluse, studying the *Zohar* and unpublished works by Cordovero on an island in the Nile. In 1569–1570, Luria moved to Safed with his family and became Cordovero's student. After Cordovero's death, he attracted disciples of his own, the most famous (as we saw) being Chaim Vital. Luria himself wrote little: only a few hymns and short commentaries to parts of the *Zohar.* In 1572 he died—just two years after arriving in Safed.

Luria's fame is extraordinary when we consider that he spent only two years in Safed and wrote hardly anything. But in contrast to Cordovero, the academic systematizer, Luria was a charismatic figure with a reputation for sanctity and supernatural abilities. He attributed his knowledge to divine revelations given him by the prophet Elijah, and he claimed the power to discern people's sins by reading the furrows of their brows. After determining the sin, he would issue the proper penance— spiritual "medicine" to cure the soul.

THE LURIANIC MYTH

While Luria was best known in his own day as an occult figure with supernatural powers, today he is famous for creating a new kabbalistic myth. He posited three stages in the creation of the world: *tsimtsum* ("contraction"), *sh'virat hakelim* ("the breaking of the vessels"), and *tikkun* ("restoration").

STEP 1: *TSIMTSUM*

Luria began with a question: How can God create the world if God is everywhere? Luria found his answer in the notion of *tsimtsum*—an idea going back to earlier kabbalists, including Nachmanides. According to Luria, God had to contract inward in order to make enough room to create the world. When God contracted, God left behind a vacuum. But this vacuum was not altogether empty.

As the names of the *sefirot* make clear, God is made up of many qualities, including judgment, which contains the root of evil. According to Lurianic Kabbalah, God's contraction was the means of separating the Divine from all things evil. God therefore left the attribute of judgment within the vacuum. But the evil does not exist there alone. A residue of divine light (called *r'shimu*, pronounced r'-SHEE-moo) adheres to the edges of the vacuum the way oil adheres to the sides of an empty bottle of dressing.

STEP 2: *SH'VIRAT HAKELIM*

God emanated back into the vacuum through a stream of undifferentiated divine light. To differentiate the light, vessels appeared to hold the light. The first three *(Keter, Chokhmah, and Binah)* were close enough to their divine source to withstand the power of the divine light. But the vessels contained primeval evil, remember, and the farther they were from the source of light, the more powerful evil became, until the seven far-off vessels, unable now to withstand the pressure, smashed into "shards" like the fragments of a shattered piece of glass.

Lest the chaos remain unchecked, a new light shone forth; it collected most of the scattered shards and restored them to the divine realm, which was then reorganized into a series of five *partsufim* (pronounced pahr-tsoo-FEEM), "faces," that correspond only in part to the ten *sefirot*:

1. *Arikh anpin*, "the long-suffering, patient One" (= the *sefirah* of *Keter*)
2. *Abba*, "Father" (= *Chokhmah*)
3. *Imma*, "Mother" (= *Binah*)
4. *Z'ir anpin*, "the impatient One" (= *Tiferet* and the five surrounding *sefirot*)
5. *Malkhut* or *Shekhinah* (also known as *nukba d'z'ir*)

STEP 3: *TIKKUN*

Restoration, however, is not complete. Shards remain in the material world, becoming *k'lipot* (pronounced k'-lee-POHT): "husks" of evil. They engulf the vestiges of the divine light that were not able to return to the divine realm, and hold them captive. Lurianic Kabbalah urges all Jews to pray and act with the intention of collecting the captured divine sparks and restoring them to their original source. This act of *tikkun*, "restoration," will restore order and unity in the sefirotic realm.

This mission of *tikkun* has been reinterpreted in a myriad of ways. One need not accept the Lurianic myth to appreciate the timeless message that good works on earth can restore the universe.

And *Kabbalat Shabbat? Kabbalat Shabbat* is the act of welcoming that single day when unity prevails over fragmentation and we have a preview of total *tikkun:* what the Rabbis called a "taste of the world-to-come."

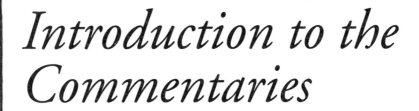

Introduction to the Commentaries

How to Look for Meaning in the Prayers

Lawrence A. Hoffman

THE ART OF JEWISH READING

I remember the day I looked at a manuscript of a prayer book that no one could identify. It had been smuggled out of Russia (then the Soviet Union) and was obviously the liturgy for Rosh Hashanah, but who had written it? And when? It was handwritten, so the style told us much, but in addition, someone had written marginal notes in another handwriting, and yet a third person had written comments to the comments—a third unknown scholar of years gone by whose name we wanted to rescue from oblivion.

Standing before the massive volume, I reflected on the sheer joy of studying a traditional Jewish text. I had seen printed versions before, but never a handwritten instance. What a wonderful habit we Jews developed once upon a time: writing a text in the middle of the page and then filling up the margins with commentaries. Every page becomes a cross-cut through Jewish history. Jewish Bibles come that way; so do the Talmud, the Mishnah, and the codes. We never read just the text. We always read it through the prism of the way other people have read it.

To be a Jewish reader, then, is to join the ranks of the millions of readers who came before us, leaving their comments in the margins, the way animals leave tracks in the woods. Go deep into the forest, and you will come across deer runs, for example: paths to water sources, carved out by hundreds of thousands of deer over time. The deer do not just inhabit the forest; they are part of the forest; they change the forest's contours as they live there, just as the forest changes them by offering shelter, food, and water. There is no virgin forest, really; it is an ecosystem, a balance between the vegetation and the animals who live there.

So, too, there are no virgin texts. They too are ecosystems, sustaining millions of readers over time. When we read our classic texts we tread the paths of prior readers in search of spiritual nourishment. *My People's Prayer Book* is therefore not just the Siddur text; it is the text as read by prominent readers from among the people. You are invited to share our path and even to break new ground yourself, passing on to others your own marginal notes, should you wish.

THE LITURGICAL TEXT WE USE

This volume begins our study of the synagogue service for Shabbat. Like previous volumes dedicated to the daily liturgy, this one too follows the Siddur text as provided by Phillip Birnbaum in 1949. Birnbaum combined the standard Ashkenazi rite with some modifications that had become popular in America, to give us the traditional liturgy in modern format. More than any other text, it is Birnbaum's that has met the test of time and represents the traditional liturgy most North Americans know best.

The final text was then translated by Joel Hoffman, in consultation with Marc Brettler. The translation strives to reproduce not only the content of the original Hebrew but also its tone, register, and style, so as to bring to modern readers the same experience (to the greatest extent possible) that the original authors would have conveyed with their words. In terms of content, we assume that by and large, words have meaning only insofar as they contribute to sentences and concepts—as, for example, "by and large," which has nothing to do with "by" or "large."

We try to reproduce a tone and register similar to the original text: formal, but not archaic; prose or poetry, depending on the Hebrew. Where the Hebrew uses obscure words, we try to do the same, and where it uses common idiom, we try to use equally common idiom. Parallelism and other literary devices found in the Hebrew are replicated as much as possible in the English. Our translations are best appreciated if they are read in conjunction with the running commentary by Joel Hoffman on why one set of words was chosen rather than another, as can be seen especially in *L'khah Dodi* (p. 115), for which he has provided a personal introduction as well. The poem owes its existence to a class in translation that Hoffman teaches to rabbinic students at the Hebrew Union College in New York. His introduction (p. 119) expresses his gratitude to his students for their collaborative effort in working through the poem with him. For his translation of Mishnah Shabbat (on candle lighting), he consulted Jacob Neusner, ed., *The Mishnah: A New Translation* (New Haven and London: Yale University Press, 1988).

Our translation has not doctored the text to make it more palatable to modern consciousness. Blatant sexisms are retained, for instance, wherever we think the author intended them. We depend upon our commentaries to bridge the gap between the translation of the original and our modern sensibilities.

THE COMMENTARIES AND THEIR SOURCES

The heart and soul of *Minhag Ami* is its choice of commentaries that surround the prayer-book text. Translator Joel M. Hoffman explains his choice of words, provides alternatives, and compares his own translation with others. As always, Marc Brettler comments on the way the Bible is embedded in the Siddur, and, in this case, expresses gratitude to Oxford University Press for allowing him to reuse and to amplify his commentary to Adele Berlin and Marc Zvi Brettler, eds., *The Jewish Study Bible* (New York: Oxford University Press, 2004). Ellen Frankel and Elliot N. Dorff provide theological reflections on what the prayers might mean, should mean, could mean, cannot mean, or have to mean (even if we wish they didn't). Alyssa Gray presents talmudic commentary, and Daniel Landes gives us the Halakhah of prayer, the rules and traditions by which this sacred liturgical drama has traditionally been carried out. Lawrence Kushner and Nehemia Polen supply a kabbalistic commentary, adding wisdom from the world of Chasidic masters, and David Ellenson surveys liberal prayer books of the past two hundred years to see how their writers agonized over attempts to update this book of Jewish books for modern times.

My own historical commentary had to deal with the fact that the Birnbaum Siddur is only for Ashkenazi Jews—more specifically the Ashkenazi version common in eastern Europe, often under the influence of Elijah ben Solomon of Vilna, known as the *Gra,* or Vilna Gaon (1720–1797). To balance the picture, I cite Sefardi practice also. But the word "Sefardi" has two distinct meanings.

Nowadays, it usually describes Jews whose liturgy was influenced by eighteenth and nineteenth-century Chasidism and, before that, the specific brands of Kabbalah initiated by people like Moses Cordovero, Solomon Alkabetz, and Isaac Luria (the *Ari*) in sixteenth-century Safed (Palestine). Master liturgist and scholar of texts E. Daniel Goldschmidt compiled a scientific edition of this variant, and I used that to represent "Sefardi practice." But "Sefardi" can also mean the old Spanish-Portuguese custom carried by Jews from Spain in 1492 and then brought to the Netherlands, whence it moved to England (among other places) and eventually to America as well. When I want to draw attention to this Spanish-Portuguese custom, I call it that, using as my guide the standard work published in England at the turn of the twentieth century by Moses Gaster, *The Book of Prayer and Order of Service According to the Custom of the Spanish and Portuguese Jews.* At times I cite *Seder Rav Amram* and *Siddur Saadiah,* the first two Jewish prayer books of which we are aware, from ninth- and tenth-century Babylonia (now Iraq). And from the same era, roughly, I use the Genizah fragments, manuscripts telling us how Jews prayed in the Land of Israel prior to the Crusades. In this volume, I am particularly indebted to Ezra Fleischer's reconstruction of the use of psalms (*Eretz-Israel Prayer and Prayer Rituals as Portrayed in the Geniza Documents* [Hebrew] (Jerusalem: Magnes Press, The Hebrew University, 1988).

This book is the richer for several guest contributors who were gracious enough to lend their expertise to background essays. *Kabbalat Shabbat* is a particularly difficult service to make sense of, not because of the overt meaning of the words (it is no harder or easier than other services, on that account) but because so much of it is kabbalistic and, therefore, dependent on a "deep" reading to get at the esoteric meaning that lies below the obvious.

We are fortunate to have Reuven Kimelman write a running commentary for us. Kimelman's recent work (*The Mystical Meaning of Lekhah Dodi and Kabbalat Shabbat* [Hebrew] (Jerusalem: The Hebrew University Magnes Press, and Los Angeles: Cherub Press, 2003) has established him as a foremost interpreter of the service.

It is particularly difficult to find an accessible but scholarly outline that provides the background readers need to make sense of Kabbalah in its historical context. But medievalist Sharon Koren has done just that. Her introductory essay "The Mystical Spirituality of Safed" is probably the best such short account available today. Readers are well advised to read it before turning to the commentaries.

Part of the *Kabbalat Shabbat* service is a reading from the Mishnah on Shabbat candle lighting. We began that topic in Volume 7, *Shabbat at Home.* Our discussion now continues with this Mishnah, which, among other things, is a primary source for our information regarding the ritual role of women at the end of the second century. But the Mishnah's cryptic reference to the fate of women who are said to die in childbirth if they fail to keep certain *mitzvot* (including candle lighting) has generated considerable controversy. In "Shedding Feminist Light on the Sabbath Candles," Wendy I. Zierler provides a feminist critique of the issues, providing (among other things) the voices of women in Jewish tradition as they have responded to the Mishnah in question.

Finally, though by no means a *guest* contributor, Marc Brettler (our regular writer from the point of view of biblical scholarship) has provided a remarkable background account of the psalms that figure so prominently in this service. His introductory essay "*Kabbalat Shabbat:* A Liturgy from Psalms" describes the unique role of "kingship psalms" in the Bible.

As in previous volumes, our commentators are likely to refer to Halakhah (Jewish law), a topic that deserves its own introduction here, since it is so essential to Judaism, but is not easily accessible to western readers. Frequently misunderstood as mere legalism, it is actually more akin to Jewish poetry, in that it is the height of Jewish writing, the pinnacle of Jewish concern, sheer joy to create or to ponder. It describes, explains, and debates Jewish responsibility, yet is saturated with spiritual importance. Jewish movements can be differentiated by their approach to Halakhah, but Halakhah matters to them all.

The topic of Halakhah is the proper performance of the commandments, said to number 613 and divided into positive and negative ones, numbering 248 and 365, respectively. Strictly speaking, commandments derived directly from Torah (*mid'ora'ita*) are of a higher order than those rooted only in rabbinic ordinance (called *mid'rabbanan*), but all are binding.

The earliest stratum of Halakhah is found primarily in the Mishnah, a code of Jewish practice promulgated about 200 C.E. The Mishnah was the foundation for further rabbinic discussion in the Land of Israel and Babylonia, which culminated in the two Talmuds, one from each center, called the Palestinian Talmud (or the Yerushalmi), and the Babylonian Talmud (or the Babli). While dates for both are uncertain, the former is customarily dated to about 400 C.E., and the latter between 550 and 650 C.E..

With the canonization of the Babli, Jewish law developed largely by means of commentary to the Talmuds, and by responsa, applications of talmudic and other precedents to actual cases. These are still the norm today, but they were initiated by authorities in Babylonia called Geonim (sing., Gaon) from about 750 to shortly after 1000. By the turn of the millennium, other schools had developed in North Africa particularly, but also in western Europe. Authorities in these centers are usually called Rishonim ("first" or "early" [ones]) until the sixteenth century, when they become known as Acharonim ("last" or "later" [ones]).

The first law code is geonic (from about 750), but it was the Rishonim who really inaugurated the trend toward codifying, giving us many works, including three major ones that are widely cited here: the *Mishneh Torah,* by Maimonides (Moses ben Maimon, 1135–1204), born in Spain but active most of his life in Egypt; the *Tur,* by Jacob ben Asher (1275–1340), son of another giant, Asher ben Yechiel, who had moved to Spain from Germany, allowing Ashkenazi and Sefardi practice to intertwine in his son's magnum opus; and the *Shulchan Arukh,* by Joseph Caro (1488–1575), who also wrote influential commentaries on both the *Mishneh Torah* and the *Tur* before composing what would become the most widely used Jewish legal corpus ever.

Several commentaries here draw centrally on these sources, not just for halakhic guidance but for historical information as well. Most of what Jews have written through the ages has been halakhic in nature, so reconstructions of Jewish ritual at any stage of its development, and even the theological assumptions that underlie Jewish practice, must often be reconstructed from legal sources that purport only to tell us what to do but end up telling us why as well.

There is no way to convey the richness of even a single one of these works, let alone the legion of other sources in Jewish tradition on which *My People's Prayer Book* draws. Suffice it to say that the commentaries that follow access many of the greatest works of our people, from the close of the geonic era (1034) to the present.

The authors of the commentaries represent a panoply of contemporary scholars, all students of the prayer-book text, and all committed to a life of prayer, but representative of left, right, and center in the Jewish world. As editor, I could not ask for a more scholarly and helpful group of colleagues; I am indebted to every one of them, who have together made the editing of this series a joy. They are matched by the many people at Jewish Lights who support this volume energetically. Emily Wichland handles all publication details with the kind of love and care that is rare. Stuart M. Matlins, founder of Jewish Lights Publishing, takes personal pride in this series—as well he should. He helped conceptualize it from the start and remains its most ardent supporter. I am grateful for the privilege of working with a publisher as astute and spiritually committed as Stuart.

The people mentioned here represent all of us, all of *Am Yisrael*, all of those God had in mind when God said to Ezekiel (34:30) "They shall know that I, Adonai their God, am with them, and they, the House of Israel, are my people." Unabashedly scholarly and religious at one and the same time, *Minhag Ami*, "A Way of Prayer for My People," will be deemed a success if it provides the spiritual insight required to fulfill yet another prophecy (Isa. 52:6), that through our prayers,

> My people [*ami*] may know my name
> That they may know, therefore, in that day,
> That I, the One who speaks,
> Behold! Here I am.

1 *From the Kabbalists of Safed*

A. 95–99, 29: PSALMS TO WELCOME SHABBAT

I. PSALM 95

[1] Let us sing to Adonai; let us trumpet our rock and deliverer. [2] Let us come before Him with praise, trumpeting Him with songs. [3] For Adonai is a great God, a king greater than all other gods. [4] In his hand are the depths of the earth and the mountainous heights. [5] The sea is his—He made it! And the land was fashioned by his hands. [6] Let us bow down low, kneeling before Adonai our maker, [7] for He is our God and we are the people of his pasture, the sheep of his hand. If only you would listen to his voice! [8] Do not be stubborn, as you were at Merivah, on the day of Massah in the wilderness [9] when your ancestors tried Me, tested Me, though they had seen my deeds. [10] For forty years I was disgusted by a generation calling them a misguided people that did not know my ways. [11] I swore in anger that they would never come to My Resting Place.

[1] לְכוּ נְרַנְּנָה לַיְיָ נָרִיעָה לְצוּר יִשְׁעֵנוּ: [2] נְקַדְּמָה פָנָיו בְּתוֹדָה בִּזְמִרוֹת נָרִיעַ לוֹ: [3] כִּי אֵל גָּדוֹל יְיָ וּמֶלֶךְ גָּדוֹל עַל־כָּל־אֱלֹהִים: [4] אֲשֶׁר בְּיָדוֹ מֶחְקְרֵי־אָרֶץ וְתוֹעֲפוֹת הָרִים לוֹ: [5] אֲשֶׁר־לוֹ הַיָּם וְהוּא עָשָׂהוּ וְיַבֶּשֶׁת יָדָיו יָצָרוּ: [6] בֹּאוּ נִשְׁתַּחֲוֶה וְנִכְרָעָה נִבְרְכָה לִפְנֵי־יְיָ עֹשֵׂנוּ: [7] כִּי הוּא אֱלֹהֵינוּ וַאֲנַחְנוּ עַם מַרְעִיתוֹ וְצֹאן יָדוֹ הַיּוֹם אִם־בְּקֹלוֹ תִשְׁמָעוּ: [8] אַל־תַּקְשׁוּ לְבַבְכֶם כִּמְרִיבָה כְּיוֹם מַסָּה בַּמִּדְבָּר: [9] אֲשֶׁר נִסּוּנִי אֲבוֹתֵיכֶם בְּחָנוּנִי גַּם־רָאוּ פָעֳלִי: [10] אַרְבָּעִים שָׁנָה אָקוּט בְּדוֹר וָאֹמַר עַם תֹּעֵי לֵבָב הֵם וְהֵם לֹא־יָדְעוּ דְרָכָי: [11] אֲשֶׁר־נִשְׁבַּעְתִּי בְאַפִּי אִם־יְבֹאוּן אֶל־מְנוּחָתִי:

BRETTLER (BIBLE)

Psalm 95 After an introductory call to worship (vv. 1–3), the psalm focuses on God as creator. This is royal activity: just as human kings were responsible for major building projects, God as king has fashioned the world (vv. 4–5) and Israel (vv. 6–7). The psalm concludes with a rebuke (vv. 8–11), but it is not clear why. Perhaps an original psalm has been expanded, or this is a (prophetic?) response to the psalm.

1, 6 "Let us sing ... Let us bow down low" The psalm has *two* calls   (p. 52)

FRANKEL (A WOMAN'S VOICE)

[11] *"My Resting Place"* How different are the moods expressed in this psalm! It begins in joy and ends in anger. In its opening lines, the people praise God for their deliverance; at its close, they are reminded that God once doomed their ancestors in the desert: "I swore in anger that they would never come to My Resting Place!"

If we read the opening lines with foreknowledge of its reproachful end, we might infer that the speaker's enthusiastic rhetoric—"Let   (p. 58)

I. PSALM 95

DORFF (THEOLOGY)

Psalm 95 The first part of *Kabbalat Shabbat*, a set of psalms and *L'khah Dodi*, was created by sixteenth-century kabbalist Moses Cordovero to welcome the Sabbath Bride. This idea comes from the talmudic metaphor of the Sabbath as a bride whom we welcome (B. Shab. 119a). The six psalms (Pss. 95–99 and 29) correspond to the six days of the week. *L'khah Dodi* was composed by Cordovero's brother-in-law, Shlomo Alkabetz.   (p. 53)

[1] Let us sing to Adonai; let us trumpet our rock and deliverer. [2] Let us come before Him with praise, trumpeting Him with songs. [3] For Adonai is a great God, a king greater than all other gods. [4] In his hand are the depths of the earth and the mountainous heights. [5] The sea is his—He made it! And the land was fashioned by his hands. [6] Let us bow down low, kneeling before Adonai our maker,

KIMELMAN (KABBALAH)

Kabbalat Shabbat Halakhically speaking, *Kabbalat Shabbat* denotes the onset of Shabbat and our acceptance of its obligations. In Kabbalah, it connotes welcoming Shabbat. Halakhah treats Shabbat as a day of divine sovereignty; Kabbalah sees it as a moment of divine intimacy. In Halakhah, Shabbat is king; in Kabbalah, Shabbat is bride. Since the coronation metaphor is matched by a marriage metaphor, welcoming Shabbat as bride parallels enthroning God as king.   (p. 59)

ELLENSON (MODERN LITURGIES)

Kabbalat Shabbat The opening prayers in *Kabbalat Shabbat* (from Psalm 95 to *L'khah Dodi*) originated in sixteenth-century Safed (see Koren, "The Mystical Spirituality of Safed," pp. 33–42). They are thoroughly kabbalistic. Most   (p. 55)

KUSHNER & POLEN (CHASIDISM)

Kabbalat Shabbat Hasidic literature is filled with tales of the miraculous deeds of the masters. The following such wonder-story is related in Rabbi Aaron of Karlin's *Bet Aharon*. It describes how the Baal Shem Tov once welcomed the Sabbath in a field wherein sheep grazed also. Soon the BeShT found himself surrounded by the entire flock. Bleating and crying out, as he offered his own prayers, one by one, all the sheep lifted up their front legs and stood on their hind legs like human beings.   *(p. 60)*

לְכוּ נְרַנְּנָה לַיי נָרִיעָה לְצוּר יִשְׁעֵנוּ: ²נְקַדְּמָה פָנָיו בְּתוֹדָה בִּזְמִרוֹת נָרִיעַ לוֹ: ³כִּי אֵל גָּדוֹל יי וּמֶלֶךְ גָּדוֹל עַל־כָּל־אֱלֹהִים: ⁴אֲשֶׁר בְּיָדוֹ מֶחְקְרֵי־אָרֶץ וְתוֹעֲפוֹת הָרִים לוֹ: ⁵אֲשֶׁר־לוֹ הַיָּם וְהוּא עָשָׂהוּ וְיַבֶּשֶׁת יָדָיו יָצָרוּ: ⁶בֹּאוּ נִשְׁתַּחֲוֶה וְנִכְרָעָה נִבְרְכָה לִפְנֵי־יי עֹשֵׂנוּ: ⁷כִּי הוּא אֱלֹהֵינוּ וַאֲנַחְנוּ עַם מַרְעִיתוֹ וְצֹאן יָדוֹ הַיּוֹם אִם־

LANDES (HALAKHAH)

Kabbalat Shabbat Kabbalat Shabbat is a halakhic anomaly. It is the only post-talmudic prayer service to achieve a permanent, popular, and nearly universal place in Jewish liturgy. What accounts for that widespread acceptance? Of all prayer services, it alone has no connection to services instituted by the patriarchs or to the Temple offerings (see Volume 2, *The Amidah*, pp. 5–7). If so, what religious requirement does *Kabbalat Shabbat* serve? And if it serves no   *(p. 60)*

L. HOFFMAN (HISTORY)

KABBALAT SHABBAT *BEGINS WITH THE MOST FAMOUS OF ITS THREE COMPONENTS: SIX PSALMS ANTICIPATING GOD'S ULTIMATE REIGN, AND A POEM* (L'KHAH DODI) *TO WELCOME THE SHABBAT QUEEN AND BRIDE.* L'KHAH DODI *IS INTRODUCED BY A MYSTICAL MEDITATION,* ANA B'KO'ACH.

Psalms 95 to 99 It is hard to imagine a time without phones, faxes, and even trains to take people to meetings and conventions. But none of that existed in the sixteenth century, so even with the invention of printing, it took time for *Kabbalat Shabbat* to spread beyond Safed. About half a   *(p. 62)*

J. HOFFMAN (TRANSLATION)

¹ *"Let us"* Literally, "go and…," a common Hebrew idiom used to introduce what is technically called cohortative or hortatory. (The actual cohortative verb comes next. The construction is similar to *hava nagilah*—"let us rejoice"—where *hava* introduces the cohortative *nagilah*, "let us rejoice.") The English idiom "let us…" is the obvious translation because it expresses exactly the same point as the Hebrew "go and…," but the imperative "go" in the Hebrew parallels the beginning of *L'khah Dodi*, "go forth," in a way we do not capture. This parallelism is reinforced immediately below, where this psalm (v. 2) and *L'khah Dodi* both use the   *(p. 62)*

⁷for He is our God and we are the people of his pasture, the sheep of his hand. If only you would listen to his voice! ⁸Do not be stubborn, as you were at Merivah, on the day of Massah in the wilderness ⁹when your ancestors tried Me, tested Me, though they had seen my deeds. ¹⁰For forty years I was disgusted by a generation calling them a misguided people that did not know my ways. ¹¹I swore in anger that they would never come to My Resting Place.

בְּקֹלוֹ תִשְׁמָעוּ: ⁸אַל־תַּקְשׁוּ לְבַבְכֶם כִּמְרִיבָה כְּיוֹם מַסָּה בַּמִּדְבָּר: ⁹אֲשֶׁר נִסּוּנִי אֲבוֹתֵיכֶם בְּחָנוּנִי גַּם־רָאוּ פָעֳלִי: ¹⁰אַרְבָּעִים שָׁנָה אָקוּט בְּדוֹר וָאֹמַר עַם תֹּעֵי לֵבָב הֵם וְהֵם לֹא־יָדְעוּ דְרָכָי: ¹¹אֲשֶׁר־נִשְׁבַּעְתִּי בְאַפִּי אִם־יְבֹאוּן אֶל־מְנוּחָתִי:

BRETTLER (BIBLE)

to worship, verses 1–2 above, and here. Each is followed by the impetus, or motivation, for that call, introduced by *ki,* "for...." A similar structure is found in other kingship psalms (Pss. 96, 98, 47) and the Song of the Sea (Exod. 15:21): "Sing to Adonai, for *(ki)* He has triumphed gloriously."

¹ *"Let us sing ... trumpet"* Modeled after the acclaim of the new king at his enthronement (similarly Pss. 98:4, 6) like the ritual reflected in 1 Kings 1:39–40: "They sounded the horn and all the people shouted, 'Long live King Solomon!' All the people then marched up behind him, playing on flutes and making merry till the earth was split open by the uproar."

¹ *"Rock"* A common biblical epithet for God, symbolizing strength enough to protect the psalmist; hence, "rock" and "salvation" appear together, not just here but elsewhere (e.g., Pss. 18:3, 47; 62:8).

² *"With praise* [todah] ... *songs* [z'mirot]" *Todah* is either the name of a sacrifice (see Ps. 50:23), or words of thanksgiving (Ps. 147:7). The parallelism to *z'mirot* ("songs") suggests the latter, but Psalm 116:17, "I will *sacrifice* a thank-offering [*todah*] to You and *invoke* the name of Adonai," indicates that prayers could accompany *todah* offerings.

Z'mirot may be a word play—the Hebrew root *z.m.r* in Hebrew can denote a type of song and a warrior. "Song" fits this verse; "warrior" anticipates the continuation of the psalm, which emphasizes God's power.

³ *"Greater than"* A claim of God's incomparability, like Exodus 15:11, but without denying the existence of other, less powerful deities.

⁵ *"He made it"* Our Bible begins with two creation stories: Genesis 1:1–2:4a (an exilic account by the author we call P [for "priestly"]) and Genesis 2:4b–3:24 (by an earlier author we call J [for the name of God he preferred]). The terms and concepts that Psalm 95 uses to discuss creation resemble those of the early account, so Psalm 95 may be very old.

⁷ *"Sheep of his hand"* Human kings were often depicted as shepherds—like David in our Bible, but outside the Bible, too, like Hammurabi, the famous Babylonian king from the eighteenth century B.C.E.

⁸⁻¹⁰ *"Merivah ... Massah ... forty years"* Later tradition sometimes looked back on the wilderness period as ideal (Jer. 2:2); not so here, which emphasizes Israel's sins at Merivah and Massah (Exod. 17:7, Deut. 33:8, Num. 20:1–13), as well as the forty years of wandering associated with the sin of the spies (Num. 14:33–34; 32:13).

⁹ *"Tried Me* [nisuni]*"* A play on words, connecting the etymology of Massah to the root *n.s.h,* "to try [put to the test]" (cf. Exod. 17:2).

¹¹ *"Resting Place* [m'nuchah]*"* Sometimes a technical term for the Land of Israel (e.g. Deut. 12:9) but also a possible pun with verse 9, "tested me"—because Israel tested God *(b'CHaNuNi),* they will not reach God's resting place *(m'NuCHati).*

———◆———

DORFF (THEOLOGY)

Psalms 95–99 are often called "the coronation psalms" because they picture God as sovereign of the universe and may have been used in ancient times at the New Year celebration (see Brettler, *"Kabbalat Shabbat:* A Liturgy from Psalms," pp. 21–25). According to the science of those times, nature does not automatically guarantee that one year follows another; instead, our lease on life must be renegotiated annually with the gods. That, of course, is a very dangerous time, for the gods might refuse to renew the lease. Therefore, in their new year's *(akitu)* festival, the Babylonians appointed a man condemned to death as king for the last day of the old year (with limited powers, of course), executed him at the end of the day, and then recrowned the real king on the first day of the new year. Some scholars suggest that these psalms were similarly used in ancient Israel and that the sovereignty verses recited during the blowing of the shofar in *Musaf* of Rosh Hashanah (called *malkuyot*—pronounced mahl-khu-YOHT) derives from these ancient roots.

Whether that thesis is true or not, these psalms clearly accent God's sovereignty. Cordovero chose them because on the Sabbath we acknowledge God's ownership of the world by desisting from weekday work that uses the world for our own ends.

How does desisting from work recognize God's sovereignty over the world? Ownership vests owners with the right to decide who may use their property and under what circumstances. In the biblical understanding of things, God permits us to use the world for six workdays, but not on Shabbat. Abiding weekly by this restriction recognizes God's sovereignty over the world.

Accepting God as the owner of the world we occupy is anything but grudging. On the contrary, Psalm 95, the first of these psalms, sets the tone from the very beginning: we are to "sing to Adonai [and] trumpet our rock and deliverer."

The initial letters of these six psalms have the numerical value of 430, the same as the Hebrew word *nefesh,* "soul" (Philip Birnbaum, *The Daily Prayerbook,* p. 237), reminding us that on the Sabbath a Jew gains "an extra soul" (Betz. 16a; Ta'an. 27b). One does not have to be a mystic to experience the extra energy, the sense of renewal, and the recovery of meaning and purpose that one gains each Friday night as one welcomes the Sabbath with these psalms.

[4] *"The depths of the earth … the mountainous heights"* A merism, a biblical literary device whereby two ends of a spectrum stand for themselves and everything in between. So God owns everything from the lowest to the highest—a common biblical theme. Deuteronomy 10:14, for example, says: "The heavens to their uttermost reaches belong to Adonai your God, the earth and all that is on it!"

[5] *"The sea is his"* Why does God own everything? The biblical answer is that God created everything. God owns sea and land—a merism (see above, "The depths of the earth … the mountainous heights")—because God created them both (and human beings as well).

How does creation convey ownership? Henry Ford's celebrated invention of the assembly line in 1908 divided the creation of things into parts. Rather than making objects in their entirety, people repeated one small task as a tiny part of the larger process. Goods could be made faster and more cheaply, but at the price of separating people from the things they were creating. So we stopped thinking of the makers as owners.

At the same time, we still recognize that when individuals create a complete thing, they own it. For example, artists own their paintings until and unless they decide to sell them, and authors own their books until they sign over rights to a publisher. Our sophisticated patent and copyright laws even protect intellectual property—that is, our ideas, apart from any particular object embodying them. So even though we are more used to cooperative efforts in which none or all of the makers of an object own it, we do have modern examples in which creating something—even just the idea of something—conveys ownership of it. The doctrine of monotheism implies God's claim to own the whole universe, because if God is one, no other party was involved in creation, and God alone is its sole creator and owner.

[7-8] *"For He is our God, and we are the people of his pasture … Do not be stubborn, as you were at Merivah"* We now get a different reason for worshiping God: God is not

only the creator of everything (see above, *"The sea is his"*) but also the People Israel's covenanted partner, who takes care of us.

This belief makes Judaism a theistic rather than a deistic religion. Deists believe that God is a creative force that brought the world into being. Most of the founding fathers of the United States were deists. Some deists believe also that after creating the world, God abandoned it. Eighteenth-century philosopher David Hume (1711–1776), for instance, thought that God and his world would be imperfect if God continually had to tinker with creation. Other deists, like twentieth-century rabbi and theologian Mordecai Kaplan, believe, on the contrary, that God is the creative force that surfaces in our lives every time an acorn becomes an oak tree or a person gets a good idea. Even for Kaplan, though, God is a force.

Theists believe that God has a personality: a will, emotions, and thoughts. The God depicted in the Bible, in rabbinic literature, and in the writings of most Jewish thinkers interacts with us personally, commanding us and even judging our behavior. Thus, the psalmist here warns that divine care will sustain us only *on condition* that we obey God's commandments. We dare not rebel the way the generation that left Egypt did. God's refusal to let them enter the Promised Land should serve as sufficient warning that God will punish us—as only a theistic God can—if we disobey the covenant.

——◆——

ELLENSON (MODERN LITURGIES)

nineteenth-century Reformers were partial to the pre-1492 Sefardi heritage because of its heightened achievements in philosophy and poetry; but as much as they loved this vaunted Spanish rationalism, they despised mysticism. They therefore looked askance at the Safed *Kabbalat Shabbat.*

There were other reasons, too, to exclude this Safed liturgy. Given their commitment to abbreviating the service, the Reformers regarded it as overly lengthy. Then too, its capstone prayer *L'khah Dodi* contained references to Zion and views of messianic redemption that were offensive to nineteenth-century Reform sensibilities.

Historical justification for rejecting the Safed set of prayers included its recent liturgical arrival, which denied it the aura of antiquity that the nineteenth century equated with authenticity. And, finally, the Reformers' ideal, the classical Sefardi model, had never contained it—not even in the liturgy of the Sefardi communities that went from Spain to Holland, England, and then the Americas. These communities may have adopted *L'khah Dodi* eventually, but not the psalms that led up to it.

Especially noteworthy nowadays is an innovation that opens the service even before any traditional prayers are considered. Beginning with the 1940 (newly revised) *Union Prayer Book* [UPB] (American Reform), we find the lighting of Shabbat candles in the synagogue. The inclusion of this traditional home custom in the synagogue has become a staple in American Reform prayer books, but also the 1995 British Liberal *Lev*

Chadash, the 1982 Israeli *Ha'avodah Shebalev,* and the 1996 Reconstructionist *Kol Haneshamah* (just as an option, however).

Rabbi A. Stanley Dreyfus links a synagogue ritual for candle lighting to the development of a late Friday night service:

> I assume that a candle lighting ritual was not included [earlier] because many Jews must have been uncomfortable at delaying the formal inauguration of Shabbat by means of lighting candles at 7:30 or 8:00 or even later, when the sun had set as much as two hours previously during much of the year. That the propriety of blessing candles so long after nightfall was debated, suggests that the practice of lighting them at the proper time in the home was diminishing, either because the mother felt self-conscious at reciting the Hebrew, or because the male members of the family had not yet closed their places of business.
>
> The 1895 edition of *UPB* does include under the rubric "Prayers for Private Devotion," a ritual entitled "Sanctification of the Sabbath," intended for home, not synagogue, use, apparently. It contains the text of the *Kiddush* in Hebrew and English, but, oddly, omits all reference to candle lighting. The revised edition of 1924 also includes the *Kiddush,* now quite clearly labeled, "Services in the Home." Here the editors have provided a home ritual taken verbatim from Henry Berkowitz's little volume *Sabbath Sentiments* (1898; second revised edition, 1921) which the CCAR (the Reform rabbinic body) reprinted by permission and which was very widely used in Reform households. The introduction to the ritual includes candles: "The ceremony of ushering in the Sabbath is begun by the kindling of the lights, during which a blessing is silently asked on the home and the dear ones." But the text of the traditional Hebrew blessing is not provided. The absence of the blessing in both cases may be due to the editors' not wishing to "insult" their constituency by suggesting that women lighting candles might need to read the blessing.
>
> Lighting candles at late Friday night services in the synagogue was actually tried before 1940. It appears in a 1935 paperback trial edition of the "revised" Friday Evening Service. Rabbi Dudley Weinberg *(Experimental Edition of a Commentary to the UPB, Newly Revised)* writes:
>
>> The kindling of Sabbath lights in the synagogue is one of the creative innovations of Reform Judaism. The ritual given here was composed especially for the *Union Prayer Book* (Newly Revised Edition). The privilege of reciting the meditation and the blessing over the lights in the synagogue is given to women in the congregation. This practice arises naturally from the tradition which assigns primary responsibility for the kindling of Sabbath lights in the home to women.
>
> In conformity with the custom of not identifying the authors of liturgical pieces, the name of the author of this candle lighting ritual is not given.

Nowadays, traditional *z'mirot* too, once sung only at home around the Shabbat table, are now part of *Kabbalat Shabbat.* We find, for instance, *Yah Ribon* by Israel Najara; *Yom Zeh L'yisrael* by Isaac Handali (but traditionally attributed, erroneously, to Isaac Luria); the Sefardi *D'ror Yikra*; and even *Shalom Aleikhem* as opening song choices in every single contemporary Reform and Reconstructionist liturgy, but also in the Israeli Masorti (Conservative) *Va'ani T'fillati.* (For thorough treatment of these *z'mirot,* see Volume 7, *Shabbat at Home,* pp. 23–30, 116–154.)

Other traditional prayers and readings—including *Mah Tovu* (which was included first by the Hamburg prayer books [see below, "Psalm 95 to 99"])—abound. The establishment of the State of Israel has found special liturgical expression here. Israeli poetry and song is regularly included, with *Shabbat Hamalkah* (by Chaim Nachman Bialik—see Volume 7, *Shabbat at Home*, pp. 147–154) by far the most popular addition.

The current emphasis on spirituality and the concomitant recovery of mystical and Chasidic texts are also in abundant evidence. Numerous meditations and *kavvanot* (pronounced kah-vah-NOHT, denoting meditations on prayers) are interspersed everywhere: for example, "Behold, I am ready and prepared to fulfill the command of my creator, 'And you shall observe the Sabbath'" *(Ha'avodah Shebalev)*. The influence of Rabbi Arthur Green upon the Reconstructionist Movement can be seen in the many *kavvanot* in *Kol han'shamah,* especially. Ironically, many of them—expressions of spiritual discipline—are adapted from the writings of the arch-rationalist Mordecai Kaplan, founder of Reconstructionism. One can only imagine how Rabbi Kaplan himself would have viewed such an adaptation of his work!

This spiritual trend can also be seen in the decision the authors of *Kol han'shamah* made to include selections from *Shir Hashirim* in their *Kabbalat Shabbat* liturgy. The Reconstructionist authors indicate that they have appropriated the kabbalistic view of Song of Songs as "a love poem of the union between male and female elements of divinity."

This newfound appreciation of the mystical elements of the tradition by contemporary authors of liberal prayer books—so at loggerheads with the approach taken by their nineteenth-century forebears—can be seen in other ways as well. *Y'did Nefesh* by Elazar Azikri of Safed is printed as an opening hymn in *Kol han'shamah, Ha'avodah Shebalev,* the 2001 German *Seder Hatefillot, Va'ani T'fillati,* and the 1998 Conservative *Sim Shalom.* (For *Y'did Nefesh,* see Volume 7, *Shabbat at Home,* pp. 135–146.) Newer liberal prayer books will undoubtedly contain this hymn as well. Indeed, preliminary galleys of *Mishkan T'fillah,* the newest proposed Siddur of American Reform Judaism, does incorporate it.

Psalms 95 to 99 The two formative Hamburg Temple Prayer Books of 1819 and 1845 went farthest by simply omitting all the psalms and replacing them with the standard introduction to Shabbat morning liturgy, *Mah Tovu* (but in German). Abraham Geiger wrote two Siddurim: a relatively traditional version (intended to be inclusive of the broad swath of German Jewry) in 1854, and a more strictly ideological Reform version in 1870. The 1854 Siddur shortened the service but retained the first and last psalms (Psalms 95 and 29) as symbols of the whole. In 1870, however, he adopted the Hamburg Reform solution: opening with *Mah Tovu* and a German reading (though he still retained Psalm 29 as a vestige of those the kabbalists had used).

In America, the titular founder of Reform, Isaac Mayer Wise, retained Psalms 95–99, but his more radical opponent from Baltimore, David Einhorn, followed the pattern of Hamburg. Quite cleverly, the 1895 *Union Prayer Book* (which followed these two founding liturgies) moves Psalm 92 (the psalm for the Sabbath) from its customary place farther into the service and features it as an introduction; it thereby begins with a traditional psalm from the service, but not the kabbalistic ones. It then carefully strings together selected snippets from Psalms 95–99, organized into a responsive reading in English on such favored themes as divine creation and justice. It labels all of this *l'khu n'ran'nah* (the first words and traditional title for the normal introductory Psalm 95) but in unpointed Hebrew, that only traditionalists who cared would be likely to recognize. By the 1940 newly revised version, unpointed titles like this one were gone.

Interestingly, the *Kabbalat Shabbat* service contained in the 1885 *Abodath Israel* (*AI*) by Rabbis Benjamin Szold and Marcus Jastrow, among the founders of Conservative Judaism in America, begins with *Mah Tovu* as well. *AI* demonstrates how much even these more traditionalist Reformers in America shared the viewpoints of their Reform colleagues.

Gates of Prayer (American Reform, 1975) displays a more general return to tradition by including all six introductory psalms, at least in its "traditional" service option (Service I). *Ha'avodah Shebalev* (Israeli Reform) opens with a choice of a meditation or (following Hamburg) *Mah Tovu,* but it then includes all of the traditional psalms. The 2001 German Reform *Seder* does likewise.

FRANKEL (A WOMAN'S VOICE)

us trumpet" God as the "a king greater than all other gods," creator of the natural world, caring shepherd of Israel—is designed expressly to placate God's wrath. Perhaps the psalmist strives to assure God that this generation, unlike the rebellious and ungrateful rabble that came out of Egypt, is faithful and reverent.

But it is not only God who needs to be convinced of Israel's change of heart and conduct in this generation. In the middle of verse 7, a voice interrupts the collective song of praise with a stern admonition: "If only you would listen to his voice!" Flattering words alone, warns this speaker, will not satisfy God's demands. To merit God's "resting place" requires that the people "know [God's] ways" (v. 10) and observe them, instead of being stubborn and provocative like the generation in the desert.

Surely Shabbat is God's true "resting place"! As we welcome it we are reminded that prayer alone will not bring us there; we must also seek God's ways and know them.

KIMELMAN (KABBALAH)

The ceremony for welcoming Shabbat developed in Safed, where kabbalists promoted Shabbat as a two-stage event: the day of royal nuptials and of coronation. The *Zohar* had understood this as a one-stage event. In Safed, however, Solomon Alkabetz (the author of *L'khah Dodi*) and his disciple and brother-in-law, Moses Cordovero, understood it as a two-stage affair: first, the marriage ceremony, and second, the confirming conjugal act. This unification takes place both humanly and sefirotically.

There were actually two separate customs regarding *Kabbalat Shabbat*: that of Isaac Luria and that of Alkabetz and Cordovero. Of the six introductory psalms, Luria said only Psalm 29. Alkabetz and Cordovero may have added Psalms 95–99. Luria himself did not say *L'khah Dodi*; Alkabetz and Cordovero probably did. Luria went out to the field to welcome Shabbat; Alkabetz and Cordovero did not. No single group went out into the fields singing *L'khah Dodi*.

In any event, *Kabbalat Shabbat*, as we now know it, comprises a unit of six psalms (95–99, and 29), *L'khah Dodi*, and two more psalms (92–93). Units of six psalms characterize also the morning *P'sukei D'zimrah* (Psalms 145–150) and the holiday *Hallel* (Psalms 113–118). (See Volume 3, *P'sukei D'zimrah—Morning Psalms*, pp. 107–146.) Still, *Kabbalat Shabbat* is unique: elsewhere, the psalms (as biblical material) are bracketed by blessings. Similarly, the reading of the Torah, *Haftarah*, and recitation of the *Sh'ma* are all bracketed with blessings. In contrast, the bracketing of *L'khah Dodi*, with psalms no less, underscores its role as the centerpiece of the service.

Psalm 95 In kabbalistic thought, the opening six psalms (95–99, 29) correspond to the six days of the week, each representing a day of creation. While reciting the psalms, one contemplates the corresponding day of the week, reflecting on ways to improve it. In so repairing each day, one's fragmented soul is made whole, a process known as *tikkun hanefesh* (pronounced tee-KOON hah-NEH-fehsh). Once whole, it can serve as a receptacle for an additional Shabbat soul, the *n'shamah y'teirah* (pronounced n'-shah-MAH y'-tay-RAH). (On this extra soul, see Volume 7, *Shabbat at Home*, pp. 167–178.) Appropriately, the numerical value of the initial letters of the six psalms is 430, the same as the numerical value of *nefesh*; and the total number of words is 702, the numerical value of *Shabbat*.

[1] *"Let us sing to Adonai* [l'khu n'ran'nah]" Literally, "Go, let us sing…." Understood by mystics as "go to *the synagogues*" in order to sing to Adonai. The first words (*l'khu n'ran'nah*) evoke the words of the first stanza of *L'khah Dodi*, *l'khu v'nelkhah* ("Let us go"), to make the point that by going to Shabbat we go to that aspect of God which, like Shabbat, is identified with the *sefirah* of *Malkhut*.

From the Kabbalists of Safed

Kushner & Polen (Chasidism)

And this, claims the legend, was because the prayers of such a holy person are so pure that they sanctify even nearby creatures and raise each soul to its source on high. In this way, even nearby animals sensed the Baal Shem's elevation and raised themselves. Rabbi Israel of Ryzhin explained it this way: Through the fervor and intensity of his prayer, the BeShT went all the way back to Adam, even before Adam's sin, and from that place of primal purity, he was able to mend the world. And, from such a place, even sheep could be brought to a consciousness of their creator. Such a return to Eden-like innocence is the legacy of each Jew as he or she welcomes the seventh day.

[6] *"Let us bow down low, kneeling* [bo'u nishtachaveh v'nivr'kha] *before Adonai our maker"* Rabbi Yehuda Aryeh Lieb of Ger (*Sefat Emet* on Psalms) offers two related observations on the core meaning of blessing *(b'rakhah)*. He begins by inquiring why there are three such apparently redundant verbs in Psalm 95:6: (1) *bo'u* ("come"), (2) *nishtachaveh* ("let us bow down"), and (3) *nivr'khah* ("kneeling"). He notes that, according to *Midrash Tanchuma,* these three verbs correspond to the three daily worship services: *Shacharit* (morning), *Minchah* (afternoon), and *Ma'ariv* (evening). The ultimate purpose of all religious behavior is to always re-attach ourselves to our heavenly root. But this fusion is a gradual, step-by-step process. In the morning (as in childhood), it begins with bowing down *(nishtachaveh)* as a kind of acknowledgment of God for the gift of life at the start of each new day. In the afternoon (as in adulthood), we progress to an act of submission to the service of God—that is, kneeling *(nivr'khah)*. Finally, by evening (as in the ripening of our years), we "come" *(bo'u)* to surrender our soul to its divine source. But this *nivr'khah* is from the same root as *b'rakhah* (blessing)—b.r.kh. Blessing, then, attains its fullness only as we progress through the years.

But he further notes that *nivr'khah* does not so much mean to kneel as it does actually to graft a branch back onto a tree. And so, on Friday evening, this yearning is the most intense because we hope to graft ourselves back onto our heavenly tree. Just this is the source of all blessing: to be grafted again back into the trunk of the heavenly tree.

———◆———

Landes (Halakhah)

religious requirement, then why is it even allowed, much less exalted?

For that matter, it is not even clear when *Kabbalat Shabbat* fully coalesced. The proper place of *Bameh Madlikin* is hotly contested by authorities, some putting it before *Kabbalat Shabbat,* others at the end of *Kabbalat Shabbat* but before *Ma'ariv,* and still others after *Ma'ariv* altogether (see below, "What may we use [2]"). And as for the six introductory psalms, Jacob Emden (Ya'avetz, 1697–1776, Altona, Germany) tells us *(Siddur Bet Ya'akov)* that his father, the great Chakham Tzvi, recited only the sixth

60

(Psalm 29). Contemporary halakhic guidebooks still describe them as just a custom. Its constituent parts (psalms, liturgical poetry, and Mishnah study) are unobjectionable, however, so it seems that *Kabbalat Shabbat* simply "slipped in" as a matter of *r'shut,* "optional" recitation.

Nonetheless, once formulated, *Kabbalat Shabbat* has halakhic import, as we see from the startling prohibition by the Gra of reciting *Kabbalat Shabbat* as a community (*b'tsibbur*), that is, in a *minyan* (see the instructions in *Siddur Eizor Eliyahu al pi Nusach HaGra* [based on the classic *Ma'aseh Rav,* the account of the Gra's religious practices, #116]). The reason seems clear enough. The Gra prohibits saying any psalms *b'tsibbur* unless they are preceded by a proper blessing. (As another example, he also prohibits reciting Psalm 30 before *Barukh she'amar,* the blessing that opens *P'sukei D'zimrah* and that follows Psalm 30 in common usage [See Volume 5, *Birkhot Hashachar—Morning Blessings,* pp. 28–34.]) For the Gra, reciting psalms in a *minyan* is a fulfillment of the Torah directive of Deuteronomy 10:21: "He is your praise and He is your God" (*hu t'hilat'kha v'hu e-lohekha*). This evidently means that, in effect, "Through 'your praise' (*t'hilat'kha*), you accept Adonai as 'your God' *(e-lohekha).*" Like all other *mitzvot,* this act therefore necessitates a blessing. And *Kabbalat Shabbat* has no such blessing. Precisely what allowed *Kabbalat Shabbat* to "slip into" the liturgy—the fact that it is merely a collection of psalms and a poem with no halakhically required blessing—is what led the Gra to prohibit its communal recitation.

The Gra stands alone in his opposition. Everyone else embraces the "custom," with some attempting to find a precedent for it. Thus, R. Shlomo Tzvi Schick of Kortzag (*Sefer Takanot Ut'filot, Siddur Rashban,* 1890) notes that the Talmud (Shab. 35b) reports shofar blasts being spaced so as to signal people to desist from their weekday activities and finalize preparations for Shabbat, and he connects the six psalms of *Kabbalat Shabbat* (Psalms 95–99, 29)—instituted (he claims) by the Geonim—to those blasts. According to this view, *Kabbalat Shabbat* is a time we enter into Shabbat, in contrast to the *Shulchan Arukh,* which places the communal time for fully accepting the Sabbath strictures later: at *Bar'khu,* the beginning of *Ma'ariv.* With the solidifying of *Kabbalat Shabbat* as a normative liturgical practice, it did indeed become the potential benchmark for Sabbath acceptance. Thus, authorities discuss exactly when within *Kabbalat Shabbat* that actually happens: relatively late, at Psalm 92 (*mizmor shir l'yom hashabbat* = "A musical psalm for the Sabbath day") or earlier. If earlier, is it (1) the end of *L'khah Dodi,* when we say *Bo'i khallah, bo'i khallah* ("Come forth O bride, come forth O bride"); (2) at the beginning of that poem; or even (3) at Psalm 95, *L'khu n'ran'nah* ("Let us sing to Adonai") which begins the service. (See Mishnah Berurah 261:31 and Bi'ur Halakhah 263, both by Israel Meir Hakohen Kagan, Poland, early twentieth century.)

The predominant Ashkenazi custom is not to recite the entire service of *Kabbalat Shabbat* when Friday is a Yom Tov, in order not to "embarrass the Yom Tov" by showing an eagerness to leave it for Shabbat. On such occasions, the service begins with Psalm 92 (*mizmor shir l'yom hashabbat* = "A musical psalm for the Sabbath day"), then *Kaddish* and then *Bar'khu* of *Ma'ariv*. The Sefardi custom is to do the same but to precede it with just the last of the six psalms prior, Psalm 29 (*mizmor l'david* = "David's psalm"), *Ana B'ko'ach* (the introduction to *L'khah Dodi*), and then only the first, third, and last stanzas of *L'khah Dodi*.

———◆———

L. HOFFMAN (HISTORY)

century later (1591), an important and relatively encyclopedic Polish author on ritual, Moses Mos (*Mateh Moshe*), still seems ignorant of it. Perhaps a decade or two later, German pietist Joseph Yuspa Hahn (1570–1637) says that *Kabbalat Shabbat* has arrived only months before and calls it "a nice custom"—not much different from our saying we have recently discovered (and like) Shlomo Carlebach's *Pitchu Li* or Debbie Friedman's *Mi Sheberakh* melodies.

By the eighteenth century, *Kabbalat Shabbat* had become standard in Ashkenaz, as had an outline of its origins. Jacob Emden (1697–1776, the *YaBeTZ*—from *Ya'akov Ben TZvi*), influential halakhist and kabbalist himself, was learned not just in matters Jewish but also in secular literature, which he could read in German, Dutch, and Latin. "In these lands," he testifies, "we begin with Psalm 95, and say six psalms in all (95 to 99 and 29), corresponding to the six days of the week, according to Moses Cordovero, the student and brother-in-law of Solomon ben Moses Alkabetz."

Today, these psalms (and what follows up to the end of *L'khah Dodi*) are said, to some degree, in most places, but Psalms 95–99 are excluded from the classic Spanish-Portuguese rite, which begins only with Psalm 29.

———◆———

J. HOFFMAN (TRANSLATION)

word "face" as part of a Hebrew idiom (see below, "Him," and "Shabbat's reception has arrived").

[1] *"Sing"* Others, "sing joyously," "exult," "laud," "shout for joy," etc. Hebrew has a handful of verbs that all generally refer to some aspect of celebrating. (But sometimes some of these verbs—in Lamentations, for example—seem to have negative implications.) Teasing apart the various nuances of the Hebrew verbs is all but impossible, and, in any event, we do not have exact English words to capture the Hebrew. Here and below we chose single verbs in English (rather than expressions) to try to match the general rhythm of the Hebrew, recognizing that we have probably not captured the exact meanings.

[1] *"Trumpet"* Others use different verbs or expressions, from "raise a shout" to "make a joyful noise." The root from which the verb here comes may have connotations of

sounding trumpets, perhaps even in war, so we somewhat arbitrarily choose the verb "trumpet" here. We would prefer a more general term for making joyous noise, but in English all the likely candidates seem to have negative connotations: "shout," "bellow," "roar," "clamor," "screech," etc.

[1] *"Rock and deliverer"* Literally, "our delivering rock" or "rock of our salvation." "Rock and deliverer," as in *JPS,* seems more poetic.

[2] *"Him"* Literally, "his face," a fact worth mentioning only because, as already noted (see above, "Let us"), the use of "face" here reinforces the parallel with *L'khah Dodi.*

[2] *"Praise"* The Hebrew is *todah,* used later by the Rabbis to mean "grateful acknowledgment" (see Volume 2, *The Amidah,* p. 42). We translate the word as it was probably understood in its original biblical context.

[2] *"Songs"* The Hebrew here (*z'mirot* from *z.m.r*) is not from the same root *(r.n.n)* as "sing" above. In this case, both our lack of vocabulary in English and our lack of specific knowledge about ancient music hamper our translation.

[3] *"A great God"* Strict adherence to the general principles of capitalization would require "a great god" here, because in English only proper nouns get capitalized, and proper nouns do not take "a" or "an." Nonetheless, we follow the common (though perhaps misleading) convention of capitalizing "God" here.

[3] *"All other gods"* Perhaps reflecting the vagaries of Hebrew idioms, or perhaps reflecting a slightly less logically coherent approach than our modern English, Hebrew commonly uses "all" where we need "all other." In this case, it is logically impossible for God to be greater than "all gods," which is why English requires "all other."

[4] *"Hand"* The more common expression, "in his hands," is probably wrong, because "in his hands" expresses general control in a way that the Hebrew probably did not.

[4] *"Depths"* More literally, "ends," but in light of the apparent contrast with "heights" that follows, "depths" seems more appropriate.

[4] *"And the mountainous heights"* Literally, "and the heights of the mountains are his." We have near but not perfect syntactic parallelism between this Hebrew line and the last, which we capture in English by changing "heights of the mountains" into "mountainous heights," thus creating near but not perfect syntactic parallelism in English, too. But in so doing we miss the segue into the next line, where we would have "...are his" leading into "The sea is his...."

[6] *"Let us"* Unlike verse 1, above, the Hebrew here has "come" instead of "go" for the cohortative "let us." It is not clear how these two expressions ("come..." and "go...") may have differed in Hebrew.

[6] *"Bow down low, kneeling"* The Hebrew has three verbs in a row, all of which more

or less mean "bow down."

[7] *"People of his pasture, the sheep of his hand"* This seems to be an expansion of the common biblical imagery that portrays the People Israel as the sheep of God's pasture. Here Israel is not the "sheep of the pasture" but the "people of the pasture" and the "sheep of his hand."

[8] *"Merivah, on the day of Massah"* "Merivah" (from the root "to quarrel") and "Massah" (from the root "to test" or "to try") are the same place when they are first mentioned together in Exodus 17:7. They may also be the same place in Deuteronomy 33:8. The account in Numbers 20:1–13 mentions "waters of Merivah" without mention of Massah. In the Exodus account, the Israelites wondered aloud, "Is God with us or not?" The place names thus represent Israel's reluctance to accept God.

[10] *"I was disgusted by"* Others, "I was provoked by" and "I hated." The Hebrew verb here *(akut)* doesn't appear often enough for us to know its exact meaning.

[10] *"A generation"* Commonly translated "this generation" or "that generation," but the Hebrew is the less specific "a generation." Perhaps we have misunderstood the whole Hebrew line, and it should be "It was forty years…. I was disgusted by a generation, calling them a misguided people."

[10] *"Calling them a misguided people that did not know my ways"* Literally: "saying, 'a misguided people are they; they did not know my ways.'" The use of the word "they" to end the first phrase and then to start the second is typical biblical "chiasmus" (or "chiasm"), from the Latinized version of the Greek *chiasma,* "crossing," as in the Greek letter *chi,* X. ("Chiasm" is "an inverted relationship between syntactic elements of parallel phrases.") But because "misguided people are they" sounds antiquated, we give up on capturing the chiasmus here.

The word for "misguided" comes from the image of "hard-hearted," but we don't translate the phrase literally because the word "heart" in ancient Hebrew functioned completely differently from our modern word "heart." (See J. Hoffman, "Mind and body and strength," Volume 1, *The Sh'ma and Its Blessings,* p. 100, for a lengthier explanation.)

[11] *"My Resting Place"* In this context, God's "resting place" is almost certainly Israel or Jerusalem. "My Resting Place" seems to have functioned as an epithet like "the Promised Land" or "The Holy Land."

II. Psalm 96

¹Sing a new song to Adonai! Sing to Adonai, all the earth! ²Sing to Adonai! Praise his name! Proclaim his victory every day. ³Recount his glory among the nations, his wonders among all peoples. ⁴For Adonai is great and highly praised, more revered than all other gods, ⁵for all of the other nations' gods are false, but Adonai made the sky.

⁶Majesty and glory are arrayed before Him, strength and splendor in his temple. ⁷To Adonai, you families of various peoples, to Adonai ascribe honor and might! ⁸To Adonai ascribe the honor of his name! Bring an offering and enter his courts. ⁹Bow down to Adonai in holy beauty. Tremble before Him, all the earth! ¹⁰Tell the nations Adonai is king. Let the world be firm, so that it not falter. He judges the peoples with equity. ¹¹Let the heavens be glad and let the earth rejoice. Let the sea thunder along with all that fills it ¹²and let the field exult along with all that is in it. Then all the trees of the forest will sing ¹³before Adonai, for He comes to judge the earth. He will judge the earth justly, and its peoples faithfully.

¹שִׁירוּ לַיָי שִׁיר חָדָשׁ שִׁירוּ לַיָי
כָל־הָאָרֶץ: ²שִׁירוּ לַיָי בָּרֲכוּ
שְׁמוֹ בַּשְּׂרוּ מִיוֹם־לְיוֹם יְשׁוּעָתוֹ: ³סַפְּרוּ
בַגּוֹיִם כְּבוֹדוֹ בְּכָל־הָעַמִּים נִפְלְאוֹתָיו:
⁴כִּי גָדוֹל יְיָ וּמְהֻלָּל מְאֹד נוֹרָא הוּא
עַל־כָּל־אֱלֹהִים: ⁵כִּי כָּל־אֱלֹהֵי הָעַמִּים
אֱלִילִים וַיָי שָׁמַיִם עָשָׂה:

⁶הוֹד־וְהָדָר לְפָנָיו עֹז וְתִפְאֶרֶת
בְּמִקְדָּשׁוֹ: ⁷הָבוּ לַיָי מִשְׁפְּחוֹת עַמִּים
הָבוּ לַיָי כָּבוֹד וָעֹז: ⁸הָבוּ לַיָי כְּבוֹד
שְׁמוֹ שְׂאוּ־מִנְחָה וּבֹאוּ לְחַצְרוֹתָיו:
⁹הִשְׁתַּחֲווּ לַיָי בְּהַדְרַת־קֹדֶשׁ חִילוּ מִפָּנָיו
כָל־הָאָרֶץ: ¹⁰אִמְרוּ בַגּוֹיִם יְיָ מָלָךְ אַף־
תִּכּוֹן תֵּבֵל בַּל־תִּמּוֹט יָדִין עַמִּים
בְּמֵישָׁרִים: ¹¹יִשְׂמְחוּ הַשָּׁמַיִם וְתָגֵל
הָאָרֶץ יִרְעַם הַיָּם וּמְלֹאוֹ: ¹²יַעֲלֹז שָׂדַי
וְכָל־אֲשֶׁר־בּוֹ אָז יְרַנְּנוּ כָּל־עֲצֵי־יָעַר:
¹³לִפְנֵי יְיָ כִּי בָא כִּי בָא לִשְׁפֹּט הָאָרֶץ
יִשְׁפֹּט־תֵּבֵל בְּצֶדֶק וְעַמִּים בֶּאֱמוּנָתוֹ:

BRETTLER (BIBLE)

Psalm 96 A kingship psalm like the previous one, opening with a call to worship, which is then repeated (vv. 1, 7), and emphasizing God's role as creator. But this psalm also emphasizes God as judge (cf. Ps. 94) and is universalistic, demanding that all nations acknowledge God (vv. 1, 7).

A variant of this psalm (1 Chr. 16:23–33) appears in connection with the installation of the ark in Jerusalem. The Greek translation (the Septuagint) introduces Psalm 96 with a similar idea, "when the house was being rebuilt after the captivity." The psalm may therefore be describing God actually "coming" (v. 13) to "his Temple" (v. 6).

Many kingship psalms *(p. 68)*

DORFF (THEOLOGY)

[2] *"Proclaim his victory* [y'shu'ato] *every day"* Although the purely biblical context of the psalm allows for the translation of *y'shu'ato* as "victory," Jewish tradition prefers the larger context of human affairs in which the best way to think of *y'shu'ato* *(p. 69)*

FRANKEL (A WOMAN'S VOICE)

[1] *"New song"* What is this "new song" *(shir chadash)* we are called upon to sing to God? In this remarkably universalist psalm, the human, earthly, and heavenly worlds are all entreated to extol and worship God. In the span of thirteen short verses, the *(p. 72)*

GRAY (OUR TALMUDIC HERITAGE)

[1] *"Sing"* The Hebrew *shiru* ("Sing!") occurs three times in these two verses. The talmudic sage R. Abbahu (third century C.E.) related them to the three daily prayer services. The first *shiru* ("Sing a new [*chadash*] song to Adonai") corresponds to the *Shacharit* (morning) service, where we praise God for renewing (*m'chadesh,* from *ch.d.sh,* the same root as *chadash*) the work of creation. The second *shiru* ("Sing ... all the earth") corresponds to the *Minchah* (afternoon) service, which *(p. 72)*

II. PSALM 96

[1] Sing a new song to Adonai! Sing to Adonai, all the earth! [2] Sing to Adonai! Praise his name! Proclaim his victory every day. [3] Recount his glory among the nations, his wonders among all peoples. [4] For Adonai is great and highly praised, more revered than all other gods, [5] for all of the other nations' gods are false, but Adonai made the sky.

[6] Majesty and glory are arrayed before Him, strength

KIMELMAN (KABBALAH)

[1] *"Sing a new song to Adonai"* Since Psalms 96 and 98 begin "Sing a new song to Adonai," and Psalms 97 and 99 begin with "Adonai is king," the four psalms together form the poetic pattern *abab.* By such repetition the worshiper realizes that *Kabbalat Shabbat* is the new song to Adonai as king.

KUSHNER & POLEN (CHASIDISM)

[6] *"Majesty and glory are arrayed before Him"* Rabbi Levi Yitzhak of Berdichev (*K'dushat Levi*) notes that the Hebrew *hadar* ("majesty") means "to return" in Aramaic. Now, if an earthly king were to give someone a garment as a gift, to return it would be insulting and unseemly. Nevertheless, God gives us *khiyyut* ("vitality, life force"), and when we bring that vitality into our *d'vekut* (our yearning to cleave to the Holy One), this is effectively returning it to God. But not only is God   *(p. 72)*

שִׁירוּ לַיְיָ שִׁיר חָדָשׁ שִׁירוּ לַיְיָ כָּל־הָאָרֶץ: [2]שִׁירוּ לַיְיָ
בָּרְכוּ שְׁמוֹ בַּשְּׂרוּ מִיּוֹם־לְיוֹם יְשׁוּעָתוֹ: [3]סַפְּרוּ בַגּוֹיִם
כְּבוֹדוֹ בְּכָל־הָעַמִּים נִפְלְאוֹתָיו: [4]כִּי גָדוֹל יְיָ וּמְהֻלָּל
מְאֹד נוֹרָא הוּא עַל־כָּל־אֱלֹהִים: [5]כִּי כָּל־אֱלֹהֵי הָעַמִּים
וַיְיָ שָׁמַיִם עָשָׂה:

[6]הוֹד־וְהָדָר לְפָנָיו עֹז וְתִפְאֶרֶת בְּמִקְדָּשׁוֹ: [7]הָבוּ לַיְיָ

L. HOFFMAN (HISTORY)

[1] *"Sing a new song"* Rashi thinks the subject is a messianic song yet to be sung, when God "will judge the earth justly" (v. 13). ReDaK (David Kimchi, 1160?–1235?) draws the same lesson from the fact that the Hebrew here for "song" is *shir* (masculine), not the more usual form, *shirah* (feminine). Less palatable to us than his grammatical observation is his logic: "The feminine is weak," corresponding to the weak and temporary nature of whatever songs of joy Jews have been   *(p. 73)*

J. HOFFMAN (TRANSLATION)

Psalm 96 Psalm 96 is repeated in slightly altered form in Chronicles 16, which appears elsewhere in the liturgy (see Volume 3, *P'sukei D'zimrah* [Morning Psalms], p. 78).

[1] *"Sing a new song to Adonai"* Others, "sing to Adonai a new song," but that word order sounds stilted. However, the phrase "sing to Adonai" appears three times at the beginning of this psalm, a pattern that our translation partially masks.

[1] *"All the earth"* The Hebrew makes it clear that "all the earth" is being addressed directly and commanded to sing. Something like "sing to Adonai, O all of earth" might make the point more clearly, but at the expense of introducing archaic language. More importantly, the verb in Hebrew is plural. Hebrew often uses a plural verb with a singular subject to refer to the people who live somewhere, as in "all of Egypt are …" or "all of Israel are…." Here we have "all of the earth." Perhaps the intent was "all (people) who live on earth," but it may also have been "all (creatures) who live on earth, including people," or "all things and creatures (trees, mountains, animals, people, etc.) on earth." The last possibility is particularly likely in light of the many passages in Psalms that specifically address physical attributes of the world, as, for example, the trees and so forth. Our   *(p. 73)*

and splendor in his temple. [7]To Adonai, you families of various peoples, to Adonai ascribe honor and might! [8]To Adonai ascribe the honor of his name! Bring an offering and enter his courts. [9]Bow down to Adonai in holy beauty. Tremble before Him, all the earth! [10]Tell the nations Adonai is king. Let the world be firm, so that it not falter. He judges the peoples with equity. [11]Let the heavens be glad and let the earth rejoice. Let the sea thunder along with all that fills it [12]and let the field exult along with all that is in it. Then all the trees of the forest will sing [13]before Adonai, for He comes to judge the earth. He will judge the earth justly, and its peoples faithfully.

מִשְׁפְּחוֹת עַמִּים הָבוּ לַיָי כָּבוֹד וָעֹז: [7]הָבוּ לַיָי כְּבוֹד שְׁמוֹ שְׂאוּ־מִנְחָה וּבֹאוּ לְחַצְרוֹתָיו: [9]הִשְׁתַּחֲווּ לַיָי בְּהַדְרַת־קֹדֶשׁ חִילוּ מִפָּנָיו כָּל־הָאָרֶץ: [10]אִמְרוּ בַגּוֹיִם יָי מָלָךְ אַף־תִּכּוֹן תֵּבֵל בַּל־תִּמּוֹט יָדִין עַמִּים בְּמֵישָׁרִים: [11]יִשְׂמְחוּ הַשָּׁמַיִם וְתָגֵל הָאָרֶץ יִרְעַם הַיָּם וּמְלֹאוֹ: [12]יַעֲלֹז שָׂדַי וְכָל־אֲשֶׁר־בּוֹ אָז יְרַנְּנוּ כָּל־עֲצֵי־יָעַר: [13]לִפְנֵי יָי כִּי בָא כִּי בָא לִשְׁפֹּט הָאָרֶץ יִשְׁפֹּט־תֵּבֵל בְּצֶדֶק וְעַמִּים בֶּאֱמוּנָתוֹ:

BRETTLER (BIBLE)

(this one included) are similar to Deutero-Isaiah, the anonymous exilic prophet who penned Isaiah 40ff., but it is hard to know which source came first. Other instances include Psalm 98:1, "His holy arm has won him victory"—similar to Isa. 52:10, "Adonai will bare His holy arm ... and the very ends of earth shall see the victory of our God."

[1] *"New song"* But what "new song": the psalm as a whole, or just the end of verse 10, "Adonai is king"? This psalm incorporates many elements of Psalms 29 and 96, so it might be called "new" because it updates the other two.

[6] *"Majesty and glory ... strength"* These are typical royal attributes (Pss. 21:6; 45:4), so they apply to God as king and are especially evident when God is at "his Temple." These attributes may also be personifications of semi-deities or ministering angels.

[9] *"All* [kol] *the earth"* The universalism of the psalm is again emphasized as "all *(kol)* the land" fears God. *Kol,* "all," appears seven times throughout the psalm, emphasizing God's great power in many contexts.

[10] *"Tell the nations Adonai is king. Let the world be firm, so that it not falter"* This is the only instance where "Adonai is king" appears in the middle of a psalm, not at the beginning! It is what we are to "tell the nations." But are we also supposed to tell them, "Let the world be firm, so that it not falter"? Perhaps we are supposed to "tell the nations" everything to the end of the psalm, in which case, "Adonai is king" really does begin a psalm—a psalm within a psalm! The nations get told two main entailments of "Adonai is king." He is creator and (last verse) judge, accomplishing both superlatively by creating a permanent, "totter-proof" world with just laws.

[11, 12] *"Let the heavens be glad ... the earth rejoice ... the sea thunder ... the field exult"* The whole universe emulates the populace gathered for the coronation: rejoicing loudly (see above, "Let us sing ... trumpet"). The progression from humanity to nature is facilitated by that fact that *ha'arets* (v. 9), like "the land," may refer to both the land and its inhabitants. The inhabitants ("the nations" of verse 10) come first; then come the heavens, and then earth, sea, field, and trees (see below, "Let the sea thunder ... the rivers clap their hands").

[13] *"He comes* [ki va]" The verb "comes" *(va)* may mean "is coming," like "Aunt Jenny is coming to visit tomorrow," that is, an event in the near future, or "has come," a completed action. If the latter, it may refer to the actual act of bringing the ark into the Temple.

[13] *"Judge the earth justly"* The end of the verse returns to the God's kingship as announced in verse 10. Human kings did not typically mete out justice fairly, so these psalms announce God's arrival as the ideal: a divine royal judge, for Israel and the entire world.

◆

DORFF (THEOLOGY)

is "his salvation," meaning actual saving. But what does God save us from?

In Christianity, Jesus saves people from sin and its punishment. The Jewish tradition never believed we could be saved from sin, for that would rob us of free will and our ability to choose right over wrong, and we would no longer be human. But we are morally imperfect, so three times each day, in the daily *Amidah,* we ask God for forgiveness.

From what, then, does God's salvation save us from? The Hebrew word is used repeatedly in the psalms to describe God extricating people from bad situations, including human enemies and illness. Thus, the psalmist here urges us to thank God "every day" for rescuing us from real and potential attackers, whether human, bacterial, or anything else. Certainly now that we know how the body's immune system saves us minute by minute from disease-carrying microbes, we have new and powerful evidence that we should, in the words of the *Amidah,* thank God daily "for your miracles that are with us on each day" (see Volume 2, *The Amidah,* pp. 164, 166).

[3] *"Recount his glory among the nations"* While other ancient peoples believed the gods had authority only over the nation that worshiped them, Israel recognized a single universal God with authority over all. Therefore (v. 10) "Tell the nations Adonai is king!" Nations who worship the sun, moon, and stars as their idols should know that "Adonai made the sky" and all that we see in it (v. 5) and so is properly "revered."

[4] *"More revered than all other gods"* The biblical books that we call the Former Prophets *(n'vi'im rishonim)*—Joshua, Judges, 1 and 2 Samuel, 1 and 2 Kings—regularly condemn the ancient Israelite practice of returning to the idolatrous worship of the surrounding nations. Thus, biblical religion—the religion of the authors of the biblical books—differs radically from Israelite religion, the religion actually practiced by many of our ancestors. (This is not so different from modern times, where rabbis' understanding and practice of Judaism often differ considerably from those of lay Jews—although hopefully no Jew is practicing idolatry!)

Even within biblical religion, however, it is not clear whether Judaism in its early stages was monotheistic or henotheistic. Monotheism is the belief that only one god exists. Henotheism is the belief in many gods, with one superior to the rest. In passages like this (and the famous verse from Exodus 15 used in our liturgy, "Who is like You among the gods, Adonai"), does the author mean that other gods exist but Israel's God is superior (henotheism), or that Israel's God is the only one and therefore superior to what other nations merely *think* are gods? It is hard to tell. What is clear, though, is that later Jewish tradition was staunchly monotheistic.

[10–13] *"He judges the people with equity … will judge the earth justly, and its peoples faithfully"* We moderns take for granted that God is moral and demands morality of us, but historically and philosophically that is not nearly as simple as it may at first seem.

Historically, the gods of the ancient world were powerful but not just. Greek and Roman myths about the gods are probably the most well known, but what was true of their gods was true of most others'. You had better obey the gods, for they could do you harm; you at least needed to find one god to defend you against other gods who might be angry with you. Not justice, but pitting one divine power against another was the name of the game.

It was the Jews who gave us the idea that God was not only powerful but just—an idea repeated regularly in *Kabbalat Shabbat:* "Righteousness and justice form the base of his [God's] throne" (Ps. 97:2); "The sky proclaims his righteousness" (Ps. 97:6); "He will judge the earth justly, and its peoples equitably" (Ps. 98:9); "The king's glory is loving justice" (Ps. 99:4); and "Adonai is upright, my rock, in whom there is no flaw" (Ps. 92:16). We find it elsewhere in our prayers, too. Our funeral service features words from Moses' last address, "The rock, his works are pure, for all his ways are just" (Deut. 32:4), and three times daily we pray (in the *Ashre*), "Adonai is righteous in all his ways" (Ps. 145:21: see Volume 3, *P'sukei D'zimrah,* p. 115).

But the same Bible forces us to question God's justice, the most discussed example being the command to Abraham to bind Isaac on an altar, presumably to sacrifice him because, as the first-born, he belongs to God—a belief typical of ancient religions. God ultimately intercedes, but God's initial instructions raise the question of whether we should obey divine commandments that appear immoral. The nineteenth-century Protestant theologian Søren Kierkegaard believed that we should; he used the story of Abraham and Isaac, in fact, to prove that sometimes there is a "teleological [or, perhaps, theological] suspension of the ethical," when we need to violate morality as we see it in obedience to an all-knowing and all-powerful (and good?) God. The Rabbis rejected that conclusion, opting instead to believe that God never intended the sacrifice of Isaac but only that Abraham bind him to the altar as a demonstration of faith and obedience. Still, one wonders why a good God would test Abraham so severely in the first place.

Other morally troubling biblical stories depict God hardening Pharoah's heart to make him incapable of doing the right thing (Ex. 10:1, 27) and punishing Saul for having mercy on the women and children of Amalek (1 Sam. 15). The Rabbis added stories of their own. For example, God shows Moses that Rabbi Akiba, despite his devotion to God and Torah, would be flayed by the Romans; when Moses protests, God answers, "Be quiet! So I have decided" (Men. 29b). The Rabbis are forced to admit that in the world God created, *tsadik v'ra lo, rasha v'tov lo,* "the righteous suffer, and the evil prosper" (Ber.7a). To preserve God's claim to justice, they formulate the belief in life after death, where God will rectify things.

Philosophically, also, the belief in God's justice raises many issues. Plato questioned the relationship between belief and morality (*Euthyphro* 9–12) through Socrates' question, "Is holiness beloved by the gods because it is holy, or is it holy only because the gods love it?" In other words, is morality independent of religion, so that we recognize goodness on non-religious grounds, or is morality a function of religion, so that the good is defined by what God wants?

American presidents Washington, Jefferson, and Eisenhower, among others, believed the latter: that people would be moral only if they were religious, and to this day most Americans associate religion with morality. At the same time, we all know religious people who act immorally. Worse yet, history and even contemporary times are replete with morally grotesque acts done in the name of religion. Conversely, we all know avowed atheists who are nevertheless moral.

There is, then, no one-to-one mapping of morality onto religion, but there are strong ties between the two. The psalmist is correct to tell us here that we should worship God because God represents morality, not just power. (I discuss the relationships between religion and morality at length in the appendices of my three books on Jewish ethics: *Matters of Life and Death* on medical ethics; *To Do the Right and the Good* on social ethics; and, especially, *Love Your Neighbor and Yourself* on personal ethics.)

◆

Frankel (A Woman's Voice)

word *amim,* "nations," appears five times; its synonym, *goyim,* twice; and *aretz,* "the earth," referring to all of the world's inhabitants, four times. How widely has the psalmist cast his net in this psalm! Even the trees, fields, and seas are bidden to rejoice before God.

But what is the cause for such universal celebration? The central theme of this psalm is the coming of God's rule on earth, a messianic vision of universal justice and order, when all nations, not just Israel, will be subject to God's righteous sovereignty. The psalmist includes in this vision "families of various peoples" *(mishpachot amim),* and promises that God will rule all peoples *(amim)* in faithfulness.

Here is a vision of God elevated above the created world but without hierarchy in the earthly sphere. Israel is not privileged among the nations but is included among them. In fact, Israel's special status is inferred only indirectly, through references to the Temple and its courts. But even these holy places are ascribed to God, not to the nation in whose midst they reside. And although the psalmist disparages "the other nations' gods [as] false," the idol-worshipers themselves receive no censure, as they typically do in many other psalms. Rather, God will judge them "with equity" *(b'mesharim).*

In such a world, who would not declare (with v. 10), "Adonai is king [*Adonai malakh*]!"

———◆———

Gray (Our Talmudic Heritage)

falls when the inhabitants of "all the earth" can see the sun at its height and offer requisite praise. The third *shiru* ("Sing to Adonai! Praise [*bar'khu*] his name") corresponds to *Ma'ariv* (evening), when we praise God with the call to prayer, *bar'khu,* the same word as in the verse (Midrash T'hillim 96:1).

———◆———

Kushner & Polen (Chasidism)

not insulted; God responds by giving us even more vitality. And, in this way, when we return life force to God every *Erev* Shabbat, then God returns it to us with even greater purity.

[12] *"Let the field exult along with all that is in it ... the trees of the forest will sing"* Rabbi Yehuda Aryeh Lieb of Ger (*Sefat Emet* on Psalms) notes that a human being is often referred to as an *olam katan,* a "microcosm." This means that each person contains within him or herself all aspects of creation. And therefore, as we rouse all parts of ourselves in the service of God, so too do we similarly awaken all of creation.

There are two kinds of trees: those that bear fruit and those that do not. Similarly, there are parts of our personalities that seem to be filled with vitality and other dimensions that seem less imbued with life. But, as we go about mending ourselves, we repair those dimensions of our being and of the cosmos in which the vitality is not so obvious.

Indeed, the Rabbis say that in messianic times, even non-fruit-bearing trees will bear fruit (Ket. 112b). In the words of our psalm, let everything "exult." Even the dimensions of our own psyche that we thought would never bear fruit are now revealed to be fertile and fecund.

L. HOFFMAN (HISTORY)

able to sing so far. "The masculine is strong," indicating the lasting nature of the messianic song at the end of days.

[4] *"Adonai is great ... more revered than all other gods"* Idolaters' "gods" have frequently been heavenly bodies, the stars themselves with their astrological portents. The Rabbis were torn: they denied divine status to the stars but acknowledged the "science" of astrology, holding that other nations might indeed be ruled by the stars, even if Jews—God's own people—were not. Nowadays, we would universalize that claim. The stars do not determine human destiny for anyone. This psalm implies, then, that even if our horoscope indicates disaster, we need not capitulate to bad fate if we link ourselves to God, who is above "all other gods."

J. HOFFMAN (TRANSLATION)

translation doesn't rule out any of these possibilities and so at least has the benefit of probably not being wrong.

[2] *"Praise"* Others, "bless." In English (by and large) we praise God and God blesses us. But in Hebrew, one verb (from the root *b.r.kh,* the same root that gives us *b'rakhah,* "blessing") covers both acts.

[2] *"Victory"* We translate the word for victory here as "salvation" elsewhere. Many words, including this one, seem to refer at times to godly matters, and at times to matters of war.

[2] *"Every day"* Literally, "day to day." The English expression "day to day" does not mean "every day," however, so we do not translate the phrase literally. But the author may have envisioned actual days, and the point may have been that we are to proclaim God's victory *to* each day, one by one, that is, first to Sunday, then to Monday, etc., giving us something like, "proclaim his victory to Sunday, then to Monday, then

Tuesday…." In Psalm 19:2, we may have another example of the personification of days (and, there, nights).

[3] *"Recount"* Once again, we run out of verbs in English. "Tell of" might work, but, as above, we prefer to avoid prepositions, to help preserve the poetic impact of the Hebrew.

[3] *"His wonders among all peoples"* "Among all peoples declare his wonders," not "take the wonders among all peoples and declare them." The Hebrew, unlike our English, is unambiguous.

[4] *"Praised"* From the root *h.l.l,* as in the prayer we call *Hallel;* not *b.r.kh,* as we had above (see above, "Praise").

[4] *"More revered than all other gods"* Yet again, English vocabulary limits our translation. Elsewhere, we translate the word for "revered" *(nora)* as "awesome." "Feared" is also common. The concept is a combination of admiration and fear. As for "than all other gods," *JPS* translates, "held in awe *by* all divine beings."

[5] *"False"* That is, false gods, often translated as "idols." The form of the word suggests a diminutive, similar to the word "god-lette," if such a word existed. *El* is "God" and *elil,* therefore, might be "little God." Modern Hebrew (along with many other languages) provides numerous examples of this doubling (technically called reduplication) used to express a diminutive. For example, *cham* is "hot"; *chamim* is "warm." *Kar* is "cold"; *karir* is "cool." Additionally, the word *elil* may have been influenced by an Akkadian word, *ilalu,* meaning "weak."

[6] *"Majesty and glory"* As with "strength and splendor" immediately following, we are faced with an almost arbitrary choice of related words. *JPS* gives us "glory and majesty" for our "majesty and glory." The Septuagint gives us something along the lines of "praise and beauty."

[10] *"Tell the nations"* More literally, "say among the nations."

[11] *"Thunder"* Others, "roar." The verb here *(yiram)* is frequently associated with the heavens, and so we guess that it has the more specific meaning of "thunder" (as in modern Hebrew), and is used metaphorically here. *JPS* agrees.

[12] *"Field"* The Hebrew *(sadai)* looks like a possessive, "my fields," but it is probably a poetic word for "field." We have no parallel poetic word for "field" in English, so we must be satisfied with the prosaic "field," probably missing a poetic subtlety in Hebrew.

[12] *"Trees of the forest"* A "tree of the forest" may have been a specific type of tree, perhaps a non-fruit-bearing tree. Elsewhere in Psalms we see the phrase "trees of the field," but a field is an odd place for a tree, so we surmise that "tree of the field" might have been a technical term, and, if so, that "tree of the forest" might likewise have been a technical term. (Modern Hebrew uses "of the field" technically in its word for

"strawberry," which is literally "berry of the field," and uses "of the tree" technically in the full name for "apple," literally "apple of the tree," in contradistinction to an "apple of the ground," which is a potato.) Additionally, in Song of Songs 2:3, the heroine's beloved is compared to a "fruit tree among trees of the forest" *(etz tapu'ach ba'atsei haya'ar)*, the point there probably being that a fruit tree is not a "tree of the forest." ("Fruit" here—*tapu'ach*—is often mistranslated as "apple.")

[12] *"Sing (y'ran'nu, from r.n.n)"* Not the word for "sing" (*shiru,* from *sh.y.r*) that started this psalm, but the less common word with which Psalm 95 began.

[13] *"For He comes"* The phrase "for He comes" appears twice, but repeating the verb in English, while copying the Hebrew structure, would create a different effect in English, because Hebrew allows for doubling where English does not.

[13] *"Its peoples"* Literally, just "peoples."

[13] *"Faithfully"* Literally, "in his faithfulness," perhaps even emphasizing "his," there being different kinds of faithfulness, among which God's is unique. But probably we just have a matter of style here.

◆ ◆ ◆

III. PSALM 97

¹Adonai is king! Let the earth exult, many islands rejoice! ²Cloud and darkness surround Him; righteousness and justice form the base of his throne. ³Fire walks before Him, burning his foes around Him. ⁴His lightning illumines the world! The earth sees and trembles. ⁵Mountains melt like wax before Adonai, before the lord of all the earth. ⁶The sky proclaims his righteousness as all peoples see his glory. ⁷All image worshipers, who glory in their false gods, are ashamed. All other gods bow down to Him. ⁸Zion hears and rejoices, as the daughters of Judah celebrate, all in your laws, Adonai. ⁹For You, Adonai, exalted over all the earth, are highly exalted over all other gods. ¹⁰Hate evil, you who love Adonai! He guards the lives of his faithful, saving them from the hands of the wicked. ¹¹Light is sown for the righteous, and for the upright, gladness. ¹²Rejoice in Adonai, you righteous, and praise his holy name.

יְיָ מָלָךְ תָּגֵל הָאָרֶץ יִשְׂמְחוּ אִיִּים רַבִּים: ²עָנָן וַעֲרָפֶל סְבִיבָיו צֶדֶק וּמִשְׁפָּט מְכוֹן כִּסְאוֹ: ³אֵשׁ לְפָנָיו תֵּלֵךְ וּתְלַהֵט סָבִיב צָרָיו: ⁴הֵאִירוּ בְרָקָיו תֵּבֵל רָאֲתָה וַתָּחֵל הָאָרֶץ: ⁵הָרִים כַּדּוֹנַג נָמַסּוּ מִלִּפְנֵי יְיָ מִלִּפְנֵי אֲדוֹן כָּל־הָאָרֶץ: ⁶הִגִּידוּ הַשָּׁמַיִם צִדְקוֹ וְרָאוּ כָל־הָעַמִּים כְּבוֹדוֹ: ⁷יֵבֹשׁוּ כָּל־עֹבְדֵי פֶסֶל הַמִּתְהַלְלִים בָּאֱלִילִים הִשְׁתַּחֲווּ־לוֹ כָּל־אֱלֹהִים: ⁸שָׁמְעָה וַתִּשְׂמַח צִיּוֹן וַתָּגֵלְנָה בְּנוֹת יְהוּדָה לְמַעַן מִשְׁפָּטֶיךָ יְיָ: ⁹כִּי־אַתָּה יְיָ עֶלְיוֹן עַל־כָּל־הָאָרֶץ מְאֹד נַעֲלֵיתָ עַל־כָּל־אֱלֹהִים: ¹⁰אֹהֲבֵי יְיָ שִׂנְאוּ רָע שֹׁמֵר נַפְשׁוֹת חֲסִידָיו מִיַּד רְשָׁעִים יַצִּילֵם: ¹¹אוֹר זָרֻעַ לַצַּדִּיק וּלְיִשְׁרֵי־לֵב שִׂמְחָה: ¹²שִׂמְחוּ צַדִּיקִים בַּיְיָ וְהוֹדוּ לְזֵכֶר קָדְשׁוֹ:

BRETTLER (BIBLE)

Psalm 97 This psalm continues the theme of kingship psalms, emphasizing God's justice and power (though not his role as creator). Structurally, it is quite different; it contains no call to worship, and it concludes rather than begins with imperatives. In contrast to the previous psalm, its utopian vision uses verbs in the past tense, indicating that this "new" world is already present.

 5, 6 *"Mountains melt … the sky proclaims"* God appears in a thunderstorm, a common biblical image that we will see again in Psalm 29. It is most familiar from God's appearance at Sinai (Exod. 19:16) but also in the song of Deborah, "When You came forth … the *(p. 80)*

DORFF (THEOLOGY)

10 *"Hate evil, you who love Adonai"* If God is just, those who love Him must also be just—an instance of *imitatio dei,* modeling ourselves after God. "You shall be holy, for I, Adonai your God, am holy" (Lev. 19:2) is another biblical instance of this theme, and the Rabbis make it more *(p. 81)*

FRANKEL (A WOMAN'S VOICE)

3–11 *"Fire walks before Him … lightning illumines the world … light is sown for the righteous"* Like a symphony with recurrent themes, the five clustered psalms inaugurating the *Kabbalat Shabbat* service, Psalms 95–99, circle back repeatedly to the theme *(p. 82)*

GRAY (OUR TALMUDIC HERITAGE)

10 *"Hate evil, you who love Adonai"* The Talmud (Ber. 10a) relates a conversation between the second-century sage R. Meir and his wife, Beruriah, about the meaning of Psalm 104:35: "May sins *(chata'im)* cease from the earth, and evildoers be no more." R. Meir was being victimized so badly that he actually prayed for his attackers' deaths, reading Psalm 104:35 as "May sinners *(chotim)* cease from the earth." Beruriah pointed out that the actual word is *chata'im,* which could *(p. 82)*

III. PSALM 97

1 Adonai is king! Let the earth exult, many islands rejoice! 2 Cloud and darkness surround Him; righteousness and justice form the base of his throne. 3 Fire walks before Him, burning his foes around Him. 4 His lightning illumines the world! The earth sees and trembles. 5 Mountains melt like wax before Adonai, before the lord of all the earth. 6 The sky proclaims his righteousness as all peoples see

KUSHNER & POLEN (CHASIDISM)

11 *"Light is sown* [or zaru'a] *for the righteous* [latsaddik]" By reading "Light is sown *(or zaru'a)* for the righteous *(latsaddik)*" literally, Rabbi Moshe Hayyim Ephraim of Sudilkov (1748–1800), in his *Degel Machaneh Ephraim,* gets "light is sown *into* a tsadik." He teaches, then, that God takes light from God's own essence and, as it were, sows it in the world. And, from those light-seeds blossom the *tsadikim,* the righteous ones of each generation. Abraham, for *(p. 83)*

L. HOFFMAN (HISTORY)

[11] *"Light is sown for the righteous"* Tenth-century philosopher Saadiah Gaon (*Beliefs and Opinions*, 9:8) differentiates degrees of happiness in this life. Some people like just being at rest (we might say, "just watching television"), while others find a higher degree of happiness in joyous activity, and still others reach the greatest bliss through discovering the study of Torah. He applied this calculus of relative good elsewhere, too. Every single good deed, for instance, is rewarded eternally (as goodness ought to be), but it does not follow that one

יְיָ מָלָךְ תָּגֵל הָאָרֶץ יִשְׂמְחוּ אִיִּים רַבִּים: [2] עָנָן וַעֲרָפֶל ¹
סְבִיבָיו צֶדֶק וּמִשְׁפָּט מְכוֹן כִּסְאוֹ: [3] אֵשׁ לְפָנָיו תֵּלֵךְ
וּתְלַהֵט סָבִיב צָרָיו: [4] הֵאִירוּ בְרָקָיו תֵּבֵל רָאֲתָה וַתָּחֵל
הָאָרֶץ: [5] הָרִים כַּדּוֹנַג נָמַסּוּ מִלִּפְנֵי יְיָ מִלִּפְנֵי אֲדוֹן
כָּל־הָאָרֶץ: [6] הִגִּידוּ הַשָּׁמַיִם צִדְקוֹ וְרָאוּ כָל־הָעַמִּים
כְּבוֹדוֹ: [7] יֵבֹשׁוּ כָּל־עֹבְדֵי פֶסֶל הַמִּתְהַלְלִים בָּאֱלִילִים

good deed is as good as a million, since even eternal reward can vary in intensity. Similarly, the righteous in the afterlife enjoy different degrees of light. Some are bright, but only like reflected sunlight. Others emit light as if from a source planted deep within them, as it says, "Light is *sown* for the righteous."

Eighteenth- and nineteenth-century Chasidim applied the same teaching to the Tzaddikim who founded and led Chasidic dynasties. Chasidism had "officially" begun with the Baal Shem Tov (BeSHT). When he died in 1760, he left a small   *(p. 83)*

J. HOFFMAN (TRANSLATION)

[1] *"The earth exult"* Above ("all the earth"), we saw "earth" used with a plural verb, probably in reference to something on the earth. Here "earth" takes a singular verb, probably because it denotes the earth itself (or perhaps land as opposed to water).

[1] *"Islands"* Or "coastlands," as in *NRSV*. "Islands" seems more likely, because "coastlands" would be part of "the earth," while the structure of the Hebrew line seems to suggest apposition (earth/island) or synonymy. (No reasonable understanding of the Hebrew word here is synonymous with "earth.") So we choose "islands." But on the other hand, it's not clear that "many islands" would have been part of the worldview of a people living in ancient Israel.

[3] *"Fire walks before Him"* *JPS*'s "Fire is his vanguard" is nice. *NRSV*'s more literal "Fire goes before him" is similar to our translation, but for the verb, and harks back to *King James,* "Fire goeth before him."

[3] *"Around"* The Hebrew repeats *saviv* here—the word used in verse 2, where "surround" seemed preferable.

[4] *"His lightning illumines"* We avoid "lights up" (as in *JPS* and *NRSV*) so as to avoid introducing the poetic affect of "lightning lights." The Hebrew word for "lightning" does not contain the word "light," and so contains no poetic doubling.   *(p. 84)*

his glory. [7] All image worshipers, who glory in their false gods, are ashamed. All other gods bow down to Him. [8] Zion hears and rejoices, as the daughters of Judah celebrate, all in your laws, Adonai. [9] For You, Adonai, exalted over all the earth, are highly exalted over all other gods. [10] Hate evil, you who love Adonai! He guards the lives of his faithful, saving them from the hands of the wicked. [11] Light is sown for the righteous, and for the upright, gladness. [12] Rejoice in Adonai, you righteous, and praise his holy name.

הִשְׁתַּחֲווּ־לוֹ כָּל־אֱלֹהִים: [8] שָׁמְעָה
וַתִּשְׂמַח צִיּוֹן וַתָּגֵלְנָה בְּנוֹת יְהוּדָה
לְמַעַן מִשְׁפָּטֶיךָ יְיָ: [9] כִּי־אַתָּה יְיָ עֶלְיוֹן
עַל־כָּל־הָאָרֶץ מְאֹד נַעֲלֵיתָ עַל־כָּל־
אֱלֹהִים: [10] אֹהֲבֵי יְיָ שִׂנְאוּ רָע שֹׁמֵר
נַפְשׁוֹת חֲסִידָיו מִיַּד רְשָׁעִים יַצִּילֵם:
[11] אוֹר זָרֻעַ לַצַּדִּיק וּלְיִשְׁרֵי־לֵב שִׂמְחָה:
[12] שִׂמְחוּ צַדִּיקִים בַּייָ וְהוֹדוּ לְזֵכֶר קָדְשׁוֹ:

BRETTLER (BIBLE)

mountains quaked" (Ju. 5:4–5), and the vision of Habakkuk, "God is coming … his majesty covers the skies … the age-old mountains are shattered" (Hab. 3:3–6). But God's power is combined with justice: "Righteousness and justice form the base of his throne" (v. 2). Unlike earthly kings, God does not abuse his power.

[7] *"All image worshipers … are ashamed … other gods bow down"* Psalm 96:4–5 announced the falseness of other gods. This psalm extends that theme, in that idolaters are ashamed and rival gods bow down.

[8] *"Daughters of Judah"* Women were included in ancient Israelite worship.

[9] *"Adonai, exalted* [elyon] *over all the earth"* In Psalm 47:3, another kingship psalm, God is "exalted … over all the earth." Oral cultures feature poetry that draws on stock phrases that are reiterated in compositions of similar genre. Antiquity did not see this as plagiarism.

Elyon was originally a Canaanite divine name; later it became an adjective describing the Canaanite high gods El and Baal; its use in reference to Adonai was originally polemical, as if to say, "Only our God is *elyon.*"

[10] *"His faithful* [chasidav]" Reference to these "faithful" occurs twenty-five times in the Psalms, referring either to righteous individuals generally or to some specific group unknown to us. In 2 Maccabees 14:6, Alcimus, a treacherous high priest, denounces

"Jews called *chasidim* [the faithful] who follow Judah the Maccabee [and] keep the war alive."

[11] *"Gladness"* The Hebrew *simchah* is a pun, meaning "gladness," but also "radiance"—like the "light [that] is sown" at the verse's beginning.

[12] *"Rejoice ... praise his holy name"* "Rejoice" designates happiness rather than fear as the proper reaction to God's power—at least for the righteous.

———◆———

DORFF (THEOLOGY)

concrete: "As God clothes the naked ... you should clothe the naked. As God visited the sick ... you should visit the sick; as God comforted those who mourned ... you should comfort those who mourn; and as God buried the dead ... you should bury the dead" (Sot. 14a).

[10] *"He guards the lives of his faithful"* After the Holocaust, this verse rings hollow. It is important to note, then, that already in biblical times, the relationship between righteousness and reward was questioned (most strongly by Job). The Rabbis admit that the righteous suffer and the evil prosper (see above, "He judges the people with equity ... will judge the earth justly, and its peoples faithfully"). Ben Azzai asserts: "Each good deed leads to another, and each bad deed leads to another, for the reward of fulfilling a commandment is [the ability and motivation to fulfill another] commandment; the result of committing a transgression is [the ability and temptation] to commit another transgression" (*Pirkei Avot* 4:2). Long before Kant but in good Kantian fashion, Ben Azzai believed that one should act morally on principle, for its own sake.

Still, what do we say to Jews who suffered the destruction of the two Temples in Jerusalem, the Crusades, the Inquisition, pogroms, and the Holocaust—and also individual tragedies for which no human actions are responsible (like a child with leukemia)? Especially where the evil use of human free will cannot be blamed, no answer suffices. At the same time, at its core, Judaism insists that acting morally matters and that we must do the right thing even if it does not always bring appropriate reward; and we hope, with the psalmist, that God will ultimately "guard the lives of his faithful."

———◆———

FROM THE KABBALISTS OF SAFED

FRANKEL (A WOMAN'S VOICE)

of God's awesome power. As in the preceding psalm, the speaker lauds God's kingship over creation, including "all other gods," but the mood in this psalm is much darker than in the other four in the series. God's power manifests in "cloud and darkness" and fire "burning [God's] foes around Him." The natural world becomes markedly agitated in God's presence: the earth "sees and trembles"; the mountains "melt like wax." Idol-worshipers, who are spared from censure in the previous psalm, are here "ashamed" when God appears to expose their disloyalty.

The violent imagery and glorification of power found in this psalm characterize God as classically masculine—a God of war, of vengeance, of harsh justice. The only softer notes sounded are in verse 8, where Zion, grammatically and figuratively feminine, and the surrounding towns of Judah, likewise feminine nouns, rejoice over God's glory. Interestingly, the Hebrew idiom for these towns ringing Jerusalem is *b'not y'hudah,* literally, the "daughters of Judah." Even if we were to understand this idiom as strictly formal—suburbs grow out from cities just as children descend from their parents—the choice of the word "daughters" rather than other equally apt metaphors such as "sons," "fledglings," "branches," or "fruit," suggests that these communities clustering around the holy city of Jerusalem function like handmaidens to a queen, or like a chorus accompanying a celebrated diva.

The psalm concludes by contrasting the fiery end awaiting the wicked (v. 3) with the blissful fate awaiting the righteous. If we extend the metaphor, we can regard light as a symbol of nature's mutability in the hands of an all-powerful creator, who can shape it into lightning to illumine the world, fire to burn evildoers, or enlightenment to gladden the righteous.

GRAY (OUR TALMUDIC HERITAGE)

be read as "sins," not "sinners." Also, the verse continues, "and evildoers be no more." R. Meir, she concluded, should pray for the attackers' repentance, as a result of which their "*sins* would cease from the earth" and they would be "wicked no more." Baruch Halevi Epstein (Russia, 1860–1942) applied Beruriah's principle to our verse also: we should hate evil, not evildoers, and do our best to cause evildoers to see the light and change their ways so that evil will ultimately disappear.

KUSHNER & POLEN (CHASIDISM)

example, was like the dawn light, clear and bright; Isaac, classically associated with the afternoon, had a reddish cast. Moses was the light of Torah itself. Other *tsadikim* have the light of one particular *mitzvah* or another. In this way, each righteous person has his or her own unique hue of light. And that is why a *tsadik* is brought into the world, that we may ask (in the words of Shabbat 118b), "With what *mitzvah* did your father shine?" We now wonder ourselves: which *mitzvah* is the source of our own personal light?

———◆———

L. HOFFMAN (HISTORY)

circle of followers, who gradually came under the control of Dov Baer (the Maggid) of Mezhirech. Another member of that (the "second") generation was Jacob Joseph of Polonnoye, whose *Toldot Ya'akov Yosef* (1780) is the first encyclopedic statement of Chasidism's philosophy and traditions. Chasidic leaders of the third generation, like Levi Yitzchak of Berdichev, Elimelekh of Lyzhansk, and Schneur Zalman of Liady carried Chasidism north to Lithuania, south through the Ukraine, and westward into central Poland. The high point of Chasidic growth followed, from 1773 to 1815, bringing to power not just the well-known authorities who had studied in Mezhirech, but also such authoritative voices as Jacob Joseph Hachozeh ("the Seer") of Lublin, and Nachman of Breslov (grandson of the BeSHT himself). By 1830, the main spread of Chasidism was over, its main schools having been established as independent and often rival entities.

It was this third generation that spawned the famous schools of Chasidism like Chabad, Belz, the Breslovers, and others, and which developed the doctrine of the Tzaddik. It varied from school to school, but generally, the Tzaddik was a leader who had merged his soul with the divine, bridging the distinction between individual and the world of the *sefirot*, and therefore able to mediate the path to God for his followers. The act of merger (*d'vekut*, as it was called) filled the Tzaddik, as it were, with divine light, or blessing (the *shefa*), which flowed to his Chasidic followers.

The image of light being sown for the Tzaddik, then, was reclaimed in Chasidic lore in a way not entirely unlike Saadiah's but with altogether novel mystical significance.

———◆———

J. HOFFMAN (TRANSLATION)

[5] *"Wax"* Probably beeswax. Certainly not candle wax.

[5] *"Lord"* The word for "lord" and the word for "Adonai" are almost identical in Hebrew, creating a poetic effect absent in our English. (This identity between Adonai and "lord" led the translators of the Septuagint to use the Greek word *Kurios,* literally "Lord," for "Adonai," and led eventually to the common English practice of calling Adonai "the Lord." We prefer to use "Adonai," assuming that the word is God's name, not to be translated.)

[6] *"As"* Literally, "and," but as we have pointed out frequently in these volumes, Hebrew often uses coordination ("and") where English requires subordination ("as," "when," "because," and so forth).

[7] *"False gods"* Others, "idols." We retain "false gods," in keeping with our translation of the word when it was used above (see Ps. 96:5).

[7] *"Ashamed"* Others, "dismayed." The verb we see here is frequently used in connection with idol worshipers, but we don't know its exact nuances.

[7] *"Other gods"* Again, the Hebrew gives us just "all gods." Because the Hebrew only implies the sense of "other," some translations interpret *elohim* here as "divine beings," that is, a category that doesn't include God. The Septuagint takes another route, translating *elohim* here as "angels" or "messengers."

[8] *"Hears and rejoices"* JPS's "Zion, hearing of it, rejoices" probably captures the original sense of the Hebrew but seems too bland for what ought to be a poetic translation.

[8] *"Daughters"* Some translations, based on phrases such as "daughter of Zion" for "Zion," assume that "daughters" here refers poetically to "towns." We disagree.

[8] *"All"* We add "all" here to make it clear that both Zion's rejoicing and the daughters' celebrating are for God's laws. Though the Hebrew is ambiguous, leaving open the possibility that only the daughters' celebrating is connected to the laws, the trope marks (probably from about 1,100 years ago) resolve the ambiguity in favor of what we have.

[8] *"In"* This is the most likely interpretation of the Hebrew based on context, but literally we have "for the sake of your laws." That is, we assume it means that the laws benefit the people, but the Hebrew, surprisingly, seems to give us just the opposite.

[9] *"Other gods"* Once again, we add "other," in keeping with modern English usage, but here, unfortunately, our choice ruins the otherwise exact parallelism between "all the earth" and what could be "all the gods."

[10] *"Hate evil, you who love Adonai"* Surprisingly, some translations have "[Adonai]

loves those who hate evil." The Hebrew does not support this interpretation, though it makes sense in context.

[10] *"Lives"* From the Hebrew *nefesh,* sometimes mistranslated as "soul." (For a detailed discussion of *nefesh,* see J. Hoffman, "Mind and body and strength," Volume 1, *The Sh'ma and Its Blessings,"* pp. 100, 102.)

[11] *"Sown"* Planted, like seeds.

[11] *"Gladness"* Or "radiance."

[12] *"Praise* [hodu]" From *y.d.h,* the same root we translated above as the noun "praise." (See above, "Praise," p. 63.) *JPS* gives us "acclaim." *NRSV* (as in *King James*) has "Give thanks to."

[12] *"His holy name"* Following *JPS.* Literally, "the memory of his holiness," which, following standard Hebrew grammar, means "his holy memory." But the word for memory, *zekher,* clearly does not function the way our modern word "memory" does (see Volume 5, *Birkhot Hashachar [Morning Blessings],* p. 194).

◆ ◆ ◆

IV. Psalm 98

[1] A psalm. Sing a new song to Adonai, for He has done wonders. His right hand, his holy arm, has won Him victory. [2] Adonai makes his victory known, revealing his triumph before the eyes of all nations. [3] He remembered his love and faithfulness toward the house of Israel. All the ends of the earth saw our God's victory. [4] Celebrate God, all the earth, with song and joyful music, [5] music with harps for Adonai, with harps and the voice of song, [6] with trumpets and the voice of the horn. Celebrate before Adonai, the king! [7] Let the sea thunder along with all that fills it, the world and its inhabitants, too. [8] Let the rivers clap their hands, the mountains sing together [9] before Adonai, for He comes to judge the earth. He will judge the earth justly, and its peoples equitably.

מִזְמוֹר. שִׁירוּ לַייָ שִׁיר חָדָשׁ כִּי־
נִפְלָאוֹת עָשָׂה הוֹשִׁיעָה־לּוֹ יְמִינוֹ
וּזְרוֹעַ קָדְשׁוֹ: [2] הוֹדִיעַ יְיָ יְשׁוּעָתוֹ לְעֵינֵי
הַגּוֹיִם גִּלָּה צִדְקָתוֹ: [3] זָכַר חַסְדּוֹ
וֶאֱמוּנָתוֹ לְבֵית יִשְׂרָאֵל רָאוּ כָל־אַפְסֵי־
אָרֶץ אֵת יְשׁוּעַת אֱלֹהֵינוּ: [4] הָרִיעוּ לַייָ
כָּל־הָאָרֶץ פִּצְחוּ וְרַנְּנוּ וְזַמֵּרוּ: [5] זַמְּרוּ
לַייָ בְּכִנּוֹר בְּכִנּוֹר וְקוֹל זִמְרָה:
[6] בַּחֲצֹצְרוֹת וְקוֹל שׁוֹפָר הָרִיעוּ לִפְנֵי
הַמֶּלֶךְ יְיָ: [7] יִרְעַם הַיָּם וּמְלֹאוֹ תֵּבֵל
וְיֹשְׁבֵי בָהּ: [8] נְהָרוֹת יִמְחֲאוּ־כָף יַחַד
הָרִים יְרַנֵּנוּ: [9] לִפְנֵי־יְיָ כִּי בָא לִשְׁפֹּט
הָאָרֶץ יִשְׁפֹּט־תֵּבֵל בְּצֶדֶק וְעַמִּים
בְּמֵישָׁרִים:

BRETTLER (BIBLE)

Psalm 98 Although more military in its emphasis, Psalm 98 parallels Psalm 96, beginning also with "Sing a new song to Adonai" and ending with "He will judge the earth justly, and its peoples equitably," mirroring Psalm 96:13, "He will judge the earth justly, and its peoples faithfully." "Recount his glory among the nations" (Ps. 96:3) becomes "Adonai makes his victory known, revealing his triumph before the eyes of all nations" (Ps. 98:2). Announcement becomes reality.

[1] *"A psalm"* So short an introduction is unique in Psalms; the Greek *(p. 90)*

FRANKEL (A WOMAN'S VOICE)

[4] *"Song and joyful music"* Building on the cumulative energy of the preceding three psalms, Psalm 98 expresses an almost ecstatic fervor of praise, beginning like Psalm 96 with a call to "sing a new song to Adonai" and ending likewise with a vision of God's ultimate just rule on earth. The recurrent themes of God's power, military triumph, and love for Israel appear in this psalm as in the previous ones. The new imagery introduced here is orchestral, conjuring up music produced by human beings (harps, trumpets, horn, and song) but also the natural sounds of the world: the sea, the earth, and all their creatures will thunder; the rivers clap hands; and the mountains sing. And this concert is meant to be loud, not merely tuneful.

Words related to the root *y.r.h,* "to shout or thunder," appear three times in the four middle verses. We are urged to reciprocate in kind for God's gifts to us. When God manifests steadfast "love and faithfulness" for Israel through shows of strength, we can respond by demonstrating our own power—with exuberant song, musical instruments, and our psalms.

———◆———

IV. PSALM 98

[1] A psalm. Sing a new song to Adonai, for He has done wonders. His right hand, his holy arm, has won Him victory. [2] Adonai makes his victory known, revealing his triumph before the eyes of all nations. [3] He remembered his love and faithfulness toward the house of Israel. All the ends of the earth saw our God's victory. [4] Celebrate God, all the earth, with song and joyful music, [5] music with harps for Adonai,

GRAY (OUR TALMUDIC HERITAGE)

[1] *"His right hand, his holy arm, has won Him victory"* The talmudic sage R. Acha said, "As long as [the People] Israel are in exile, it is as if the Holy Blessed One's right arm is subjugated. But when Israel is redeemed, see what is written: 'His right hand, his holy arm, has won Him victory'" (Midrash T'hillim 98:1).

———◆———

LANDES (HALAKHAH)

4–6 *"Celebrate God ... with song and joyful music ... harps ... trumpets ... horn"* This psalm has inspired a few rigorously halakhic communities to have musical accompaniment to the early part of *Kabbalat Shabbat*—the psalms only, ending before *L'khah Dodi* (Sefer Noheg K'tson Yosef [Joseph Kosman, Israel, mid-late twentieth century], Shab. 16). In this view, *Kabbalat Shabbat* is an approach to Shabbat, but still distinctly part of the workweek (one would have to be careful to start *Kabbalat Shabbat* well

מִזְמוֹר. שִׁירוּ לַיְיָ שִׁיר חָדָשׁ כִּי־נִפְלָאוֹת עָשָׂה ¹
הוֹשִׁיעָה־לּוֹ יְמִינוֹ וּזְרוֹעַ קָדְשׁוֹ: ²הוֹדִיעַ יְיָ יְשׁוּעָתוֹ
לְעֵינֵי הַגּוֹיִם גִּלָּה צִדְקָתוֹ: ³זָכַר חַסְדּוֹ וֶאֱמוּנָתוֹ לְבֵית
יִשְׂרָאֵל רָאוּ כָל־אַפְסֵי־אָרֶץ אֵת יְשׁוּעַת אֱלֹהֵינוּ:
⁴הָרִיעוּ לַיְיָ כָּל־הָאָרֶץ פִּצְחוּ וְרַנְּנוּ וְזַמֵּרוּ: ⁵זַמְּרוּ לַיְיָ
בְּכִנּוֹר בְּכִנּוֹר וְקוֹל זִמְרָה: ⁶בַּחֲצֹצְרוֹת וְקוֹל שׁוֹפָר

before candle-lighting time). This practice is vigorously opposed by R. Eliezer Waldenberg, contemporary authority and head of Jerusalem Court (Tzitz Eliezer, 14:34).

——◆——

J. HOFFMAN (TRANSLATION)

¹ *"A psalm"* The usual Hebrew word for "psalms" is *t'hillim,* from the root *h.l.l* meaning "to praise." Here we see a different word, from the root *z.m.r,* perhaps meaning "to sing." Many psalms begin with one or two introductions or attributions, of the sort "David's Psalm" or "for the conductor," but the role of these introductions is not clear. Additionally, the Septuagint often contains introductions that our Hebrew text does not. In this case, the Septuagint gives us "David's Psalm." In Psalm 97, the Septuagint begins "For David, for when his land is established." In Psalm 96, "When the house was built after the captivity, David's song." In Psalm 95, something along the lines of "David's song of praise." Psalm 99 starts with "David's Psalm."

¹ *"Done"* JPS gives us the poetic "worked," but "working wonders" seems to us more mundane and therefore less accurate than "doing wonders."

¹ *"His right hand, his holy arm, has"* Following JPS. Other translations tend toward "his right hand and his holy arm have...," as though the two are distinct. We assume that God's right hand is God's holy arm. Either way, apparently God is right-handed. It is clear from other contexts that "right" was good and "left" was bad. For example, the Latin word for "right," *dexter,* became our "dexterous," while the *(p. 91)*

with harps and the voice of song, [6] with trumpets and the voice of the horn. Celebrate before Adonai, the king! [7] Let the sea thunder along with all that fills it, the world and its inhabitants, too. [8] Let the rivers clap their hands, the mountains sing together [9] before Adonai, for He comes to judge the earth. He will judge the earth justly, and its peoples equitably.

הָרִיעוּ לִפְנֵי הַמֶּלֶךְ יְיָ: [7] יִרְעַם הַיָּם וּמְלֹאוֹ תֵּבֵל וְיֹשְׁבֵי בָהּ: [8] נְהָרוֹת יִמְחֲאוּ־כָף יַחַד הָרִים יְרַנֵּנוּ: [9] לִפְנֵי־יְיָ כִּי בָא לִשְׁפֹּט הָאָרֶץ יִשְׁפֹּט־תֵּבֵל בְּצֶדֶק וְעַמִּים בְּמֵישָׁרִים:

BRETTLER (BIBLE)

translation of the Bible (the Septuagint) introduces this (and all other kingship psalms) with "A psalm of David," reflecting the late post-exilic belief that David authored not only the psalms explicitly attributed to him but others as well.

[1] *"His right hand"* God is right-handed, the biblical norm, although exceptional "lefties" appear in Judges 3:15 and 1 Chronicles 12:2.

[3] *"Love and faithfulness"* A word-pair, which appears eleven times in Psalms, often connected to covenant obligations.

[4] *"Celebrate God"* Mirroring the noisy coronation acclaim, and (like Psalm 96) drawing in all of nature (see above "Let the heavens be glad ... the earth rejoice ... the sea thunder ... the field exult").

[6] *"The horn* [shofar]" At Solomon's coronation, "They sounded the horn [shofar] and all the people shouted, 'Long live King Solomon!'" (1 Kings 1:39). Such affinities to the coronation ritual suggest the possibility of an annual ritual where God was declared king (see Brettler, *"Kabbalat Shabbat:* A Liturgy from Psalms," pp. 21–25).

[7, 8] *"Let the sea thunder ... the rivers clap their hands"* Paralleling Psalm 96:11–12, possibly alluding to a myth describing a time when the waters personified rival deities and rebelled (as in Psalm 93:3, where "The ocean sounds its thunder" in opposition to God). Here, we see the end of the mythic tale, when the "sea" and "rivers" have been subdued and "thunder" out homage to God.

[8] *"Mountains sing"* Another strong connection to Deutero-Isaiah (see above "Psalm 96"), Isaiah 55:12: "You shall leave in joy and be led home secure. Before you, mount and hill shall shout aloud."

◆

J. HOFFMAN (TRANSLATION)

Latin word for "left," *sinister,* became our "sinister." Similarly, our English "right" comes from the Anglo-Saxon root for "just, correct, proper," while "left" comes from the Anglo-Saxon root for "weak." (It is commonly assumed that the preference for right-handed agility came from the need to wield one's weapon in the right hand, so that the left hand would be free to hold a shield over the heart.)

[2] *"All nations"* More literally, "the nations."

[3] *"Remembered his love and faithfulness toward the house of Israel"* Or, "to the benefit of the house of Israel, he remembered his love and faithfulness."

[4] *"Celebrate"* This is the same verb we translated (somewhat arbitrarily) as "trumpet" above (see Psalm 95, "trumpet," p. 62).

[4] *"Song and joyful music"* The Hebrew has three verbs here, all used, as nearly as we can tell, in the general sense of "celebrate musically." Some word-by-word translations include "sing," "exult," "sing joyously," and "sing psalms." (The last one, "sing psalms," is particularly interesting. It is based on the fact that the root of the verb is also used in one of the words for "psalm" and raises the possibility that there was a special verb for singing psalms.) We abandon any hope of a word-by-word translation. *JPS*'s "break into joyous songs of praise" is similar. But because the following lines place so much emphasis on instruments, we prefer to include "music" in addition to "song."

[5] *"Music with"* As above, we recognize the paucity of English verbs regarding music, so we must try to convey the poetry through nouns. The Hebrew verb used here seems to be the equivalent of "play" (as in "play the harp"), but broad enough to include singing. We would like to begin the next line "play harps for Adonai," but then we would have to continue, "[play] harps and the voice of song," which is ungrammatical in English.

[5] *"Harps"* Our modern instruments do not correspond with instruments of old. Certainly, they didn't have the modern free-standing stringed instrument with pedals at the bottom that comes to mind when a modern reader thinks of a harp. For this reason, some translations *(JPS, NRSV)* prefer "lyre" here, but that word seems not to conjure up any image in the mind of a modern reader. In older translations, "harp" was common (*King James,* 1899 *Douay-Rheims,* and 1917 *JPS*). Whatever we call it, the instrument was probably a stringed instrument played by plucking the strings. Also, as

a technical matter, the Hebrew is singular, but the plural is called for in English.

Alternatively, these lines may be describing a specific instrumentation, in which case the translation would be something like, "[a musical piece to be performed] with one harp: one harp, voice, trumpets, and one horn."

[6] *"Horn"* Shofar, in Hebrew. But in the Hebrew of the Bible, the word meant any sort of horn, not specifically the ram's horn we use nowadays on Rosh Hashanah. In later dialects of Hebrew, the Hebrew word matched our usage. (It is not unusual for words to progress in meaning from general to specific as they move from one language or dialect to another. A similar process took the Spanish word *sombrero*—which in Spanish means any kind of hat—and turned it into the English word "sombrero," which means "Mexican hat.")

[7] *"The world and its inhabitants, too"* We add "too" to improve the readability of the English. Hebrew in general allows additional subjects (as, in this case, "the world and its inhabitants") to follow the verb in a way that English does not. So we need the extra word in English.

[8] *"Sing"* Yet again, we have a verb in Hebrew with no clear equivalent in English. Other translations make the joy of the singing more explicit, translating variously "exult," "sing joyously," and "sing for joy," but we prefer to keep to a single verb.

[9] *"Equitably"* Except for this word, Psalm 98 ends like Psalm 96, where we saw "faithfully" instead of "equitably."

◆ ◆ ◆

V. PSALM 99

¹ Adonai is king! Let the peoples shudder. He sits on a throne of cherubim. Let the earth tremble! ² In Zion, Adonai is the Great One. He is exalted above all peoples. ³ Let them praise your name, Great One, Awesome One. He is holy! ⁴ The king's glory is loving justice. It was You who established equity, You who acted justly and righteously through Jacob. ⁵ Exalt Adonai our God and bow down toward his footstool. He is holy! ⁶ Moses and Aaron were among his priests, and Samuel among those who called on his name. They all called on Adonai and He answered them. ⁷ In a pillar of cloud He spoke to them, and they kept his decrees and the laws He gave them. ⁸ Adonai our God, You answered them; You were a forgiving God to them, avenging the deeds done them. ⁹ Exalt Adonai our God and bow down at his holy mountain, for Adonai our God is holy.

יְ֭יָ מָלָךְ יִרְגְּז֣וּ עַמִּ֑ים יֹשֵׁ֥ב כְּרוּבִ֗ים תָּנ֥וּט הָאָֽרֶץ: ²יְיָ֭ בְּצִיּ֣וֹן גָּד֑וֹל וְרָ֥ם ה֝֗וּא עַל־כָּל־הָעַמִּֽים: ³יוֹד֣וּ שִׁמְךָ֣ גָּד֑וֹל וְנוֹרָ֖א קָד֣וֹשׁ הֽוּא: ⁴וְעֹ֥ז מֶלֶךְ֮ מִשְׁפָּ֪ט אָ֫הֵ֥ב אַ֭תָּה כּוֹנַ֣נְתָּ מֵישָׁרִ֑ים מִשְׁפָּ֥ט וּ֝צְדָקָ֗ה בְּיַעֲקֹ֤ב ׀ אַתָּ֬ה עָשִֽׂיתָ: ⁵רֽוֹמְמ֡וּ יְיָ֪ אֱלֹ֫הֵ֥ינוּ וְֽהִשְׁתַּחֲו֗וּ לַהֲדֹ֥ם רַגְלָ֗יו קָד֥וֹשׁ הֽוּא: ⁶מֹ֘שֶׁ֤ה וְאַהֲרֹ֨ן ׀ בְּֽכֹהֲנָ֗יו וּ֖שְׁמוּאֵל בְּקֹרְאֵ֣י שְׁמ֑וֹ קֹרִ֥אים אֶל־יְ֝יָ וְה֣וּא יַֽעֲנֵֽם: ⁷בְּעַמּ֣וּד עָ֭נָן יְדַבֵּ֣ר אֲלֵיהֶ֑ם שָׁמְר֥וּ עֵ֝דֹתָ֗יו וְחֹ֣ק נָֽתַן־לָֽמוֹ: ⁸יְיָ֣ אֱלֹהֵינוּ֮ אַתָּ֪ה עֲנִ֫יתָ֥ם אֵ֣ל נֹ֭שֵׂא הָיִ֣יתָ לָהֶ֑ם וְ֝נֹקֵ֗ם עַל־עֲלִילוֹתָֽם: ⁹רֽוֹמְמ֡וּ יְיָ֪ אֱלֹ֫הֵ֥ינוּ וְֽהִשְׁתַּחֲו֗וּ לְהַ֥ר קָדְשׁ֑וֹ כִּֽי־קָ֝ד֗וֹשׁ יְיָ֥ אֱלֹהֵֽינוּ:

BRETTLER (BIBLE)

[1] *"Throne of cherubim"* Like Psalms 93 and 97, this opens with "Adonai is king," and then fills in the implications of God's kingship. The new element added here is where God (as king) actually sits. God is enthroned within the Temple on the ark of the covenant above which there sat cherubim: mythic beings, part human, part animal.

[2] *"Exalted above all peoples"* God is superlative relative to all "peoples," but (as in Pss. 95:3, 96:4, 97:9) not necessarily to other gods. Some Septuagint manuscripts therefore read "gods, divine beings" rather than "peoples." *(p. 96)*

FRANKEL (A WOMAN'S VOICE)

[6] *"Moses and Aaron ... and Samuel"* Noticeably absent from this list of flawed leaders is Miriam, the sister of Moses and Aaron, who also called upon God's name at the Red Sea and, according to rabbinic legend, conjured up a miraculous well that healed and restored the Israelites throughout their long and arduous desert journey. She too experienced divine retribution—for speaking out against Moses—and was forgiven when God healed the leprosy-like illness (Num. 12:10) with which she had been stricken for her rebellious words. Why, then, is she not listed here? Was it so inconceivable to the psalmist that a woman might merit inclusion in this small society of divinely blessed and cursed men?

[8] *"A forgiving God ... [but] avenging"* Although the initial verses of this psalm parallel the themes and images expressed in the four preceding psalms, it departs from the others in verses 6–8, where the speaker refers to three biblical leaders—Moses, Aaron, and Samuel—and their special relationship to God. They enjoyed a unique intimacy with God, who answered them when they called and gave them the law *(chok),* but they paid a high price for it. *(p. 97)*

V. PSALM 99

[1] Adonai is king! Let the peoples shudder. He sits on a throne of cherubim. Let the earth tremble! [2] In Zion, Adonai is the Great One. He is exalted above all peoples. [3] Let them praise your name, Great One, Awesome One. He is holy! [4] The king's glory is loving justice. It was You who established equity, You who acted justly and righteously through Jacob. [5] Exalt Adonai our God and bow down toward his footstool.

KIMELMAN (KABBALAH)

[9] *"Bow down ... for Adonai our God is holy"* A segue into Psalm 29, which follows, because Psalm 29:2 reads, similarly, "Bow down to Adonai in holy beauty."

[1] *"Shudder"* Or "tremble," but we want to reserve tremble for use below ("earth trembles") so that we can avoid "earth quakes" there, which would mistakenly specifically suggest an earthquake.

[1] *"On a throne of cherubim"* The Hebrew is unclear, referring to God as the "cherub sitter," an appellation that also appears elsewhere. The Septuagint gives us the clearer "sits with/above/on cherubim." In English, too, we add a preposition. A cherub (plural, "cherubim") is a multiwinged angelic

[2] *"All peoples"* It's not clear why Adonai is being compared to peoples, rather than, as is more common, to their gods.

[3] *"Them"* Presumably the peoples of verse 2.

[3] *"Great One, Awesome One"* As in "Great One" (above). The other possibility runs along the lines of "Let them praise your name as great and awesome."

[3] *"He"* God. Another reasonable understanding of the Hebrew would be "it"—that is, "God's name."

[4] *"The king's glory is loving justice"* One possible understanding of enigmatic Hebrew. *JPS* offers "Mighty king who loves justice," but with the note that the meaning of the Hebrew "is uncertain." A third option is *NRSV*'s "mighty king, lover of justice."

[4] *"Equity"* Equitable treatment. Above we saw that God judges the people of the earth "equitably."

[4] *"Acted justly and righteously"* Or, "created justice and righteousness." Either way, it's not clear how this concept relates to "Jacob," mentioned next. *JPS*'s "worked righteous judgment in Jacob" seems devoid of meaning, as does the most straightforward translation of the Hebrew: "made justice and righteousness in Jacob." We seem to have classic biblical chiasmus here (i.e., an inverted relationship between syntactic elements

¹יְיָ מָלָךְ יִרְגְּזוּ עַמִּים יֹשֵׁב כְּרוּבִים תָּנוּט הָאָרֶץ:
²יְיָ בְּצִיּוֹן גָּדוֹל וְרָם הוּא עַל־כָּל־הָעַמִּים: ³יוֹדוּ שִׁמְךָ
גָּדוֹל וְנוֹרָא קָדוֹשׁ הוּא: ⁴וְעֹז מֶלֶךְ מִשְׁפָּט אָהֵב אַתָּה
כּוֹנַנְתָּ מֵישָׁרִים מִשְׁפָּט וּצְדָקָה בְּיַעֲקֹב אַתָּה עָשִׂיתָ:
⁵רוֹמְמוּ יְיָ אֱלֹהֵינוּ וְהִשְׁתַּחֲווּ לַהֲדֹם רַגְלָיו קָדוֹשׁ הוּא:
⁶מֹשֶׁה וְאַהֲרֹן בְּכֹהֲנָיו וּשְׁמוּאֵל בְּקֹרְאֵי שְׁמוֹ קֹרְאִים

creature, but almost all references are to statues of them that adorn holy places like the tabernacle and, here, God's throne. *King James*, and before it the 1599 Geneva Bible, gave us "between" cherubim, reflecting the notion that the cherubim flanked the throne's occupant.

[2] *"Great One"* This is one understanding of difficult Hebrew. We assume that *gadol* ("great") is an epithet here and immediately below. Another possibility is the almost universal (*JPS*, e.g.) "[Adonai] is great in Zion."

(p. 97)

He is holy! [6] Moses and Aaron were among his priests, and Samuel among those who called on his name. They all called on Adonai and He answered them. [7] In a pillar of cloud He spoke to them, and they kept his decrees and the laws He gave them. [8] Adonai our God, You answered them; You were a forgiving God to them, avenging the deeds done them. [9] Exalt Adonai our God and bow down at his holy mountain, for Adonai our God is holy.

אֵל־יְיָ וְהוּא יַעֲנֵם: [7]בְּעַמּוּד עָנָן יְדַבֵּר אֲלֵיהֶם שָׁמְרוּ עֵדֹתָיו וְחֹק נָתַן־לָמוֹ: [8]יְיָ אֱלֹהֵינוּ אַתָּה עֲנִיתָם אֵל נֹשֵׂא הָיִיתָ לָהֶם וְנֹקֵם עַל־עֲלִילוֹתָם: [9]רוֹמְמוּ יְיָ אֱלֹהֵינוּ וְהִשְׁתַּחֲווּ לְהַר קָדְשׁוֹ כִּי־קָדוֹשׁ יְיָ אֱלֹהֵינוּ:

BRETTLER (BIBLE)

[3] *"Let them praise your name … He is holy"* Change from second person ("your") to third ("He") is common biblical style. Alternatively, "He is holy!" may be the actual words of praise recited by the people, as in Isaiah's famous vision (Isa. 6:3), where the angels declare: "Holy, holy, holy! Adonai of Hosts! His presence fills all the earth!"

[5] *"Exalt Adonai"* A call to worship, but in the middle of the psalm! Since Psalm 99 concludes the psalm collection that began at Psalm 93, it may once have ended here, with verses 6–9 a later addition. This would explain why "Exalt Adonai" of verse 5 is repeated in verse 9. Such "resumptive repetitions" (as they are called) are common when later insertions interrupt the flow. Leviticus, for example, once ended at verse 26:46. Some time later, Chapter 27 was added, so an extra verse (27:34) was appended as a resumptive repetition of verse 26:46.

[8] *"You answered them"* Possibly just a request for a divine answer, but perhaps more. Amos 8:11 predicted a time when people would "wander … to seek the word of Adonai, but they shall not find it." If the psalm is post-exilic (see above, "Exalt Adonai"), it may reflect that time when prophecy has disappeared.

[8] *"You were a forgiving God"* Exodus 34:6 ("forgives iniquity, transgression, and sin") provides the attributes of God that play such an important part in our festival and Yom Kippur liturgy. It was important to the psalmist, too, who paraphrases it here and elsewhere. "You … avenge[ed] the deeds done them" reworks "He does not remit all punishment," the negative part of the thirteen attributes that our liturgy purposely omits! (See Volume 4, *Seder K'riat Hatorah—The Torah Service*, pp. 64–69.)

FRANKEL (A WOMAN'S VOICE)

In an ambivalent expression of praise, the speaker declares to God—and indirectly to the listeners—"You were a forgiving God to them (v. 8); but the end of verse 8, "avenging the deeds done them" can equally be read as "avenging their own deeds," that is, exacting retribution for the misdeeds they committed!

———◆———

J. HOFFMAN (TRANSLATION)

of parallel phrases). Here, the verb "established" *(konanta)* precedes the object "equity"; so the following line puts the verb "created" or "acted" *(asita)* at the end, with the object "justice and righteousness" at the beginning. But that leaves no place for "Jacob." A final possibility is that "Jacob" is used here to mean Israel, the place.

5 *"Exalt"* The verb is plural, addressing more than one person.

6 *"All"* The Hebrew reads "they called...."

8 *"Avenging the deeds done them"* Or "their deeds," leading *JPS* to say, "exacting retribution for their misdeeds." We assume that God avenges the wrongs done *to* those who "called on Adonai," but another possibility is that God exacts retribution for the wrongs done *by* them.

———◆ ◆ ◆———

VI. PSALM 29

David's psalm: To Adonai, you heavenly beings, to Adonai ascribe honor and might! [2] Ascribe the honor of his name to Adonai. Bow down to Adonai in holy beauty. [3] Adonai's voice peals across the water—the thunder of the God of honor—across great water. [4] Adonai's voice is mighty. Adonai's voice is glorious. [5] Adonai's voice can break cedar trees, and Adonai can smash the cedar trees of Lebanon [6] and make them dance like a calf, Lebanon and Sirion like a wild ox. [7] Adonai's voice can carve out flames of fire. [8] Adonai's voice can make the desert tremble. Adonai can make the Kadesh desert tremble. [9] Adonai's voice can pierce oak trees and strip forests. In his palace, everything says "Honor." [10] Adonai reigned during the flood, and Adonai will reign supreme forever. [11] Adonai will give strength to his people. Adonai will bless his people with peace.

מִזְמוֹר לְדָוִד: הָבוּ לַיְיָ בְּנֵי אֵלִים הָבוּ לַיְיָ כָּבוֹד וָעֹז: [2] הָבוּ לַיְיָ כְּבוֹד שְׁמוֹ הִשְׁתַּחֲווּ לַיְיָ בְּהַדְרַת־קֹדֶשׁ: [3] קוֹל יְיָ עַל־הַמָּיִם אֵל־הַכָּבוֹד הִרְעִים יְיָ עַל־מַיִם רַבִּים: [4] קוֹל־יְיָ בַּכֹּחַ קוֹל־יְיָ בֶּהָדָר: [5] קוֹל־יְיָ שֹׁבֵר אֲרָזִים וַיְשַׁבֵּר יְיָ אֶת־אַרְזֵי הַלְּבָנוֹן: [6] וַיַּרְקִידֵם כְּמוֹ־עֵגֶל לְבָנוֹן וְשִׂרְיֹן כְּמוֹ בֶן־רְאֵמִים: [7] קוֹל־יְיָ חֹצֵב לַהֲבוֹת אֵשׁ: [8] קוֹל יְיָ יָחִיל מִדְבָּר יָחִיל יְיָ מִדְבַּר קָדֵשׁ: [9] קוֹל יְיָ יְחוֹלֵל אַיָּלוֹת וַיֶּחֱשֹׂף יְעָרוֹת וּבְהֵיכָלוֹ כֻּלּוֹ אֹמֵר כָּבוֹד: [10] יְיָ לַמַּבּוּל יָשָׁב וַיֵּשֶׁב יְיָ מֶלֶךְ לְעוֹלָם: [11] יְיָ עֹז לְעַמּוֹ יִתֵּן יְיָ יְבָרֵךְ אֶת־עַמּוֹ בַשָּׁלוֹם:

99

BRETTLER (BIBLE)

Psalm 29 God appears as at Sinai, in earthquake and thunderstorm (Exod. 19:16, 18). This psalm is probably a monotheized version of a Canaanite poem praising Baal for his power. It localizes the storm in the Lebanon mountain range (v. 6), where Baal was worshiped, and refers to the mythic conquest of the rebellious water deity (v. 3) (see above, "Let the sea thunder … the rivers clap their hands"). The ultimate result of God's great power is that He "will reign supreme forever" (v. 10), and that is why this psalm follows Psalms 95–99 in *Kabbalat Shabbat!*

The Book of Psalms came together gradually. Psalm 72:20, in fact, announces itself as "the *(p. 102)*

DORFF (THEOLOGY)

[1] *"You heavenly beings"* See above, "More revered than all other gods."

---◆---

FRANKEL (A WOMAN'S VOICE)

[3] *"Voice [kol]"* Echoing the themes of the previous five psalms—but out of sequence with them—this psalm circles back yet again to the subject of God's awesome power, expressed here seven times as *kol,* which can be translated both as "voice" and as "thunder." This mighty sound issuing from heaven can "break cedar trees," make mountains and deserts "dance like a calf," "strip forests," and even induce labor *(p. 103)*

GRAY (OUR TALMUDIC HERITAGE)

Psalm 29 R. Hillel, the son of R. Shmuel b. Nahmani, explains that the eighteen benedictions of the daily *Amidah* correspond to the eighteen times God's ineffable name (Y-H-V-H) is mentioned in this psalm (Ber. 28b). The Talmud stipulates further (R. H. 32a, Meg. 17b) that the source for *Avot* ("Patriarchs," the first blessing of the *Amidah*) is Psalm 29:1: "To Adonai, you heavenly beings *(b'nei elim),*" which Rashi (France; ca. 1040–1105) explains does not literally mean "heavenly beings" but rather "strong ones," *(p. 104)*

VI. PSALM 29

[1] David's psalm: To Adonai, you heavenly beings, to Adonai ascribe honor and might! [2] Ascribe the honor of his name to Adonai. Bow down to Adonai in holy beauty. [3] Adonai's voice peals across the water—the thunder of the God of honor—across great water. [4] Adonai's voice is mighty. Adonai's voice is glorious. [5] Adonai's voice can break cedar trees, and Adonai can smash the cedar trees of Lebanon [6] and make

KIMELMAN (KABBALAH)

[1] *"Adonai"* The Midrash saw in the eighteen mentions of the divine name a link with the daily eighteen-blessing *Amidah.* Every time we pronounce "Adonai" in the psalm we advance one more blessing in the *Amidah.* Thus as Psalm 29 ends with "May Adonai bless his people with *shalom*" so the final blessing of the *Amidah* ends with "Adonai who blesses his people with *shalom.*"

Kabbalah intensified the search for the meaning of Psalm 29. *(p. 105)*

KUSHNER & POLEN (CHASIDISM)

[3] *Adonai's voice* [kol adonai]" Noting that there are seven occurrences of the Hebrew word *kol* ("voice") in Psalm 29, Rabbi Ze'ev Wolf of Zhitomir (*Or Hama'ir*, s.v. Shavuot), following classical rabbinic exegesis, concludes that perhaps there are seven different kinds of voices. These, in turn, would therefore correspond to the seven *midot*, the characteristics of the psyche, which in turn are associated with the seven lower (of the ten) *sefirot* (*Chesed*, love; *G'vurah*, rigor; *Tiferet*, harmony; *Netsach*, achievement; *Hod*,   *(p. 106)*

J. HOFFMAN (TRANSLATION)

[1] *"David's Psalm [Ps. 29]"* Often translated, "a Psalm by David," but the title in Hebrew leaves the exact connection between David and the psalm ambiguous: is it "of David" or "by David"? Our English translation retains the ambiguity. On the other hand, "a Psalm by David" makes it clear that this is but one psalm of many, and that is a fact clearly indicated by the Hebrew but not by our English.

As with most psalms, Psalm 29 praises God with poetic language and loose meter. While our translation contains hints of the poetic language, we make no attempt to capture the meter.

[1] *"Heavenly beings"* Literally, "children of the gods."

[3] *"Adonai's voice peals across"* Taken from Birnbaum. The Hebrew literally reads "is on," but the next line, which is in apposition and thus parallel in meaning, refers to "thunder … across great water," suggesting that in both cases we have images of sound waves moving across an expanse. The English "peals across" thus best captures the poetic flavor of the Hebrew. Other possibilities, though less likely, are "Adonai's voice is above" or even "Adonai's voice is better than." *JPS* and *NRSV* both read, "The voice of the Lord is over the waters; the God of glory thunders, the Lord, over the mighty waters."   *(p. 106)*

¹מִזְמוֹר לְדָוִד: הָבוּ לַיְיָ בְּנֵי אֵלִים הָבוּ לַיְיָ כָּבוֹד וָעֹז: ²הָבוּ לַיְיָ כְּבוֹד שְׁמוֹ הִשְׁתַּחֲווּ לַיְיָ בְּהַדְרַת־קֹדֶשׁ: ³קוֹל יְיָ עַל־הַמָּיִם אֵל־הַכָּבוֹד הִרְעִים יְיָ עַל־מַיִם רַבִּים: ⁴קוֹל־יְיָ בַּכֹּחַ קוֹל־יְיָ בֶּהָדָר: ⁵קוֹל־יְיָ שֹׁבֵר אֲרָזִים וַיְשַׁבֵּר יְיָ אֶת־אַרְזֵי הַלְּבָנוֹן: ⁶וַיַּרְקִידֵם כְּמוֹ־עֵגֶל לְבָנוֹן וְשִׂרְיֹן כְּמוֹ בֶן־רְאֵמִים: ⁷קוֹל־יְיָ חֹצֵב לַהֲבוֹת אֵשׁ:

L. HOFFMAN (HISTORY)

Psalm 29 Classic Spanish-Portuguese ritual begins here and is followed by "What may we use for the Sabbath light…." The latter occurs at the end of our service, but its placement has always been a matter of debate (see Landes, "What may we use for the Sabbath light").

them dance like a calf, Lebanon and Sirion like a wild ox. [7] Adonai's voice can carve out flames of fire. [8] Adonai's voice can make the desert tremble. Adonai can make the Kadesh desert tremble. [9] Adonai's voice can pierce oak trees and strip forests. In his palace, everything says "Honor." [10]Adonai reigned during the flood, and Adonai will reign supreme forever. [11]Adonai will give strength to his people. Adonai will bless his people with peace.

קוֹל יְיָ יָחִיל מִדְבָּר יָחִיל יְיָ מִדְבַּר [8]
קָדֵשׁ: קוֹל יְיָ יְחוֹלֵל אַיָּלוֹת וַיֶּחֱשֹׂף [9]
יְעָרוֹת וּבְהֵיכָלוֹ כֻּלּוֹ אֹמֵר כָּבוֹד: יְיָ [10]
לַמַּבּוּל יָשָׁב וַיֵּשֶׁב יְיָ מֶלֶךְ לְעוֹלָם: יְיָ [11]
עֹז לְעַמּוֹ יִתֵּן יְיָ יְבָרֵךְ אֶת־עַמּוֹ בַשָּׁלוֹם:

BRETTLER (BIBLE)

end of the prayers of David son of Jesse," as if there is nothing else to come. Psalm 29 was written long before Psalms 93–99; that is why it does not appear alongside them in the Psalter.

[1] *"Heavenly beings"* Clearly not entirely a monotheistic psalm—"heavenly beings" serve alongside God as his cabinet.

[1] *"Honor* [kavod]" Psalm 24 calls God "king of honor" five times in four verses, so "honor" is a quality intrinsic to God, but what exactly is it? God promises Solomon "honor" (1 Kings 3:13), so it may be some specifically royal quality.

[3] *"Adonai's voice* [kol]" As a celebration of God's awesome power over nature, the psalm uses *kol* as "voice" or "thunder" no fewer than seven times.

[3] *"Great water"* A reference specifically to the water of Chaos subdued by Baal according to the Canaanite myth—changed to Adonai by the Israelites (see further Hab. 3:15; Pss. 77:20, 93:4).

[5] *"Cedar trees of Lebanon"* In typical biblical style, the second half of the verse repeats the first half but intensifies it—it is not mere cedars that Adonai's "thunder" breaks, but even the cedars of Lebanon, renowned for their height and strength (and thus chosen by Solomon for his Temple).

[5] *"Lebanon ... Sirion"* "Lebanon" refers to the mountain range in the modern

country of Lebanon, and Sirion is Mount Hermon there, where Lebanon, Syria, and Israel now meet.

[8] *"Kadesh desert"* "Kadesh" means "sanctified site," so several locations go by that name. Here, "Kadesh" is a wilderness in southern Israel. God's power extends from Lebanon in the north to Kadesh in the south (making this a literary device known as merism—reference to two polar opposites to imply both them and all points in between).

[9] *"In his palace* [heikhal], *everything says 'Honor'"* Heikhal is a loanword, originally Sumerian, meaning "big house," namely the royal palace. The Bible uses it for King Ahab's palace (e.g., 1 Kings 21:1) but usually God's palace, the Temple. The ascription of "honor" to God here occurs either in God's earthly (Jerusalem) Temple, or the parallel, God's Temple in heaven.

[10] *"Adonai reigned during the flood"* We would have expected "Adonai reigned at creation," not just "during the flood." The flood must therefore not be the later one of Noah's but a leftover reference to the Canaanite myth of Baal subduing primeval waters and becoming king.

[10] *"Adonai will reign supreme forever"* Like the conclusion to the Song of the Sea (Exod. 15:18; *Mi Kamokha* in our liturgy): "Adonai will reign for ever and ever." Human beings, like King David, also receive the blessing: "May my master King David live forever" (1 Kings 1:31), but only hyperbolically. With God, it is meant literally.

[11] *"Adonai will give strength … peace"* God's power is not just abstract; God shares it with Israel. But Israel's "strength" should be expended not on endless war but on *shalom*—peace and well-being.

◆

FRANKEL (A WOMAN'S VOICE)

in wild beasts. In the presence of such impressive power, can human beings do anything but proclaim, as the psalmist does (v. 10): *Kavod* ("Honor").

Yet, the word *kol* also conjures up another scene from the Bible: Elijah's encounter with God at Horeb (1 Kings 19:9–18). From his refuge in a cave, Elijah witnesses awesome displays of God's power: wind, earthquake, and fire, reminiscent of the revelation on Mt. Sinai (known also as "Horeb") many generations earlier. But Elijah does not interpret these natural wonders as signs of God's presence. Three times the text says: God was not there. Only when Elijah hears *kol d'mama daka,* "a still, small voice," does he emerge from his cave to speak with God.

Why is the *kol* that Elijah hears so different from the *kol* celebrated here in this psalm? As we prepare to encounter God through this Shabbat service, how does our situation differ from Elijah's?

Elijah goes to the wilderness of Horeb to flee the wrath of Jezebel and Ahab, the idolatrous and cruel rulers of the northern kingdom of Israel. Motivated by fear, religious zeal, and guilt, he ultimately finds God appearing in the guise of compassion, not power. Only when Elijah hears himself addressed by this gentle voice does he dare venture forth from his hiding place.

How do we appear before God each *Erev Shabbat?* Do we come, as Elijah did, filled with fear and trembling? Perhaps it is only an encounter with God's power—thunder, earthquake, fire, and storm—that can make us shed our pride so that we can address God in humility and be receptive to God's compassion.

———◆———

GRAY (OUR TALMUDIC HERITAGE)

namely, our patriarchs Abraham, Isaac, and Jacob. *G'vurot* ("[God's] might," the second blessing of the *Amidah*), comes from the end of the verse "Ascribe honor and might." Finally, the source of *K'dushat Hashem* ("God's holiness," the third blessing of the *Amidah*) is verse 2: "Ascribe the honor of his name to Adonai. Bow down to Adonai in holy beauty."

[1] *"Honor and might"* The Talmud notes (Suk. 55a) that in Temple times, the Levites would sing this psalm on the first of the intermediate days *(Chol Hamo'ed)* of Sukkot. The link with Sukkot (according to Rashi) is verse 1, "honor and might," which is taken to refer to the ancient Temple's Sukkot water libation, which the Mishnah (M. Suk. 5:1–4) calls the "joy of the Place of Water-Drawing." Rashi links that ritual also to verse 3: "Adonai's voice peals across the water."

[3] *"Adonai's voice peals across the water"* See above, "Honor and might."

[4] *"Adonai's voice is mighty"* Baruch Halevi Epstein was puzzled by this phrase, which, taken literally, can simply mean that God's voice is the product of some kind of exertion—a trivial truth about every voice, so hardly worth mentioning. But Epstein points out that the Talmud (Ber. 3a) describes God's voice in diametrically opposed ways: on one hand, God roars like a lion over the destruction of the Temple; on the other hand, as reported by R. Yose, the heavenly voice coos sorrowfully like a dove over the People Israel's long exile. Epstein thus interprets our verse to mean that God's voice reaches us in a manner appropriate to every situation, whether a roar or a coo (or, one might add, a "still, small voice"—1 Kings 19:12).

[8] *"Adonai can make the Kadesh desert tremble"* R. Yose b. R. Chanina (Shab. 89a) says that Mt. Sinai had five names. One of these—derived from our verse—was Kadesh, because Israel was sanctified (*nitkadshu,* from the same root, *k.d.sh*) on Mt. Sinai by means of Torah and *mitzvot.*

[10–11] *"Adonai reigned during the flood ... will bless his people with peace"* The Talmud

(Zev. 116a) recounts that when Israel stood at Sinai, the kings of the idolatrous nations heard loud noises and asked Balaam the seer whether the noises meant that God was bringing another great flood on the world, as in the days of Noah. Balaam responded, "Adonai will reign supreme forever," explaining that God had already sworn to rule over all humanity forever and not destroy them with a flood. When the kings pressed for an explanation of the noises, Balaam told them that for 574 generations even before the creation of the world, God had been hiding a great treasure—the Torah, which was now being given to God's people, Israel. Balaam pointed to verse 11, "Adonai will give strength to his people" as proof of this divine gift to Israel. The kings replied, "Adonai will bless his people with peace."

[11] *"Adonai will bless his people with peace"* In the context of the priests' blessing of Israel, God says (Num. 6:27), "Place my name on the children of Israel and I will bless them." The Talmud (Meg. 18a) identifies this blessing as peace, since "Adonai will bless his people with peace."

KIMELMAN (KABBALAH)

The tetragrammaton, or four-letter divine name (Y*[od]* H*[eh]* V*[av]* H*[eh]*), multiplied by its eighteen appearances in the psalm (4×18) makes 72, the number of letters in one of the divine names that kabbalists recognized, and also the numerical value of Chesed, "lovingkindness," for God gave Israel Shabbat as an act of *chesed*.

The eleven verses of Psalm 29 equal VH (6+5), the last two letters of the tetragrammaton, while the ninety-one words in the whole psalm correspond to the sum of two names of God, YHVH (= 26) and Adonai (= 65). Praying the psalm with the proper intention integrates the two names, a process known as *yichud*. This process corresponds to the union of "The Holy one, blessed be He" *(Tiferet)* and his bride, the *Shekhinah*.

[1] *"Ascribe ... might"* Shabbat celebrates the union of male and female. Sometimes this is seen as uniting two aspects of God; other times as uniting God and Israel. This union involves a reciprocal exchange of potency. In verse 1, we "ascribe might" to God. In turn (v. 11), "Adonai will give [back] strength to his people."

[3] *"Adonai's voice"* Psalm 29 was midrashically transformed to celebrate the anniversary of Sinai. The sevenfold voice of God recalls the seven-fold use of "voice" *(kol)* at the Sinaitic revelation (in Exodus 18–19), which also took place on the Sabbath. Since Shabbat becomes a wedding anniversary, seven also evokes the seven-blessing wedding ceremony, which in turn evokes the seven-blessing Shabbat *Amidah*, which in turn evokes the seven-fold mention of Adonai in "the musical psalm for the Sabbath day" (Psalm 92). The repetitive staccato-like "voice ... voice ... voice ... voice ..." pounds the multiple messages into our consciousness.

[11] *"With peace"* This ending of Psalm 29 anticipates the final verse of *L'khah Dodi*: "Come forth in peace," for Shabbat is God's gift of peace.

———◆———

KUSHNER & POLEN (CHASIDISM)

reverberation; *Y'sod*, connectivity; and *Malkhut*, the presence of God). (The *sefirot* receive many translations, corresponding to the many ways they are manifest in the universe. That is why the translations here differ somewhat from those used elsewhere in this book.)

———◆———

J. HOFFMAN (TRANSLATION)

[5] *"Can break … can smash"* The modal verb "can" is often, as here, merely implied in Hebrew. Literally, the verbs are imperfect, implying "will," but they are best translated as modal forms. The Hebrew for "smash" is closely related to the Hebrew for "break," creating a verbal pun we fail to capture in the English.

[5] *"Cedar trees of Lebanon"* The "cedar trees of Lebanon" were used symbolically to denote might and beauty.

[6] *"Make them dance"* "Them" refers to Lebanon and Sirion. The following line, "Lebanon and Sirion like a wild ox," is in apposition to "makes them dance like a calf," allowing us to identify "them" in the first line with "Lebanon and Sirion" in the second.

[7] *"Carve out"* Birnbaum: "strike." *JPS:* "kindles." *NRSV:* "flashes forth flames of fire."

[8] *"Kadesh"* The name of a place, with no relation to the prayer spelled identically. It occurs as part of the name of a biblical city, Kadesh Barnea (Num. 34:4), but usually as the name of a desert. The Rabbis identify it as another name for the Sinai (see Rashi to Ps. 29:8). Here, it is used in apposition to "the desert," possibly because the addition of the word Kadesh in the second half of the verse provides metric parallelism with the first half.

[9] *"Pierce oak trees [y'cholel ayalot]"* The Hebrew is hard to fathom. Our line is in parallelism with "strips the forests" *(yechesof y'arot)*. *JPS* takes *y'cholel ayalot* to mean "causes hinds to calve," seeing *ayalot* as the plural of *ayil*, "a hind [deer]." But then the phrase has no parallelism, so *JPS* has to suggest an alternative reading of *y'cholel ayalot*, "brings ewes to early birth." *NRSV* isn't sure, so prefers "causes oaks to whirl" but supplies the alternative, "causes the deer to calve." Birnbaum follows the latter. Probably we have all missed something.

[9] *"Everything says* [kulo omer]*"* This is the most likely interpretation of the Hebrew, followed by *JPS* and *NRSV* ("all say"), but it's not immediately clear why the Hebrew is grammatical, raising the possibility that again we have missed something.

[10] *"Reigned"* Literally, "sat."

[11] *"Peace"* Or "peacefulness."

◆ ◆ ◆

B. Greeting the Sabbath Queen and Bride

I. Ana *B'kho'ach* ("By the Might..."): A Mystical Meditation

[1] By the might of your great right hand set free the captive.

[2] Accept the song of your people. Strengthen and purify us, Awesome One.

[3] Mighty One, guard those who seek You like the apple of your eye.

[4] Bless them, purify them, and have mercy on them, forever granting them your righteousness.

[5] Strong One, Holy One, in your greatness guide your people.

[6] Only One, Exalted One, turn to your people who remember your holiness.

[7] Accept our prayer, hear our cry, knower of secrets.

[8] Blessed is the One the glory of whose kingdom is renowned forever.

אָ֫נָּא, בְּכֹחַ גְּדֻלַּת יְמִינְךָ תַּתִּיר צְרוּרָה, [1]

קַבֵּל רִנַּת עַמְּךָ, שַׂגְּבֵנוּ, טַהֲרֵנוּ, נוֹרָא. [2]

נָא, גִבּוֹר, דּוֹרְשֵׁי יִחוּדְךָ כְּבָבַת שָׁמְרֵם. [3]

בָּרְכֵם, טַהֲרֵם, רַחֲמֵם, צִדְקָתְךָ תָּמִיד גָּמְלֵם. [4]

חָסִין קָדוֹשׁ, בְּרֹב טוּבְךָ נַהֵל עֲדָתֶךָ. [5]

יָחִיד גֵּאֶה, לְעַמְּךָ פְּנֵה, זוֹכְרֵי קְדֻשָּׁתֶךָ. [6]

שַׁוְעָתֵנוּ קַבֵּל, וּשְׁמַע צַעֲקָתֵנוּ, יוֹדֵעַ תַּעֲלֻמוֹת. [7]

בָּרוּךְ שֵׁם כְּבוֹד מַלְכוּתוֹ לְעוֹלָם וָעֶד. [8]

BRETTLER (BIBLE)

[2] *"Song* [rinah]*"* A biblical synonym for prayer (cf. 1 Kings 8:28; Ps. 61:2).

———◆———

DORFF (THEOLOGY)

[7] *"Knower of secrets"* Uniquely gifted with knowledge of even our most private thoughts, God can surpass the limits of human justice. President Jimmy Carter once expressed guilt for lusting in his heart. Jewish tradition is, frankly, wiser: We are responsible only for what we do, not for what we think or desire. Even the last of the Ten Commandments, forbidding coveting what belongs to someone else, is, according to the Rabbis, punishable only if one longs for something unattainable by legal means, and then only if one acts on that *(p. 112)*

ELLENSON (MODERN LITURGIES)

Ana B'kho'ach This kabbalistic poem that pleads for Israel's redemption from exile was omitted from every single liberal prayer book of the past two centuries. It just did not comport with the rational ethos of the modern period. However, because of the contemporary turn to spirituality, and in view of the popularity that Jewish mysticism enjoys at present, this prayer has been included in the 1998 edition of *Sim Shalom* and the Masorti (Israeli Conservative) *Va'ani T'fillati.* Renewed *(p. 112)*

FRANKEL (A WOMAN'S VOICE)

[3] *"The apple of your eye"* This short prayer is one of the most intimate in the prayer book. Even though it is spoken in the first person plural (as is true of most Hebrew prayers), the sentiments expressed are very personal: "Accept the song of your people"; "in your greatness, guide your people"; "hear our cry, knower of secrets."

The speaker refers to a "captive" *(ts'rurah)*—literally, "one who is bound." (Paradoxically, the same word is used in our funeral liturgy to refer to the dead, whose soul, we pray, will be

I. ANA B'KHO'ACH ("BY THE MIGHT…"): A MYSTICAL MEDITATION

[1] By the might of your great right hand set free the captive.

[2] Accept the song of your people. Strengthen and purify us, Awesome One.

[3] Mighty One, guard those who seek You like the apple of your eye.

"bound up [*ts'rurah*] in the bond of life [*bits'ror hachayim*].") And although no specific captive is mentioned, we can assume that the speaker is referring to himself or herself, held captive by the human body, by mortality, by the frailties and failings inherent in human existence.

Particularly poignant is the plea that God "guard those who seek You like the apple of your eye [*bavat*]." Generally, it is only doting parents who refer to their children as "the apple of their eye," a charming idiom that describes the pupil of the eye *(p. 112)*

L. Hoffman (History)

HAVING COMPLETED SIX PSALMS ANTICIPATING GOD'S ULTIMATE REIGN, WE PREPARE TO GREET THE SHABBAT BRIDE AND QUEEN WITH A MYSTICAL MEDITATION.

"Ana B'kho'ach ['By the might...']" This work appears in the Hebrew as a poem, and by some standards it is. Other than the last line, "Blessed is the One..." it contains seven lines of six words each. But the point of the composition is the acrostic formed by the initials of the forty-two words, which spell out what

J. Hoffman (Translation)

[1] *"By the might"* Literally, "*ana* by the might...," where *ana* simply adds a poetic or formal sense. We have no English word for *ana*, here, or for *na*, below, so we omit these words in our translation. At any rate, the Hebrew words were chosen not for their meaning but to form the requisite acrostic (see L. Hoffman).

[2] *"Song* [rinah]" Or "prayer." The word is from the same root as the word we translated as "sing" in Psalm 95.

[3] *"Apple of your eye"* Literally, just "pupil." The phrase occurs elsewhere in liturgical poetry (see Volume 7, *Shabbat at Home*, p. 130).

[7] *"Prayer* [Shav'ah]" The Hebrew refers to a specific kind of prayer asking for something. Here, presumably, we hope that in accepting the prayer, God will grant what we ask. But again, meaning is secondary to acrostic (see L. Hoffman).

[1] אָנָּא, בְּכֹחַ גְּדֻלַּת יְמִינְךָ תַּתִּיר צְרוּרָה.

[2] קַבֵּל רִנַּת עַמְּךָ, שַׂגְּבֵנוּ, טַהֲרֵנוּ, נוֹרָא.

[3] נָא, גִבּוֹר, דּוֹרְשֵׁי יִחוּדְךָ כְּבָבַת שָׁמְרֵם.

[4] בָּרְכֵם, טַהֲרֵם, רַחֲמֵם, צִדְקָתְךָ תָּמִיד גָּמְלֵם.

[5] חֲסִין קָדוֹשׁ, בְּרֹב טוּבְךָ נַהֵל עֲדָתֶךָ.

kabbalists considered the forty-two-letter name of God.

The names of God have always occasioned more than simple interest. The Bible itself accents the various names. God tells Abraham, for example (Gen. 15:7), "I am YHVH [Adonai])." Two chapters later (17:1), God announces, "I am El Shaddai." To Moses (Ex. 3:14) God says, "I am *ehyeh asher ehyeh*. This shall be my name forever." Post-biblical Jews preferred the name Adonai—the Talmud (Kid. 71a) quotes God as saying, "I am not written the way I am pronounced; I (p. 113)

4 Bless them, purify them, and have mercy on them, forever granting them your righteousness.

5 Strong One, Holy One, in your greatness guide your people.

6 Only One, Exalted One, turn to your people who remember your holiness.

7 Accept our prayer, hear our cry, knower of secrets.

8 Blessed is the One the glory of whose kingdom is renowned forever.

⁶יָחִיד גֵּאֶה, לְעַמְּךָ פְּנֵה, זוֹכְרֵי קְדֻשָּׁתֶךָ.

⁷שַׁוְעָתֵנוּ קַבֵּל, וּשְׁמַע צַעֲקָתֵנוּ, יוֹדֵעַ תַּעֲלֻמוֹת.

⁸בָּרוּךְ שֵׁם כְּבוֹד מַלְכוּתוֹ לְעוֹלָם וָעֶד.

DORFF (THEOLOGY)

longing (B.M. 5b). Furthermore, if we intend to do the right thing but fail through no fault of our own, God still rewards us; conversely, if we intend evil but fail despite our best efforts to pull it off, God does not hold us responsible (Kid. 40a).

◆——

ELLENSON (MODERN LITURGIES)

interest in Jewish mysticism is truly international! Still, despite the attraction that mysticism has for today's Reconstructionist Movement, *Kol han'shamah* does not reinstate this prayer.

◆——

FRANKEL (A WOMAN'S VOICE)

as something especially precious, also referred to as the "window of the soul." So, too, we wish to be the window to God's soul and to see into God's "secret thoughts."

The speaker alternates between God's perspective ("Your people") and Israel's, "Accept our prayer, hear our cry" and "purify us." How like a child pleading with a parent: "You promised! I need, I want! Help me, please!" Though we address God as

"Almighty," wielding "the might of your great right hand," we still hope that God will care for us as our mothers do, cleansing and having compassion *(rachamim)* upon us.

———◆———

L. HOFFMAN (HISTORY)

am written YHVH, but I am spoken ADONAI." But YHVH is only how Torah writes the name. Medieval Jews tended to use individual letters, Y"Y (*yod, yod,* with a double apostrophe in the middle), or just a *dalet* or a *hey,* for example. By the time of the Kabbalah, a plethora of names was in use.

The prophet Zechariah (14:9) had predicted, "On that day, Adonai will be one and his name will be one" (a line that also found its way into our *Alenu;* see Volume 6, *Tachanun and Concluding Prayers,* p. 136). In its time, it probably meant only that some day, God alone would be recognized by all humanity—as *JPS* translates it, "On that day, there shall be one LORD with one name." But kabbalists took the prediction literally. Consumed with their own historical sense of exile and fragmentation, and convinced that God suffered similarly, they had developed an elaborate theory of *sefirot,* different aspects of God that were thrown into exile from one another during the process of creation but that would be reunited at the end of time. (See Koren, "The Mystical Spirituality of Safed," pp. 33–42, and L. Hoffman, "The *Sod* of Shabbat Liturgy," Volume 7, *Shabbat at Home,* pp. 18–21.) The whole point of Jewish existence was to effect that state by repairing creation's flaws *(tikkun olam).* With every *mitzvah,* the correct intention *(kavvanah)* would bring about such a unification (a *zivug),* even in the interim.

Kabbalists expanded the permutations and combinations of God's name. Different letters from the name were assigned to the *sefirot,* for instance, on the theory that reassembling the letters was tantamount to unifying the *sefirot* (a *zivug).* Vowels are often variable in Hebrew, so the *Zohar* (for example) divides ELoHIM into ELeH ("these") and MI (IM reversed, meaning "Who"). *Binah,* one of the highest and least knowable *sefirot,* is MI ("Who?"). ELeH ("these"—a demonstrative pronoun that assumes the act of pointing out) becomes the knowable *sefirot,* the bottom seven that descend from *Binah.*

Similarly, since Hebrew letters have numerical value (the first letter is 1, the second 2, and so on) the letters of each name can be added to provide a numerical tally. The possibilities are endless. Names can be spelled out. For instance, YHVH becomes *yod hey vav hey.* Then each letter of the spelled-out name can be added up. Kabbalists thereby arrived at many more names of God, with many more letters constituting them.

Kabbalists were not the first to experiment with the names, however. A discussion in the Talmud (Kid. 71a) already speculates on their sanctity, holding, for instance, that God's promise to Moses, "This [YHVH] shall be my name forever," can be read midrashically as "This shall be my concealed name" (*l'olam,* "forever," is read *l'aleim=l'ha'alim,* "to hide"). If so, it must have been passed down esoterically, from teacher to student, perhaps only once every seven years. But the Rabbis there know also of a twelve-letter name of God, and a forty-two-letter name as well, which is passed along only to mature, discreet, and modest people, fully in charge of their emotions and not likely to use it for personal gain. Rashi (d. 1095) admits he does not know any of these elaborated names, as do others, like Hai Gaon (d. 1034), who answered similarly, knowing neither what letters they contained nor how to pronounce them. The Tosafot (Chag. 11b), however, think it can be formulated by manipulating the opening words of Genesis, and master kabbalist Moses Cordovero (d. 1570) was able to shuffle the four-letter name to arrive at it. In any event, our poem is the recapitulation of one version of this forty-two-letter name of God.

Many rites omit it, however, even those that otherwise favor mysticism, like the Siddur of Jacob Emden (1697–1776). By contrast, many rites expand its recitation, saying it not only here but also in conjunction with the sacrificial readings at the end of the early morning service, and as part of the ritual for counting the *omer* (the days between Passover and Shavuot).

Tradition ascribes *Ana B'kho'ach* to the second-century rabbi Nechunya ben Hakanah, who is otherwise known for his piety and ethical relationships: "Never have I sought honor based in the degradation of others," he says (Meg. 28a). But the author is more likely an anonymous kabbalist living centuries later.

[8] *"Blessed is the One"* According to the Mishnah, "Blessed is the One" began in the Temple as a congregational response to hearing the four-letter ineffable name of God. So, here, it appears as a congregational response to the forty-two-letter name (see L. Hoffman, Volume 1, *The Sh'ma and Its Blessings*, p. 93).

II. *L'khah Dodi* ("Go Forth My Love..."): THE DIVINE UNION OF BRIDE AND GROOM

¹Go forth my love to meet the bride.
Shabbat's reception has arrived!

²"Observe" and "remember"—two words
  as one,
Proclaimed by the Only, forgotten by none.
Adonai is One. His name is One.
Praised, and renowned, and glorified.

  ³Go forth my love…

⁴To meet Shabbat, come, let us go
For she is the source from which blessings
  flow.
From creation's beginning a royal veiled
  glow
The last thought created, the first sanctified.

  ⁵Go forth my love…

⁶Regal city, the king's holy shrine,
Rise up and leave your upheaval behind.
Too long in the valley of tears have you
  pined.
The Compassionate One will compassion
  provide.

  ⁷Go forth my love…

⁸Shake off the ashes. Rise up from them!
Wear glorious clothes, my people, my gem.
Through the son of Yishai of Bethlehem
Redeem my soul. Draw near to my side.

  ⁹Go forth my love…

¹⁰Awake, awake! Your light is here.
Arise, shine out light bold and clear.
Wake up! Wake up! Sing verse to hear.
Through you the presence of God comes
  alive.

  ¹¹Go forth my love…

לְ֒כָה דוֹדִי לִקְרַאת כַּלָּה, ¹
פְּנֵי שַׁבָּת נְקַבְּלָה.

שָׁמוֹר וְזָכוֹר בְּדִבּוּר אֶחָד ²
הִשְׁמִיעָנוּ אֵל הַמְּיֻחָד;
יְיָ אֶחָד וּשְׁמוֹ אֶחָד
לְשֵׁם וּלְתִפְאֶרֶת וְלִתְהִלָּה.

לְכָה דוֹדִי לִקְרַאת כַּלָּה... ³

לִקְרַאת שַׁבָּת לְכוּ וְנֵלְכָה ⁴
כִּי הִיא מְקוֹר הַבְּרָכָה;
מֵרֹאשׁ מִקֶּדֶם נְסוּכָה
סוֹף מַעֲשֶׂה בְּמַחֲשָׁבָה תְּחִלָּה.

לְכָה דוֹדִי לִקְרַאת כַּלָּה... ⁵

מִקְדַּשׁ מֶלֶךְ עִיר מְלוּכָה ⁶
קוּמִי צְאִי מִתּוֹךְ הַהֲפֵכָה;
רַב לָךְ שֶׁבֶת בְּעֵמֶק הַבָּכָא
וְהוּא יַחֲמֹל עָלַיִךְ חֶמְלָה.

לְכָה דוֹדִי לִקְרַאת כַּלָּה... ⁷

הִתְנַעֲרִי מֵעָפָר קוּמִי ⁸
לִבְשִׁי בִּגְדֵי תִפְאַרְתֵּךְ עַמִּי;
עַל יַד בֶּן יִשַׁי בֵּית הַלַּחְמִי
קָרְבָה אֶל נַפְשִׁי גְאָלָהּ.

לְכָה דוֹדִי לִקְרַאת כַּלָּה... ⁹

הִתְעוֹרְרִי הִתְעוֹרְרִי ¹⁰
כִּי בָא אוֹרֵךְ קוּמִי אוֹרִי;
עוּרִי עוּרִי שִׁיר דַּבֵּרִי
כְּבוֹד יְיָ עָלַיִךְ נִגְלָה.

לְכָה דוֹדִי לִקְרַאת כַּלָּה... ¹¹

115

¹²Be not despondent. Be not cast down.
Why be dejected; why face the ground?
In a city rebuilt on its own ancient mound,
The poor of my people find shelter inside.

¹³Go forth my love…

¹⁴Shunned are all who would shun you.
Gone are those who'd overrun you.
The joy of your God shines upon you
Like the joy of a groom and a bride.

¹⁵Go forth my love…

¹⁶Spread out to the left and the right
Proclaiming the Holy One's might.
We'll revel in our delight
Through Peretz's son magnified.

¹⁷Go forth my love…

*[Worshipers rise and turn toward the
sanctuary door to welcome Shabbat. They bow
in welcome at "Come forth O bride; come forth
O bride!"]*

¹⁸Come forth in peace her husband's pride,
Joyful, happy, gratified.
Into the midst of the faithful tribe,
Come forth O bride; come forth O bride!

¹⁹Go forth my love…

*[Traditionally, mourners observing their period
of shivah now join the community in Shabbat
worship. As they enter the room they are
greeted as follows.]*

²⁰May God comfort you with the rest of
Zion and Jerusalem's mourners.

לֹא תֵבֹשִׁי וְלֹא תִכָּלְמִי ¹²
מַה תִּשְׁתּוֹחֲחִי וּמַה תֶּהֱמִי;
בָּךְ יֶחֱסוּ עֲנִיֵּי עַמִּי
וְנִבְנְתָה עִיר עַל תִּלָּהּ.

לְכָה דוֹדִי לִקְרַאת כַּלָּה... ¹³

וְהָיוּ לִמְשִׁסָּה שֹׁאסָיִךְ ¹⁴
וְרָחֲקוּ כָּל מְבַלְּעָיִךְ;
יָשִׂישׂ עָלַיִךְ אֱלֹהָיִךְ
כִּמְשׂוֹשׂ חָתָן עַל כַּלָּה.

לְכָה דוֹדִי לִקְרַאת כַּלָּה... ¹⁵

יָמִין וּשְׂמֹאל תִּפְרֹצִי ¹⁶
וְאֶת יְיָ תַּעֲרִיצִי;
עַל יַד אִישׁ בֶּן פַּרְצִי
וְנִשְׂמְחָה וְנָגִילָה.

לְכָה דוֹדִי לִקְרַאת כַּלָּה... ¹⁷

*[Worshipers rise and turn toward the
sanctuary door to welcome Shabbat. They bow
in welcome at "Come forth O bride; come forth
O bride!"]*

בּוֹאִי בְשָׁלוֹם עֲטֶרֶת בַּעְלָהּ ¹⁸
גַּם בְּשִׂמְחָה וּבְצָהֳלָה;
תּוֹךְ אֱמוּנֵי עַם סְגֻלָּה
בֹּאִי כַלָּה, בֹּאִי כַלָּה.

לְכָה דוֹדִי לִקְרַאת כַּלָּה... ¹⁹

*[Traditionally, mourners observing their period
of shivah now join the community in Shabbat
worship. As they enter the room they are
greeted as follows.]*

הַמָּקוֹם יְנַחֵם אֶתְכֶם בְּתוֹךְ שְׁאָר ²⁰
אֲבֵלֵי צִיּוֹן וִירוּשָׁלָיִם.

BRETTLER (BIBLE)

L'khah Dodi The Bible has no equivalent prayer; it does not view the Sabbath as a bride and never uses the rhyme scheme AAAB (or with the refrain, AAABBB). The poem draws on biblical language, however, changing it where necessary to fit the rhyme scheme, and using it creatively to mean new things.   *(p. 122)*

DORFF (THEOLOGY)

[1] *"Go forth my love to meet the bride"* The metaphor of marriage goes back to the Prophets (Hos. 2:4, 18, 21–22; Isa. 54:5–8, 62:4–5), who see God as the groom and Israel as God's bride. Rabbi Akiba (*Avot D'Rabbi Natan*, 1) expands the metaphor by   *(p. 122)*

ELLENSON
(MODERN LITURGIES)

[1] *"Go forth my love"* The patent mysticism of *L'khah Dodi* was anathema to early Reform rationalists. So was its blatant imagery of a desolate Jerusalem awaiting redemptive restoration at the   *(p. 123)*

FRANKEL (A WOMAN'S VOICE)

[1] *"Go forth my love to meet the bride"* Shabbat here becomes a feminine expression of the divine will manifest in our lives. Such, of course, was the intention of the kabbalist who wrote this poem, Solomon Alkabetz, who was intoxicated, as were his mystic   *(p. 126)*

GRAY (OUR TALMUDIC HERITAGE)

[1] *"Go forth my love to meet the bride"* The opening line of *L'khah Dodi* is reminiscent of R. Chanina's practice of wrapping himself in his cloak close to sunset on Friday and saying, "Come and let us go out to greet the Shabbat Queen," and of R. Yannai's similar practice of saying "Come O bride! Come O bride!" (Shabbat 119a; see Volume 7, *Shabbat at Home*, pp. 148, 152: Gray, *"Shabbat Hamalkah"*).

[2] *"'Observe' and 'remember'—two words as one"* The first version   *(p. 127)*

II. *L'KHAH DODI* ("GO FORTH MY LOVE…"): THE DIVINE UNION OF BRIDE AND GROOM

[1] Go forth my love to meet the bride.
Shabbat's reception has arrived!

[2] "Observe" and "remember"—two words as one,
Proclaimed by the Only, forgotten by none.
Adonai is One. His name is One.
Praised, and renowned, and glorified.

KIMELMAN (KABBALAH)

L'khah Dodi Other kabbalistic Sabbath songs are characterized by Aramaisms and technical kabbalistic terminology, but *L'khah Dodi* is written in virtually pure biblical Hebrew, along the model of Spanish Hebrew poetry. The masking of its kabbalistic message is so successful that only a kabbalist attuned to its theology can unlock its meaning. Much depends on prior understanding of the kabbalistic system of *sefirot* (see Koren, pp. 33–42).

Since the six introductory   *(p. 128)*

KUSHNER & POLEN (CHASIDISM)

L'khah Dodi Gematria is an ancient system of assigning a numerical equivalent to each Hebrew letter based on its sequential place in the alphabet. (It is the most popular, but by no means the only, system of extracting additional meaning from the letters and words of the holy language.) Thus, *aleph*, the first letter, is 1; *bet*, the second letter, is 2; *gimel*, the third letter, 3; and so forth until we get to *yod*, which is 10. From then on, letters increase by tens until we reach *kuf*, which is 100. The   *(p. 132)*

L. HOFFMAN (HISTORY)

L'KHAH DODI CONCLUDES THE KAB-BALISTIC SECTION OF KABBALAT SHABBAT. IT FOLLOWS IMMEDIATELY UPON ANA B'KHO'ACH (THE MYSTICAL MEDITATION ABOVE) AND IS MEANT TO COINCIDE WITH SUNSET, SERVING AS A WELCOME FOR SHABBAT.

L'khah Dodi This poem contains multiple esoteric meanings (see Kimelman). Probably the best-loved composition in all of Jewish liturgy, it appears in almost every rite. None other than Heinrich Heine translated it into German.   *(p. 134)*

¹לְכָה דוֹדִי לִקְרַאת כַּלָּה,

פְּנֵי שַׁבָּת נְקַבְּלָה.

²שָׁמוֹר וְזָכוֹר בְּדִבּוּר אֶחָד

הִשְׁמִיעָנוּ אֵל הַמְיֻחָד;

יְיָ אֶחָד וּשְׁמוֹ אֶחָד

לְשֵׁם וּלְתִפְאֶרֶת וְלִתְהִלָּה.

J. HOFFMAN (TRANSLATION)

L'khah Dodi I cannot resist a personal note about the almost unbelievable beauty of *L'khah Dodi*, in my mind the most perfect poem in our liturgy. The structure of the poem is flawless, adhering to strict rhyme and meter. The words themselves are composed almost entirely of biblical passages, sometimes rearranged for variety, yet they convey outstanding novel imagery and kabbalistic nuances beyond compare. Further investigation into the poem reveals not only an acrostic of the author's name but an oblique numeric reference to the unification of God (see Kimelman). Any one of these qualities would be enough to make *L'khah Dodi* a gem. Their combination puts the poem at the apex of our liturgy—our   *(p. 135)*

LANDES (HALAKHAH)

"'Observe' and 'remember'" "Observe" (*shamor*) refers to the thirty-nine categories of prohibited labor. "Remember" (*zakhor*) is the articulated proclamation of Shabbat's sanctity via (1) *Kiddush* at the beginning of the Shabbat ("over wine, for the nature of man is that he is stirred greatly when he feasts and makes merry"—Sefer Hachinukh, *Mitzvah* 31) and (2) *Havdalah* at its conclusion.

For Rabbi Samson Rafael Hirsch, the leader of nineteenth-   *(p. 133)*

³Go forth my love…

⁴To meet Shabbat, come, let us go
For she is the source from which
blessings flow.
From creation's beginning a royal
veiled glow,
The last thought created, the first
sanctified.

⁵Go forth my love…

⁶Regal city, the king's holy shrine
Rise up and leave your upheaval
behind.
Too long in the valley of tears have
you pined.
The Compassionate One will
compassion provide.

⁷Go forth my love…

⁸Shake off the ashes. Rise up from
them!
Wear glorious clothes, my people, my
gem.
Through the son of Yishai of
Bethlehem
Redeem my soul. Draw near to my
side.

⁹Go forth my love…

¹⁰Awake, awake! Your light is here.
Arise, shine out light bold and clear.
Wake up! Wake up! Sing verse to
hear.
Through you the presence of God
comes alive.

¹¹Go forth my love…

¹²Be not despondent. Be not cast
down.

לְכָה דוֹדִי לִקְרַאת כַּלָּה...³

לִקְרַאת שַׁבָּת לְכוּ וְנֵלְכָה⁴
כִּי הִיא מְקוֹר הַבְּרָכָה;
מֵרֹאשׁ מִקֶּדֶם נְסוּכָה
סוֹף מַעֲשֶׂה בְּמַחֲשָׁבָה תְּחִלָּה.

לְכָה דוֹדִי לִקְרַאת כַּלָּה...⁵

מִקְדַּשׁ מֶלֶךְ עִיר מְלוּכָה⁶
קוּמִי צְאִי מִתּוֹךְ הַהֲפֵכָה;
רַב לָךְ שֶׁבֶת בְּעֵמֶק הַבָּכָא
וְהוּא יַחֲמֹל עָלַיִךְ חֶמְלָה.

לְכָה דוֹדִי לִקְרַאת כַּלָּה...⁷

הִתְנַעֲרִי מֵעָפָר קוּמִי⁸
לִבְשִׁי בִּגְדֵי תִפְאַרְתֵּךְ עַמִּי;
עַל יַד בֶּן יִשַׁי בֵּית הַלַּחְמִי
קָרְבָה אֶל נַפְשִׁי גְאָלָהּ.

לְכָה דוֹדִי לִקְרַאת כַּלָּה...⁹

הִתְעוֹרְרִי הִתְעוֹרְרִי¹⁰
כִּי בָא אוֹרֵךְ קוּמִי אוֹרִי;
עוּרִי עוּרִי שִׁיר דַּבֵּרִי
כְּבוֹד יְיָ עָלַיִךְ נִגְלָה.

לְכָה דוֹדִי לִקְרַאת כַּלָּה...¹¹

לֹא תֵבוֹשִׁי וְלֹא תִכָּלְמִי¹²
מַה תִּשְׁתּוֹחֲחִי וּמַה תֶּהֱמִי;
בָּךְ יֶחֱסוּ עֲנִיֵּי עַמִּי
וְנִבְנְתָה עִיר עַל תִּלָּהּ.

לְכָה דוֹדִי לִקְרַאת כַּלָּה...¹³

וְהָיוּ לִמְשִׁסָּה שֹׁאסָיִךְ¹⁴
וְרָחֲקוּ כָּל מְבַלְּעָיִךְ;

Why be dejected; why face the
  ground?
In a city rebuilt on its own ancient
  mound,
The poor of my people find shelter
  inside.

[13]Go forth my love…

[14]Shunned are all who would shun
  you.
Gone are those who'd overrun you.
The joy of your God shines upon you
Like the joy of a groom and a bride.

[15]Go forth my love…

[16]Spread out to the left and the right
Proclaiming the Holy One's might.
We'll revel in our delight
Through Peretz's son magnified.

[17]Go forth my love…

[Worshipers rise and turn toward the
sanctuary door to welcome Shabbat. They bow
in welcome at "Come forth O bride; come forth
O bride!"]

[18]Come forth in peace her husband's
  pride,
Joyful, happy, gratified.
Into the midst of the faithful tribe,
Come forth O bride; come forth O
  bride!

[19]Go forth my love…

[Traditionally, mourners observing their period
of shivah now join the community in Shabbat
worship. As they enter the room they are
greeted as follows.]

[20]May God comfort you with the rest
  of Zion and Jerusalem's mourners.

יָשִׂישׂ עָלַיִךְ אֱלֹהָיִךְ
כִּמְשׂוֹשׂ חָתָן עַל כַּלָּה,

[15]לְכָה דוֹדִי לִקְרַאת כַּלָּה...

[16]יָמִין וּשְׂמֹאל תִּפְרוֹצִי
וְאֶת יְיָ תַּעֲרִיצִי;
עַל יַד אִישׁ בֶּן פַּרְצִי
וְנִשְׂמְחָה וְנָגִילָה.

[17]לְכָה דוֹדִי לִקְרַאת כַּלָּה...

[Worshipers rise and turn toward the
sanctuary door to welcome Shabbat. They bow
in welcome at "Come forth O bride; come forth
O bride!"]

[18]בּוֹאִי בְשָׁלוֹם עֲטֶרֶת בַּעְלָהּ
גַּם בְּשִׂמְחָה וּבְצָהֳלָה;
תּוֹךְ אֱמוּנֵי עַם סְגֻלָּה
בֹּאִי כַלָּה, בֹּאִי כַלָּה.

[19]לְכָה דוֹדִי לִקְרַאת כַּלָּה...

[Traditionally, mourners observing their period
of shivah now join the community in Shabbat
worship. As they enter the room they are
greeted as follows.]

[20]הַמָּקוֹם יְנַחֵם אֶתְכֶם בְּתוֹךְ שְׁאָר
אֲבֵלֵי צִיּוֹן וִירוּשָׁלָיִם.

BRETTLER (BIBLE)

[1] *"My love"* From Song of Songs 7:12, "Come, my love, let us go into the open." In medieval Safed, *L'khah Dodi* was recited "in the open," outside in the fields (see Koren, "The Mystical Spirituality of Safed," pp. 33–42).

[2] *"Praised ... renowned"* Stock biblical descriptions (see Deut. 26:19; Jer. 13:11, 33:9), but always in reference to Israel, never God, as here.

[4] *"Come, let us go"* Used twice in the Bible, in 1 Samuel 9:9, of seeking a prophet, and in Isaiah 2:5, of seeking God's light.

[4] *"From creation's beginning* [merosh ... n'suchah]*"* A paraphrase of Proverbs 8:23.

[10] *"Wake up!... Sing verse* [uri ... daberi]*"* From the Song of Deborah (Jgs. 5:12), but radically recontextualized. Words addressed to Deborah are here addressed to Jerusalem.

[10] *"The presence of God comes alive* [k'vod niglah]*"* A modification of Isaiah 40:5, predicting the return from Babylonian exile, and used here for a still later hoped-for restoration, perhaps modeled after the biblical one.

[16] *"We'll revel in our delight* [v'nism'chah v'nagilah]*"* Similar to Isaiah 25:9, Psalm 118:24, and Song of Songs 1:4; but the poet flips the verbal order for the sake of rhyme.

[16] *"Peretz's son"* Several biblical texts name Peretz as David's ancestor.

[18] *"Faithful* [s'gulah]*"* From Akkadian, meaning "private possession;" Deuteronomy (7:6; 14:2; 26:18) describes Israel as *am s'gulah,* God's "private possession."

[20] *"God* [Hamakom] *comfort you"* Before the Babylonian exile, even secular inscriptions contained the tetragrammaton (the four-letter name of God, YHVH). People started avoiding it in the Second Temple period, after which the Rabbis felt the need to develop surrogates. This one, "the place," may come from the fact that God resides in a sacred place. It may also reflect Esther 4:14, where "from another place" refers to divine intervention.

◆

DORFF (THEOLOGY)

defining the biblical book Song of Songs as a graphic depiction of their love. Separately, however, a second tradition emerged. Genesis Rabbah (11:8) tells us that every day of the week was given a partner, except for Shabbat. God rectified the injustice by making Israel the Sabbath's husband, and the Sabbath Israel's bride. Kabbalists expanded the wedding imagery further by applying it to the *sefirot* (see Koren, "The Mystical Spirituality of Safed," pp. 33–42)

[2] *"'Observe' and 'remember'—two words as one"* The two versions of the Ten Commandments bid us to "remember" the Sabbath day (Exod. 20:8) and to "observe" it (Deut. 5:12), leading the Rabbis to declare that God uttered both commands at once. This duality emphasizes the need to approach the Sabbath with both *keva* and *kavannah,* observing the commandments governing the day but doing so with full intention of remembering to make it holy.

[2] *"Adonai is One. His Name is One"* Since the Sabbath is "a foretaste of the world to come" (Gen. Rab. 17:5 [17:7 in some editions]; *Mekhilta* to Exod. 31:13), this Shabbat song emphasizes Jewish messianism. According to the prophet Zechariah (14:9), "On that day [in messianic times] Adonai shall be one and his name shall be one"—that is, all peoples on earth will recognize Adonai as God. We repeat this messianic line daily to conclude *Alenu* (see Volume 6, *Tachanun* and Concluding Prayers, p. 133) and repeat the idea in the *Minchah* service for Shabbat, where the middle section of the Shabbat *Amidah* for *Minchah* begins: "You are one and your name is one" (see above, "More revered than all other gods" for comments on monotheism and henotheism).

[6] *"Regal city ... rise up"* Prophetic messianism promised a rebuilding of Jerusalem and an ingathering of the exiles. As an inhabitant of Safed, and knowing first hand exactly how downtrodden Jerusalem was, the poet describes its hoped-for renaissance in powerful, poetic terms.

◆

ELLENSON (MODERN LITURGIES)

hands of a personal messiah, all of which made early modern Jews nervous lest their liturgy imply they did not feel fully at home in their host countries.

As a result, the pioneering Hamburg Temple Prayer Books of 1819 and 1845 replaced *L'khah Dodi* with a creative composition in German. Most nineteenth-century liberal prayer book authors followed suit in one way or another. In his earlier (and more traditional) liturgy, Abraham Geiger included at least a truncated version (see below for commentary on these selections), as did the 1940 *Union Prayer Book* (American Reform), but earlier versions of that book (1895, 1924) had omitted it, following both Isaac Mayer Wise and David Einhorn, the two primary liturgical influences from the nineteenth century here.

Interestingly, in their 1885 *Abodath Israel,* one antecedent for American Conservative liturgy, Benjamin Szold and Marcus Jastrow provided even a more abbreviated version of *L'khah Dodi* than that presented by Geiger. They too had hesitations about the poem's traditional theology. The full version was restored to American Reform liturgy with its 1975 *Gates of Prayer* and then found its way into Israeli (*Ha'avodah Shebalev,* 1982) and German (*Seder Hatefillot,* 2001) Reform. But an abbreviated version still marks the 1977 British Reform *(Forms of Prayer for Jewish Worship)* as well as the British Liberal Movement's *Lev Chadash.*

[1] *"My love"* In her *Book of Blessings,* feminist author Marcia Falk substitutes *re'ot* ("friends," feminine) in the first line and *re'im* ("friends," masculine) in the second, for "my love." In accord with her preference for non-hierarchical relationships, Falk translates the refrain, "Let us go, friends, to greet the bride, let us welcome the Sabbath."

[2] *"'Observe' and 'remember'"* In his 1854 Siddur, Abraham Geiger selected five stanzas of *L'khah Dodi,* including this one, for inclusion. The other four were verses 4, 10, 12, and 18. In light of his omission of *L'khah Dodi* altogether in his 1870 prayer book, and in view of the decision made by most nineteenth-century Reform prayer book authors to delete this prayer altogether, Geiger's decision to include so many of the traditional stanzas in 1854 is notable. It reflects the role that Geiger then played as a community rabbi in Breslau who felt that Reform must proceed with caution lest it be deemed too radical. The complete removal of *L'khah Dodi* would have shocked the many Jews who regarded this prayer as a staple of Friday night worship.

But he omitted verses 6, 8, 14, and 16. Geiger was clearly balancing his anti-messianic and anti-nationalistic sensibilities against received and expected liturgical practice. He obviously selected those stanzas that focus on the Sabbath itself, while eschewing those that expressed a belief in a personal messiah and the restoration of Zion and Jerusalem. Where necessary (see below, "Awake awake!... Be not despondent"), he employed "translation" as a means for obviating the manifest content of prayers he felt he had to include even though he disagreed with what they had to say.

Interestingly, several other Reform and liberal prayer books that have included *L'khah Dodi* have followed Geiger's 1854 pattern by offering their own abbreviated versions. For example, early Conservative rabbis Szold and Jastrow—and the *UPB* of 1940, too—included stanzas 4, 6, and 18. This newly revised version of *UPB* at least included that much: its 1895 and 1921 predecessors had omitted the poem altogether.

In the contemporary period, virtually all liberal Siddurim—all Reconstructionist and Conservative prayer books as well as most present-day Reform ones (like *GOP* and *Ha'avodah Shebalev*)—include all the stanzas. Clearly, nineteenth-century liberal opposition to classical notions of redemption and Jewish nationalism has been muted, if not overturned altogether.

The two current British non-Orthodox prayer books, *Forms of Prayer for Jewish Worship* and *Lev Chadash,* are the exceptions to this rule. In each, only four stanzas (2, 3, 10, and 18) have been included.

Part of the poem's popularity (and a good reason in itself to include it) is the plethora of popular "singable" melodies that are used for it. When *UPB* 1924 introduced it, the editors were careful to assign it to the choir. Congregations today insist on singing it.

[10, 12] *"Awake, awake!... Be not despondent"* One of the most notable facets of Geiger's editorship was his decision to include these two stanzas in 1854. He apparently also felt the need to mute the meaning even of the stanzas he included, especially here! To

do so, he employed the time-honored method of creatively "translating" the Hebrew to obviate its plain meaning. "Awake, awake" by itself was not necessarily troublesome, since it contains reference to light, a favorite liberal image of the "Enlightenment" and, therefore, universal overtones of redemption and hope. Still, the obvious reference was to Jerusalem lying asleep and awaiting messianic light to dawn. "Be not despondent" (v. 12) is an equally clear personification of Jerusalem in ruins. Seeing their common theme, Geiger collapsed the two stanzas together and offered a paraphrase that removed all references to Zion. Instead, he spoke of "God's kingdom *(Gottesreich)*" being built for all peoples and emphasized how "the love and unity of mankind *(die Menschen)*" would one day emerge (see below, "A city rebuilt").

[12] *"A city rebuilt"* Like "Awake, awake" and "Be not despondent" (see above), Geiger included this line in 1854 but avoided its particularistic meaning as a prayer for the rebuilding of Zion and Jerusalem by paraphrasing it in universal terms. (Geiger went the easier route of omitting the whole prayer from his 1870 prayer book.)

One hundred years after Geiger's initial liturgy, Jewish nationalism was no longer a scandal. In the wake of Hitler, almost all Jews were ardent Zionists. Conservative Judaism had always been so, and its 1945 Rabbinical Assembly Siddur speaks clearly of Zionist dreams when it renders the line "Zion, my city, in thee shall find rest." More recently, Falk's *Book of Blessings* states directly, "Jerusalem will be rebuilt on its hill." The controversy surrounding references to Zion that so wracked nineteenth-century liberal Judaism has long since passed.

[14] *"The joy of your God shines upon you"* Seeing "God" as necessarily masculine in popular consciousness, Marcia Falk substitutes *ziv hashekhinah alayich niglah,* which she translates as *"Shekhinah's* radiance is revealed in you," for the traditional "joy of your God." Her choice also bespeaks her emphasis upon immanence, rather than the distance inherent in traditional transcendent imagery. Joy need not shine on us from without. It can be "revealed in" us.

[18] *"Her husband's pride"* Falk substitutes *ateret shekhinah,* which she translates "crown of *Shekhinah."* The 1985 Conservative *Sim Shalom* provides "soul mate, sweet gift of the Lord." By 1998, "the Lord" was too sexist, so the revised version translates "soul mate, sweet bride so adored." The Reconstructionist *Kol han'shamah* answers the gender issue by using "divine crown." Sexism was not perceived as an issue for British Reform in 1977 (which, however, uses a poetic paraphrase for the whole poem). Nor, quite obviously, did sexism matter for the various editions of the Union Prayer Book (1895, 1924, 1940). But the Chicago Sinai modern rendering of the book (2000), which frequently alters the English to demonstrate gender sensitivity, nonetheless leaves "crown of your husband" untouched. Current British Liberal liturgy (1995) selects "creation's crown."

[20] *"Mourners"* The conclusion of the 1985 *Sim Shalom* (Conservative) offers the following instruction: "Mourners do not observe public forms of mourning on Shabbat.

On the Shabbat during the period of *shivah,* when mourners attend synagogue services, they are greeted after the singing of *L'khah Dodi,* by all other members of the congregation, with these words...." The traditional greeting offered to mourners during the *shivah* period follows, with a literal translation, "May God comfort you together with all the other mourners of Zion and Jerusalem." The Israeli Masorti *Va'ani T'fillati* includes this greeting as well, but so, already, did 1945 Conservative liturgy. However, the Israeli *Va'ani T'fillati* considers the classical greeting inappropriate for a world in which the Jewish State has been rebuilt. Consequently, it alters the Hebrew to read, *Hamakon y'nakhem etchem b'tokh sh'ar ha'avelim b'tziyon u'vi'rushalayim:* "May God comfort you among the mourners *who are in* Zion and Jerusalem." One should no longer mourn *for* Zion and Jerusalem. These are no longer "dead."

——◆——

FRANKEL (A WOMAN'S VOICE)

companions in Safed, with the notion of God as a multitude of divine selves, acting upon the world in various ways. The self closest to our own experience is the *shekhinah,* God's feminine dimension, here associated with Shabbat as a bride. Although God is also depicted in masculine form—as a bridegroom—the mystic tone of the poem suggests that we, as the People Israel, are guests at a heavenly wedding, witnessing the union of two aspects of divine holiness.

Women are also present at this wedding, either at the synagogue on Friday night or at home, where many Sabbath hymns likewise adopt this metaphor. Yet, until now it was believed that Jewish men alone could fathom the deeper kabbalistic secrets only hinted at in poems such as *L'khah Dodi.* Women, traditionally seen as more earthbound to the world of materiality, and intellectually incapable of understanding esoteric mysteries, were to be excluded from mystic study and practice. However, it has recently come to light that between 1648 and 1720, many editions of Jewish prayer books throughout the Ashkenazi world were printed with a Yiddish supplement intended specifically for women, and that this supplement is infused with kabbalistic content. Known as *Seyder Tkhines* and of anonymous authorship, this collection of Yiddish prayers expressed the widespread belief that the coming of the messiah was at hand, if only Jewish men *and women* would turn to God in prayer and devotion. This inclusive outlook was short-lived, however. Following the devastating conversion of the false messiah Shabbetai Zevi in 1666 and the scandal of religious heresies in its wake, Jewish messianic hopes became suspect, and by 1720, *Seyder Tkhines* was no longer being added to the standard Siddur. With its absence, we lost the widespread acceptance of Jewish women as valued spiritual partners in hastening redemption.

Following is a stanza from a prayer from *Seyder Tkhines,* to be recited by a Jewish woman after lighting the Shabbat candles.

You have singled out
The Sabbath for rest,
So we may honor it
And rejoice in it,
And illuminate it
With candle light,
To serve you joyfully today
On Your holy Sabbath,
Which we are bound to honor
And keep in all things,
Like a king his queen
Or a bridegroom his bride,
Because in the words of our sages:
The Sabbath is queen and bride.

(Translated by Devra Kay, *Seyder Tkhines: The Forgotten Book of Common Prayer for Jewish Women* [Philadelphia: Jewish Publication Society, 2004], p. 256.)

The speaker in this prayer, like those who recite *L'khah Dodi,* identifies herself with king and bridegroom as she welcomes the Sabbath. She is not allowed to lead the congregation in the public worship that formally initiates Shabbat, but she sees herself as empowered to invite in Shabbat anyway, on behalf of the People Israel.

———◆———

GRAY (OUR TALMUDIC HERITAGE)

of the Ten Commandments (Exodus 20:8) says, "Remember the Sabbath day," but the second version (Deuteronomy 5:15) says, "Observe the Sabbath day." The Talmud (Shev. 20b) reconciles the two by saying that God proclaimed them simultaneously, something that "the [human] mouth cannot say, nor the ear bear to hear."

[4] *"The source from which blessings flow"* When properly observed, Shabbat bestows blessing on Israel (Shab. 119a; see Volume 7, *Shabbat at Home,* p. 84: Gray, *"Eshet Chayil"*).

[4] *"From creation's beginning a royal veiled glow ... the first sanctified"* The last line is usually translated literally as "last in creation, first in God's plan." Baruch Halevi Epstein paraphrases a midrash according to which the purpose of the creation of the days of the week was to lead up to the creation of Shabbat. Shabbat is thus the ultimate purpose behind the creation of the week; in that sense, although it was the last created, it was first in God's thoughts. Epstein further compares this to preparations for a wedding: first we prepare all the wedding necessities, and only then do we bring the bride underneath the *chuppah.* As the ultimate purpose of the wedding preparations is the entrance of the bride, so was the ultimate purpose of the creation of the week the entrance of Shabbat.

———◆———

KIMELMAN (KABBALAH)

psalms correspond to the six days of the week, the end of Psalm 29 (the last of them) marks the end of Friday. It should have immediately ushered us into Psalm 92, "A musical song for the Sabbath day," instead of *L'khah Dodi*. By coming between Psalm 29 (p. 29) and Psalm 92 (p. 139), *L'khah Dodi* serves as the bridge between the end of Friday and the beginning of Shabbat, thereby linking profane and holy time.

How is *L'khah Dodi* a bridge between the profane and the holy? Since the profane represents the unredeemed, or not-yet-redeemed, and the holy the redeemed, the question becomes, How does *L'khah Dodi* create a bridge to redemption? To answer this, much needs to be known about *L'khah Dodi*. We can begin it here, but all the comments that follow, regarding individual verses, bear on the subject.

The poem's language speaks to us on four levels. Its explicit subjects are Shabbat and Jerusalem, which address the dimensions of time and space. Its implicit subjects are the People Israel and the realm of the *sefirot* (which mirrors the other three). The goal is to bring all four under the canopy of the holy. Its redemptive vision is both utopian (looking toward the end of time) and restorative (recapitulating the perfection of Eden).

To impart this message, *L'khah Dodi* weaves together strands of biblical verses, rabbinic midrash, liturgical *piyyut*, Spanish Hebrew poetry, Renaissance meditative poetry, and marriage madrigals into a kabbalistic lyric of redemption. A comparable poem is Edmund Spenser's "Epithalamion," composed a generation later in 1595.

Poetically speaking, *L'khah Dodi* has nine stanzas, corresponding to the nine lower *sefirot*, and a repeating refrain corresponding to the tenth *sefirah*, *Keter*. As the refrain energizes each stanza, so too, in the kabbalistic system, *Keter* energizes each *sefirah*.

Each stanza contains four lines. Assigning letters to the closing sounds of each line (a = *ah*, b = *ee*, and c = *ayikh*), we can see a carefully laid out rhyme scheme. The refrain (vv. 1, 3, 5, etc., here) is *aa*; verses 2, 4, 6, and 18 (stanzas 2, 3, and 9) are *aaaa*; verses 8, 10, 12, and 16 (stanzas 4, 5, 6, and 8) are *bbba*; and verse 14 (stanza 7) is *ccca*.

The poem is attributed to Solomon Alkabetz. There is, however, no direct evidence from the period that he or Cordovero actually recited it. It first appears in a Moroccan document from 1577 and a prayer book from 1584. Nonetheless, other liturgical poetry from their time—especially by Mordecai Dato, who studied with Cordovero from 1555 to 1560—is so similar that there is no reason to suspect the traditional attribution of authorship to Alkabetz. Moreover, all the ideology implicit in it had already been applied by the kabbalists to the Shabbat recitation of the Song of Songs.

[1] *"Go forth my love [1]"* On one level the love expressed here is the love of Israel for God, the love of God for Israel, and the love of both for Shabbat, which is both the *sefirah Shekhinah* and Israel's bride.

On another level, the poem is about the love of groom and bride. Both levels converge in the word *Dodi*, "my love," for *Dodi* is not just an earthly husband but the divine groom too. Indeed, reversing the Hebrew letters of *Dodi* (DVDY ➝ YDVD) and exchanging the *dalet* for a *heh* (both common abbreviations for the divine name) results in YHVH: the divine name applied to *Tiferet* (the masculine principle in the sefirotic realm).

[1] *"Go forth my love [2]"* Both Israel (collectively and individually) and God are urged to welcome Shabbat by approaching their brides. As the earthly husband greets his earthly wife, so *Tiferet* greets *Binah,* the *sefirah* in the upper triad that corresponds to *Malkhut* in the final triad below (also called *Shekhinah*). Both husbands also greet *Shekhinah,* the sefirotic equivalent of Shabbat. The two movements occur in tandem. Both the human and sefirotic male *(Tiferet)* are surrounded by two females, one lower and one higher. The earthly husband is situated between wife (lower) and *Shekhinah* (higher). *Tiferet* is situated between *Shekhinah* (lower) and *Binah* (higher). It is the link with the respective lower female that allows for merging with the upper one. Ultimately, the souls of husband and wife will merge with *Shekhinah,* which itself merges with *Tiferet,* which in turn merges with *Binah.* Ultimate redemption is this merging of all into *Binah.* In the meantime, *Shekhinah* is the bride of both God and Israel. Her temporal expression is Shabbat. There are three partners in the marriage metaphor for Shabbat: God, Shabbat, and Israel. Since the Hebrew "to sanctify" also means "to marry," when God sanctified Shabbat and Israel, God took them as brides. Similarly, when Israel sanctifies Shabbat, Israel takes Shabbat as bride. Thus, Shabbat becomes the rendezvous of God and Israel. On Shabbat both human and divine meet. The meeting that takes place with *Shekhinah* in this world takes place on a grander scale with *Binah* (known as *Shabbat Hagadol,* the Great Sabbath) in the world to come. Hence, Shabbat is a foretaste of the world to come, *Shabbat Hagadol.*

The theme of union is reflected in the number of letters in the seven Hebrew words of the refrain, which add up to twenty-six, the numerical value of the tetragrammaton. These twenty-six letters are divided between two lines, the first with fifteen and the second eleven, reflecting the unification of the divine name (YH = 15, VH = 11; YH+VH = 15+11).

Each time we verbalize the refrain, we perform—in love—the unification of the divine by bringing together what was once torn asunder. Nothing can be whole without having been rent.

[2] *"'Observe* [shamor]' *and 'remember* [zakhor]'" Shabbat is really composed of three Shabbats. The Hebrew for masculine is *zakhar,* so *zakhor* represents the masculine. *Shamor* is then the feminine. The feminine *shamor* is identified with the Shabbat of Sabbath eve, represented by *Malkhut* and called "name" *(shem).* The masculine *zakhor* is identified with the Shabbat of Sabbath day, represented by *Tiferet* and called YHVH. As night precedes day, so *shamor* precedes *zakhor.* By observing Shabbat properly, through incorporating both feminine and masculine, *Malkhut* and *Tiferet* unite with each other, bringing about redemption. This is the third Shabbat which occurs at the end of the Sabbath, represented by *Binah.* That is why in the last service of Shabbat, *Minchah,* the *Amidah* states: "You *(Tiferet)* are one *(atah echad)* and your name *(Malkhut)* is one *(v'shimkha echad).*" Unification makes Shabbat the day of redemption,

as it says: "On that day YHVH (= *Tiferet*) shall be one and His name (= *Malkhut*) one" (Zec. 14:8). The human parallel is the verse "Therefore a man should ... cleave to his wife and become *one* flesh" (Gen. 2:24). When God is one and humanity is one, they meet as one. Some rites even cite the *Zohar* (II, 135a–b) to expound this idea of oneness. It states: "The secret of Shabbat: she is Shabbat, united in the secret of One to draw down upon Her the secret of One." Shabbat enables one and one to be one.

[6] *"Regal city"* Jerusalem. The opening two stanzas and closing ninth (vv. 2, 4, 18) spotlight Shabbat (sacred time), whereas the middle six (vv. 6, 8, 10, 12, 14, 16) feature Jerusalem (sacred space). Though human beings perceive time and space as separate dimensions, Kabbalah sees them as one continuum. Jerusalem is the *spatialization* of the holy; Shabbat is its *temporalization*. Desacralizing Shabbat brings about the destruction of Jerusalem and exile from the holiness of space. Sanctifying Shabbat brings about the rebuilding of Jerusalem and restoration to the holiness of space. *L'khah Dodi* thus allocates exactly six stanzas to reversing a Jerusalem destroyed, for a Jerusalem in ruins is to space what the six days of the week are to time. Jerusalem rebuilt, however, is to space what Shabbat is to time. As Jerusalem is a holy day in space, Shabbat is a sanctuary in time.

[14] *"Shunned"* The last of five stanzas (vv. 6, 8, 10, 12, 14) all deal with Jerusalem, *Shekhinah,* and the People Israel—they are interchangeable. Each stanza seeks a reversal of the lachrymose present, which it contrasts with redemption. Verse 6 commands, "Rise up.... Too long in the valley of tears have you pined." Verse 8 beseeches, "Shake off the ashes.... Wear glorious clothes." Verse 10 pleads, "Awake, awake ... Arise, shine." Verse 12 continues, "Be not despondent," and verse 14 predicts the riddance of all would-be despoilers, "who'd overrun you." Taken together, the five stanzas spell out the remedy: "The Compassionate One will compassion provide.... Through the son of Yishai of Bethlehem ... Through [Jerusalem] the presence of God comes alive ... The poor of my people find shelter inside.... The joy of your God shines upon you like the joy of a groom and a bride." The glory of God will thus be revealed to Jerusalem, the soul, and (in the sefirotic realm) the *Shekhinah,* too, for Jerusalem rebuilt signifies repair of the soul and the reconstitution of the divine name. To consummate the process, verse 14 reiterates the poem's primary metaphor: God will rejoice over Jerusalem/soul/*Shekhinah* as a groom over the bride.

[14] *"The joy of your God ... like the joy of a groom and a bride"* Genesis 1:27 explains, "God created *Adam* in his image, in the image of God did He create it, male and female did He create them." As the original human being was both male and female, so too is God. As the human image was divided into male and female, so is its divine counterpart split into "King" and "Bride." The unification of earthly husband and wife can prompt a corresponding unification in God. Connubial life can thus be an insight into divine reality.

[16] *"Left and right ... the Holy One ... We'll revel ... Peretz"* Here all four kabbalistic dimensions of *Shekhinah* are addressed: (1) Jerusalem, (2) the Sabbath, (3) the People

Israel, and (4) the *sefirah* of *Malkhut*. All four function as centers of their respective domains. Jerusalem is the sacred center of the world; Shabbat is the sacred center of the week; Israel is the sacred center of the nations. And *Malkhut*, which is portrayed as the center of ten encircling *sefirot*, stands for all of the above: Jerusalem (spatially), Shabbat (temporally), and the People Israel (humanely).

Expanding "left and right" is a spatial reference to the way the *sefirot* are arranged:

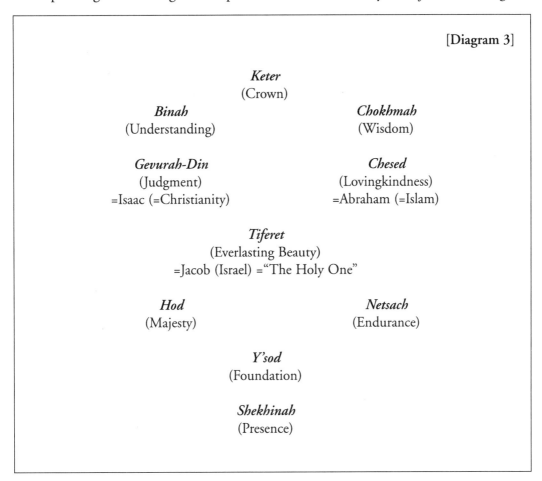

[Diagram 3]

Keter
(Crown)

Binah
(Understanding)

Chokhmah
(Wisdom)

Gevurah-Din
(Judgment)
=Isaac (=Christianity)

Chesed
(Lovingkindness)
=Abraham (=Islam)

Tiferet
(Everlasting Beauty)
=Jacob (Israel) ="The Holy One"

Hod
(Majesty)

Netsach
(Endurance)

Y'sod
(Foundation)

Shekhinah
(Presence)

The *sefirot* are said to correspond to biblical personalities. Thus, *Chesed* (on the right) is Abraham; *G'vurah* (on the left) is Isaac; *Tiferet* (in the middle) is Jacob—that is, the People Israel. Israel (through Jacob) expands to the right and left of the sefirotic structure embracing the *sefirot* of *Chesed* and *G'vurah* respectively. By virtue of its link with Abraham and thus his first-born, Ishmael, *Chesed* stands for Islam; similarly, by virtue of its link with Isaac and thus his first-born, Esau, *G'vurah* stands for Christianity. *Chesed* and *G'vurah* are, as it were, the arms of the sefirotic structure and thus cannot break through the restraining shoulders to get to the head, the uppermost *sefirah* of *Keter*. Only *Tiferet* can do so by virtue of being located in the middle.

Peretz (verse 16) is the messiah who will repair the breach created by Adam and restore things to their original state. Restoration of the pre-Adamic situation creates a world in which evil (the *k'lipot*) will be redeemed. As Israel brings about redemption through *Tiferet*, it spreads out to the left and right sides of the diagram, encompassing the rest of the universe. Thus, all of humanity, epitomized by Islam and Christianity, will return to the worship of God, for which, verse 16 says, "We'll revel in our delight."

Appropriately, the Sabbaths of Islam (Friday) and of Christianity (Sunday) are the first days to the right and to the left of the Sabbath of creation. In sum, the spatial sanctity of Eretz Yisrael will expand throughout the world; the temporal sanctity of Shabbat will radiate through the week; the human sanctity of Israel will extend to all nations from right to left (see J. Hoffman, "Left and right"); the divine *sefirot* will reunite; and redemption will have occurred.

16 *"Peretz"* Peretz, the messiah who brings redemption, precedes his descendant King David by ten generations. As David stands for the *sefirah* of *Malkhut*, Peretz stands for *Keter*, ten *sefirot* above. Redemption radiates down from Peretz to David, encompassing all ten *sefirot*.

18 *"Come forth in peace"* Stanza 9 (v. 18) brings everything to consummation. All four dimensions of the feminine, the Sabbath, Jerusalem, the People Israel, and the *Shekhinah*, are invited in/with/by means of *shalom*, for they are at once crown and spouse of their consort, human and divine. "Come forth O bride" occurs twice: for bride and queen, for just married and consummated; and for human and divine. Some make this explicit by adding: "Come my bride, the Sabbath queen."

KUSHNER & POLEN (CHASIDISM)

increments now progress by hundreds until we reach the last letter, *tav*, which is 400.

Perhaps the single most commonly noted *gematria* is the numerical equivalent for the *shem ham'forash*, the ineffable name of God, the tetragrammaton: *yod, hey, vav,* and *hey*. The numeric value of God's most awesome name is thus 10+5+6+5, totaling 26. And, while it strikes most moderns as arcane, it is difficult for even a beginning student of Kabbalah to encounter this number without taking pause. It is, in other words, a very significant number. Kabbalistic tradition furthermore often explains the broken state of our present world as a manifestation of the brokenness of God's ineffable name into its first two letters (*yod* and *hey*: 10+5=15) and its last two letters (*vav* and *hey*: 6+5=11). The messianic goal then would be to reunite the two broken halves, bringing them back to the ultimate total of 26, and thereby repair the cosmos.

Professor Reuven Kimelman (see "Go forth my love [2]"), in his *The Mystical Meaning of Lekhah Dodi and Kabbalat Shabbat*, points out that the four Hebrew words in the first line of the stanza *(L'khah dodi likrat kallah)* have 15 Hebrew letters, while the three words of the second line *(p'nai shabbat n'kablah)* have 11, totaling 26, the divine name. At last the unity is restored!

---

century modern Orthodoxy, *zakhor* is verbal expression, while *shamor* is physical demonstration. Since they were "uttered as one expression" at Sinai, they remain inseparable. *Zakhor* alone would be a "mere 'theoretical' observance of the Sabbath," while *shamor* alone would mean that Shabbat would "neither be taken to heart nor accepted by the spirit" (commentary on the Siddur).

[18] *"Come forth in peace"* As they say this line, some communities move, physically, to an antechamber or even outside, to greet the Shabbat Bride (Chaim ben Israel Benveniste, 1603–1673, Smyrna, Turkey: K'nesset Hag'dolah to Sh. A., O. Ch. 262).

Our general custom is to stand for this stanza even if praying alone (Chaim Kanevsky, B'nei B'rak, Israel, contemporary authority). One faces west (Mishnah Berurah 262:10). According to Yechiel Michael Halevi Epstein (nineteenth and twentieth centuries, Lithuania; *Arukh Hashulchan*, O. Ch. 262:5), one faces the door of the room. Rabbi Moshe Feinstein (*Ig'rot Moshe*, O. Ch. Vol. 5, #16) holds that if the door is not in the west, one should turn westward anyway. "People will do what they wish, and as long as the intent is to honor Shabbat, it is fine, but, in my humble opinion, turning specifically toward the door has no significance" (O. Ch. 263:45). These practices derive from Shabbat 119a: "R. Chanina would wrap himself in his cloak and stand at sunset of Sabbath eve, proclaiming, 'Come, let us go forth to welcome Queen Shabbat!' R. Yannai put on his Sabbath cloak on Sabbath eve and exclaimed: 'Come forth, O Bride, Come forth, O Bride!'"

From this quotation, authorities also conclude that one should dress up in one's Sabbath finery at this point (*Tzitz Eliezer* vol. 14:34) and that *Kabbalat Shabbat* should be chanted *b'simchah*, "joyfully" (*M'kor Chayim Hashalem*, Vol. 3: 112:6, by R. Chayim David Halevi, Chief Sefardi Rabbi of Tel Aviv, mid- to late twentieth century).

[18] *"Come forth O bride; come forth O bride [bo'i khallah]"* Repetition of *bo'i khallah* is a sign of affection (*Barukh she'amar*, commentary on the Siddur by R. Baruch Halevi Epstein, Pinsk, Russia, late nineteenth and early twentieth centuries).

[20] *"May God comfort you"* During *shivah* (pronounced shee-VAH, but, popularly, SHIH-vah), the week of mourning that follows burial, mourners remain home and worship services take place there with them. They are not present at synagogue services during *Kabbalat Shabbat*, either, because it is service of joy, and it is not yet Shabbat. After *L'khah Dodi*, however, Shabbat has been accepted and they can no longer publicly display their mourning (*Siddur Y'sodei Yeshurun—Shabbat*, p. 262; by Rabbi Gedalia Felder, Canada, mid-to late twentieth century).

[20] *"God (hamakom)"* Rabbi Meir Juzient (mid- to late twentieth century, Lithuania and Chicago) a master of Musar (pronounced moo-SAHR, but, popularly, MOO-sahr), the traditional Jewish ethical literature rooted in Halakhah, explained that we call God *Hamakom* ("The Place") here because mourners have "no place." Traditionally, during *shivah* (the first seven days of their mourning period), they sit on the floor, and

when they come to synagogue, it is customary for them not to sit in their regular seats for all eleven months of mourning. Understanding the feelings of dismay occasioned by having lost their bearings, we bless the mourners with the prayer that the source of *place* should grant them a renewed place among family, community, and Israel (conversation as I sat *shivah* for my father, Chicago, 1987).

———◆———

L. HOFFMAN (HISTORY)

It was composed by Solomon ben Moses Halevi Alkabetz (ca. 1505–1584), whose grave in a haunting medieval cemetery in Safed is still clearly marked and visited. Along with Joseph Caro, author of the *Shulchan Arukh,* Alkabetz is also credited with initiating the custom of spending the entire night before the festival of Shavuot in Torah study (*Tikkun leil shavuot*).

[18] "*Her husband's pride* [ateret ba'alah]" The sexual metaphor is graphic. "Pride" is literally "crown." Shabbat (which is also the last of the *sefirot,* God's feminine part, *Shekhinah*) is designated "crown." As a crown circles the head of a king, so the feminine aspect of God, *Shekhinah,* circles the divine phallus belonging to *ba'alah* ("her husband").

[20] "*May God comfort you with the rest of Zion and Jerusalem's mourners*" The syntax of the sentence leaves ambiguity as to whether the subject is "people who are part of Zion and Jerusalem [who] are mourning, or people [who] are mourning for Zion and Jerusalem" (see J. Hoffman). But a similarly worded prayer for comforting the sick is given in the Talmud (Shab. 12b): not "May God *(hamakom)* comfort *(y'nachem)* you with the rest of Zion and Jerusalem's mourners" but "May God *(hamakom)* show compassion *(y'rachem)* to you with the rest of Israel's sick." If our prayer for mourners is based on the similarly structured sentence of the Talmud, as it seems to be, the sense can only be "people [who] are mourning for Zion and Jerusalem."

That is what we would have expected. "Mourners of Zion" is a technical term, corresponding to a medieval movement of ascetics mourning the Temple's destruction. The trend went back to the years following the destruction itself, as can be seen by the Talmud's concern with people who mourn overly much. By the eighth or ninth century, many of these people were Karaites, the geonic opponents who denied the oral law by, among other things, darkening their homes on Friday night instead of celebrating with Shabbat joy *(oneg)* (see L. Hoffman, "Introduction to the Liturgy of *Kabbalat Shabbat:* Politics, Piety and Poetry," p. 1–20; and below, "What may we use").

With Kabbalah, "mourning for Zion" was given a new twist. "Zion and Jerusalem" were identified with the tenth *sefirah* (also known as *Malkhut* and *Shekhinah,* the feminine aspect of God). More than bemoaning the physical destruction of geographical sites, it meant mourning the alienation of God's feminine aspect from her male consort (the *sefirah Tiferet*).

Our custom of welcoming mourners to the service just before *Ma'ariv* is probably kabbalistic. Asking God to comfort them "along with the rest of Zion and Jerusalem's mourners" was tantamount to welcoming them into the worshiping congregation, where *everyone* was a mourner of Zion, but where such mourning ceased with the coming of Shabbat, because Shabbat as *Shekhinah* was reunited with *Tiferet* now, so there was nothing to mourn for. On a personal level, mourners were shown that their loss would not be permanent; their personal trauma was part and parcel of God's own sorrow, shared by every other Jew as well.

[20] *"God [hamakom]"* Calling God *hamakom* is talmudic. But kabbalists emphasize its numerological consequences: If YHVH is divided letter by letter (Y=10 + H=5 + V=6 + H=5), and if each of these is squared (100 +25 +36 + 25), the *gematria* adds up to *MaKOM*. In Hebrew—מקום—the "a" is a vowel but the "o" is the consonant *vav*. Only consonants get counted. So we get M=40 + K=100 + V=6 + M=40.)

◆

J. HOFFMAN (TRANSLATION)

liturgy's crown, as it were. It is therefore especially appropriate, it seems to me, that it is this poem that celebrates the arrival of Shabbat.

I am particularly grateful to my students Ethan Franzel, Wendi Geffen, Elisa Koppel, Eric Lazar, and Julie Saxe, who created this poetic translation of *L'khah Dodi* with me. As with *Y'did Nefesh* (Volume 7, *Shabbat at Home*, p. 135), we felt that the poetic impact of *L'khah Dodi* was more important than the literal meaning of the words. Accordingly, we set out to find an English translation that, at least in part, conveyed not only the words of the poem but its poetry. Because the version presented here follows the poetry of the original so closely, it can be sung to any of the melodies composed for *L'khah Dodi* in the original Hebrew. It also mostly captures not just the poetry but also the meaning of the original.

In terms of rhythm, all the verses (except verses 7, 8, and 9) consist of four lines, each with four heavy syllables and no more than two light syllables between each heavy syllable. The chorus consists of two such lines. In verses 7, 8, and 9, each line lacks one heavy syllable. Our translation similarly follows this strict rhythm. In terms of rhyme, the first three lines of each verse rhyme with each other, and the last lines of all the verses rhyme with each other. The rhyme that ends the last lines of all the verses also ends both lines of the chorus, and indeed all four lines of the last verse. Although we resorted occasionally to weak rhymes, our translation follows the same rhyme scheme.

We hope we have captured at least some of the lyric beauty of the original. We have done our best to include the kabbalistic references in the poem, but many of these depend on technical terms in Hebrew that we felt could not be translated into English; we have noted our omissions in the notes. Additionally, in Hebrew, the first two lines form a mystical reference to the unification of God (see Kimelman), a trick we could not replicate.

The first letter of each of the verses in Hebrew spells out the original author's name. If our verses spell anything, we have been unable to discern it.

[1] *"My love"* Often translated "my beloved," probably in at attempt to remove sexual love from the liturgy.

[1] *"Shabbat's reception has arrived!"* More accurately, "Let us welcome Shabbat," or, literally, "Let us accept the face of Shabbat." To "accept the face" is a common idiom in Hebrew, meaning "to welcome." In Psalm 95 we saw similar language. We chose "reception" here in keeping with the imagery of a wedding that pervades *L'khah Dodi.*

[2] *"Two words as one"* There are two versions of the Ten Commandments in the Torah. They are mostly the same, but in Exodus the command is to "remember" the Sabbath, while in Deuteronomy it is to "observe" it. Tradition holds that both words were uttered simultaneously as part of the same command. The Hebrew literally reads "as one speech act."

[2] *"Only"* The Hebrew *M'yuchad,* or "united," reflects the kabbalistic notion that God is composed of male and female parts, which must be united to form one complete God. The Hebrew word for "united" *(m'yuchad)* is related to the Hebrew word for "one" *(echad)* in much the same way that our English word "only" relates to the English word "one." Hence our choice of "Only" as a description of God here.

[2] *"Forgotten by none"* We added this concept for euphony; it does not appear in the original, which reads simply "proclaimed to us by the 'united' God."

[2] *"Renowned"* The Hebrew word for "renown" is actually the same as the word for "name," reflecting an ancient ontology that conflated the two concepts. Our translation misses that play on words.

[2] *"Glorified"* Hebrew: *Tiferet,* one of the ten *sefirot.*

[4] *"Creation's beginning"* Hebrew: *merosh mikedem,* "from the beginning, from *kedem." Kedem* means "before," but also "east," and (according to Genesis 2:8) is where God planted the Garden in Eden. In light of the rest of this verse, it is likely that *kedem* here forms a play on words that refers to creation.

[4] *"A royal veiled glow"* The Hebrew is simply *n'sukhah,* a word that has two relevant meanings. The root letters *n.s.kh* form the words for "prince" *(nasikh)* and "princess" *(n'sikha)* but also the word for "mask" *(massekha*—the "n" assimilates to the following "s"). Our translation spells out the play on words, which suggests that Shabbat was both "hidden" and "princely" (or, more accurately, "princessly"). In the next verse, we will see that Jerusalem is a "kingly city."

[4] *"The last thought created, the first sanctified"* More literally, "the last created, the first thought."

[6] *"Regal city"* Following the theme of "princess" above, in which Shabbat is "princely," the city is now "kingly."

[6] *"Shrine"* Literally, "city."

[6] *"Valley of tears"* More literally, "valley of Bacca." Bacca is a type of tree, but its name sounds like *bakhah,* the Hebrew word for "crying." The reference is to Psalms 84:7. "Valley of weeping willows" is a tempting translation that unfortunately rhymes with nothing.

[6] *"The Compassionate One will compassion provide"* From Jeremiah 15:5, in which the author, after describing the horrors of the time when God will abandon Jerusalem, asks, "Who will be compassionate to you, Jerusalem?" Hebrew often prefers doubling of roots (as in "He dreamed a dream") and that is what we get here: "He will compassion you with compassion." We try to double the word in English, too.

[8] *"My gem"* Added only for euphony.

[8] *"Yishai"* Or "Jesse." King David, who built Jerusalem and who, according to the liturgy, will rebuild it, is the son of Yishai.

[10] *"Bold and clear"* Added for euphony.

[10] *"Wake up! Wake up! Sing verse"* The Hebrew for "awake" in the line above *(hitor'ri)* and "wake up" here *(uri)* come from the same root, as do their English translations.

[10] *"Through you the presence of God comes alive"* Adapted from Isaiah 60:1. The original quote from Isaiah reads, "The presence of God shines upon you" while the Hebrew in *L'khah Dodi* is "The presence of God is revealed through you." (The Hebrew word for "upon" and "through" is the same, making the two versions seem closer in Hebrew than in English.)

[12] *"Why be dejected; Why face the ground?"* More literally, as in Birnbaum, "Why are you downcast? Why do you moan?"

[12] *"In a city rebuilt on its own ancient mound"* Its "ancient mound" is a *tel,* a technical term (identical in English and in Hebrew, though more familiar in Hebrew) for a city repeatedly rebuilt on its older ruins so as to form a hill.

[12] *"The poor of my people find shelter inside"* Isaiah 14:32. In the original poem, this line precedes Jeremiah 30:18. We reversed the order to make the rhyme work.

[14] *"Shunned are all who would shun you"* This line sets the stage for a word play that permeates the entire verse. The original reads, "Destroyed are those who would destroy you." But the words for "destroy" both times contain the sounds "sh" and "s" *(m'shi'sah* and *shosayich),* a use of sibilance that is continued in the following line, where the words for "joy" are *yasis* and *m'sos.* ("She sells sea shells by the sea shore" comes to mind.) We

try to capture the same word play in English with "shun" and "shine."

[14] *"Overrun"* Literally, "devour."

[14] *"The joy of your God ... Like the joy of a groom and a bride"* In the Hebrew, the parallelism of the last two lines is complete. "The joy of your God shines upon you like the joy of a groom shines upon a bride" would better capture the close relationship, but contains too many syllables.

[16] *"Left and right"* Literally, "right and left."

[16] *"Proclaiming the Holy One's might"* More literally, "Proclaiming Adonai's glory," but "glory" doesn't rhyme with "right" (or "left").

[16] *"We'll revel in our delight* [nagilah v'nism'chah]" From Isaiah 25:9, where, however, the verse reads, *nagilah v'nism'chah bishu'ato,* making it clear that the delight here is occasioned by God's deliverance, which Peretz, David's descendant, will bring.

[16] *"Through Peretz's son magnified"* A continuation of the messianic allusion from Isaiah 25:9 (see above, "We'll revel in our delight"). In the original poem, this line comes first, so that the reference to Peretz precedes Isaiah 25:9. We reversed them to complete the rhyme scheme.

[18] *"Her husband's pride"* Literally, "her husband's crown." It is particularly unfortunate that we couldn't keep the word "crown," but we needed "pride" to rhyme with all the other words ending in "-ide."

[18] *"Faithful"* Hebrew, *s'gulah,* a word whose exact meaning (see Brettler) has been lost.

[18] *"Tribe"* Literally, people.

[20] *"God"* Literally, "the place." *Hamakom* ("The Place") is one of God's appellations.

[20] *"Zion and Jerusalem's mourners"* Like the Hebrew, our English translation leaves open two possibilities: people who are part of Zion and Jerusalem are mourning, or people are mourning for Zion and Jerusalem.

◆ ◆ ◆

2 *From Medieval Eretz Yisrael*

Psalms for Sacred Occasions

A. PSALM 92: A PSALM FOR THE SABBATH DAY

[1] A musical psalm for the Sabbath day. [2] It is good to praise Adonai, to sing to your name, O Most High, [3] to announce your love by morning, and by night your faithfulness, [4] on harps of many strings, on melodious lutes. [5] For your creations make me happy, and I celebrate at the work of your hands. [6] How great are your works, Adonai! Your thoughts are very deep. [7] A simpleton will not know, nor a fool understand this: [8] When the wicked sprout like weeds and all evildoers flourish, it is that they be destroyed forever. [9] But You are exalted forever, Adonai. [10] For surely your enemies, Adonai, surely your enemies will perish, all evildoers scatter. [11] You raise my horn like a wild ox. I am soaked in fresh oil. [12] My eyes shall see those who lie in wait for me, as those who rise up against me to do evil will be heard by my ears. [13] The righteous bloom like a date tree, thrive like a Lebanese cedar. [14] Planted in God's house, they blossom in our God's courtyard. [15] Even in old age they will produce fruit, being invigorated, and fresh, [16] to be able to say Adonai is upright, my rock, in whom there is no flaw.

מִזְמוֹר שִׁיר לְיוֹם הַשַּׁבָּת: [2] טוֹב
לְהֹדוֹת לַיָי וּלְזַמֵּר לְשִׁמְךָ עֶלְיוֹן:
[3] לְהַגִּיד בַּבֹּקֶר חַסְדֶּךָ וֶאֱמוּנָתְךָ בַּלֵּילוֹת:
[4] עֲלֵי־עָשׂוֹר וַעֲלֵי־נָבֶל עֲלֵי הִגָּיוֹן
בְּכִנּוֹר: [5] כִּי שִׂמַּחְתַּנִי יְיָ בְּפָעֳלֶךָ
בְּמַעֲשֵׂי יָדֶיךָ אֲרַנֵּן: [6] מַה־גָּדְלוּ מַעֲשֶׂיךָ
יְיָ מְאֹד עָמְקוּ מַחְשְׁבֹתֶיךָ: [7] אִישׁ־בַּעַר
לֹא יֵדָע וּכְסִיל לֹא־יָבִין אֶת־זֹאת:
[8] בִּפְרֹחַ רְשָׁעִים כְּמוֹ עֵשֶׂב וַיָּצִיצוּ כָּל־
פֹּעֲלֵי אָוֶן לְהִשָּׁמְדָם עֲדֵי־עַד: [9] וְאַתָּה
מָרוֹם לְעֹלָם יְיָ: [10] כִּי הִנֵּה אֹיְבֶיךָ יְיָ כִּי־
הִנֵּה אֹיְבֶיךָ יֹאבֵדוּ יִתְפָּרְדוּ כָּל־פֹּעֲלֵי
אָוֶן: [11] וַתָּרֶם כִּרְאֵים קַרְנִי בַּלֹּתִי בְּשֶׁמֶן
רַעֲנָן: [12] וַתַּבֵּט עֵינִי בְּשׁוּרָי בַּקָּמִים עָלַי
מְרֵעִים תִּשְׁמַעְנָה אָזְנָי: [13] צַדִּיק כַּתָּמָר
יִפְרָח כְּאֶרֶז בַּלְּבָנוֹן יִשְׂגֶּה: [14] שְׁתוּלִים
בְּבֵית יְיָ בְּחַצְרוֹת אֱלֹהֵינוּ יַפְרִיחוּ:
[15] עוֹד יְנוּבוּן בְּשֵׂיבָה דְּשֵׁנִים וְרַעֲנַנִּים
יִהְיוּ: [16] לְהַגִּיד כִּי־יָשָׁר יְיָ צוּרִי וְלֹא־
עַוְלָתָה בּוֹ:

BRETTLER (BIBLE)

[1] *"A musical psalm [mizmor]"* Verse 4 specifies a *mizmor* as a melody sung to the accompaniment of a stringed instrument.

[1] *"For the Sabbath day"* Appropriate to the Sabbath because it deals with the wonders of the creation, which were only manifest fully on the eve of the Sabbath. The psalm also specifies the tetragrammaton (YHVH) seven times—an allusion to the seventh day of creation (PT Ber. 4.3 and parallels).

[2] *"Good to praise Adonai"* A simple but profound religious expression, in contrast to petitions, where God is praised to achieve some desired result, and *(p. 142)*

DORFF (THEOLOGY)

[4] *"On harps of many strings, on melodious lutes"* Musical instruments were part of the celebration of Shabbat in Temple times. When the Second Temple fell, it became customary to avoid instruments on Shabbat in remembrance and in mourning of it and of the *(p. 143)*

ELLENSON (MODERN LITURGIES)

Psalm 92 Even the liberal liturgies that omitted the kabbalistic Psalms 95–99 and 29 tended to include Psalm 92 and, in some cases, Psalm 93 (that follows) also. These are ancient (they are psalms) but lack kabbalistic connotations (they had been used liturgically *(p. 144)*

FRANKEL (A WOMAN'S VOICE)

[15] *"Even in old age ... being invigorated, and fresh"* On Yom Kippur, we earnestly entreat God not to "cast us away when we are old / When our strength is gone, do not abandon us" *(Sh'ma kolenu)*. That prayer resonates especially urgently in our youth-worshiping American culture, where wrinkles, sags, and diminished vigor loom as threats to be warded off at all costs. Of course, human beings have always feared old age, since it is the harbinger of our decline and death. But in *(p. 144)*

A. PSALM 92

[1] A musical psalm for the Sabbath day. [2] It is good to praise Adonai, to sing to your name, O Most High, [3] to announce your love by morning, and by night your faithfulness, [4] on harps of many strings, on melodious lutes. [5] For your creations make me happy, and I celebrate at the work of your hands. [6] How great are your works, Adonai! Your thoughts are very deep. [7] A simpleton will not know, nor a fool understand this:

GRAY (OUR TALMUDIC HERITAGE)

Psalm 92 This psalm presents two puzzles. Mishnah Tamid 7:4 claims that this was the psalm that the Levites used to sing in the Temple on Shabbat. But aside from this Mishnaic observation and the title of the psalm ("A musical psalm for the Sabbath day"), there is nothing about this psalm that remotely suggests Shabbat. Second, the psalm is not attributed to a particular biblical character, and there is no historical referent within it that could link it to anyone—a gap that typically *(p. 145)*

KIMELMAN (KABBALAH)

[1] *"A musical psalm for the Sabbath day"* "A musical psalm for the Sabbath day" can equally be translated "A song to the Sabbath day." As "a song to the Sabbath day," Psalm 92 functions like the song to a bride as she enters: "Here comes the bride." Upon the bride making her debut, the groom appears, so the next psalm (93) states, "Adonai is king, majestically robed." Together, the two psalms make the point that the Sabbath is not only the bride of Israel and the day of their nuptials, but also *(p. 146)*

L. HOFFMAN (HISTORY)

THE SECOND OF THE THREE COMPONENTS IN KABBALAT SHABBAT IS A PAIR OF PSALMS, PSALMS 92 AND 93. PSALM 92 IS EXPRESSLY LABELED IN THE BIBLE ITSELF: *"A MUSICAL PSALM FOR THE SABBATH DAY."*

J. HOFFMAN (TRANSLATION)

[1] *"A musical psalm"* Or "A psalm. A song." At any rate, the implication here is not that other psalms lack music (but see Brettler on the connection to musical instruments specifically here).

[2] *"Sing"* The Hebrew for "sing" here *(l'zamer)* is from the same root *(z.m.r)* as "psalm" *(mizmor)* immediately above. The verb may have meant specifically to "sing/recite psalms."

[2] *"O Most High"* We usually try to avoid the archaic "O," but here we see no choice.

[3] *"Love"* Hebrew, *chesed*, which frequently occurs with *emunah*, "faithfulness," in the Hebrew expression "love and faithfulness." In this psalm we find an expanded form of that ancient image, with "love *(chesed)* by morning and faithfulness *(emunah)* by night" expanding on the simpler "love and faithfulness."

[4] *"Harps of many strings"* Literally, "ten-stringed instrument and harp." Once again (see above, *(p. 146)*

¹מִזְמוֹר שִׁיר לְיוֹם הַשַּׁבָּת: ²טוֹב לְהֹדוֹת לַיְיָ וּלְזַמֵּר לְשִׁמְךָ עֶלְיוֹן: ³לְהַגִּיד בַּבֹּקֶר חַסְדֶּךָ וֶאֱמוּנָתְךָ בַּלֵּילוֹת: ⁴עֲלֵי־עָשׂוֹר וַעֲלֵי־נָבֶל עֲלֵי הִגָּיוֹן בְּכִנּוֹר: ⁵כִּי שִׂמַּחְתַּנִי יְיָ בְּפָעֳלֶךָ בְּמַעֲשֵׂי יָדֶיךָ אֲרַנֵּן: ⁶מַה־גָּדְלוּ מַעֲשֶׂיךָ יְיָ מְאֹד עָמְקוּ מַחְשְׁבֹתֶיךָ: ⁷אִישׁ־בַּעַר לֹא יֵדָע וּכְסִיל לֹא־יָבִין אֶת־זֹאת: ⁸בִּפְרֹחַ רְשָׁעִים כְּמוֹ עֵשֶׂב וַיָּצִיצוּ

[8] When the wicked sprout like weeds and all evildoers flourish, it is that they be destroyed forever. [9] But You are exalted forever, Adonai. [10] For surely your enemies, Adonai, surely your enemies will perish, all evildoers scatter. [11] You raise my horn like a wild ox. I am soaked in fresh oil. [12] My eyes shall see those who lie in wait for me, as those who rise up against me to do evil will be heard by my ears. [13] The righteous bloom like a date tree, thrive like a Lebanese cedar. [14] Planted in God's house, they blossom in our God's courtyard. [15] Even in old age they will produce fruit, being invigorated, and fresh, [16] to be able to say Adonai is upright, my rock, in whom there is no flaw.

כָּל־פֹּעֲלֵי אָוֶן לְהִשָּׁמְדָם עֲדֵי־עַד: [9] וְאַתָּה מָרוֹם לְעֹלָם יְיָ: [10] כִּי הִנֵּה אֹיְבֶיךָ יְיָ כִּי־הִנֵּה אֹיְבֶיךָ יֹאבֵדוּ יִתְפָּרְדוּ כָּל־פֹּעֲלֵי אָוֶן: [11] וַתָּרֶם כִּרְאֵים קַרְנִי בַּלֹּתִי בְּשֶׁמֶן רַעֲנָן: [12] וַתַּבֵּט עֵינִי בְּשׁוּרָי בַּקָּמִים עָלַי מְרֵעִים תִּשְׁמַעְנָה אָזְנָי: [13] צַדִּיק כַּתָּמָר יִפְרָח כְּאֶרֶז בַּלְּבָנוֹן יִשְׂגֶּה: [14] שְׁתוּלִים בְּבֵית יְיָ בְּחַצְרוֹת אֱלֹהֵינוּ יַפְרִיחוּ: [15] עוֹד יְנוּבוּן בְּשֵׂיבָה דְּשֵׁנִים וְרַעֲנַנִּים יִהְיוּ: [16] לְהַגִּיד כִּי־יָשָׁר יְיָ צוּרִי וְלֹא־עַוְלָתָה בּוֹ:

BRETTLER (BIBLE)

reminiscent of common post-exilic liturgical formulas: "Praise Adonai for He is good; His steadfast love is eternal" (e.g., Pss. 106:1, 107:1, 118:1; 1 Chr. 16:41; 2 Chr. 7:6).

[2] *"Most High"* See above, "Exalted," p. 80.

[3] *"Morning ... night"* Perhaps referring to specific times of day when God was praised in the Temple, but possibly a merism (see above, "Kadesh desert") meaning "always."

[6] *"How great are your works"* Like Psalm 104:24, which praises creation also as "works" ("How numerous are your works, Adonai; You made all of them in wisdom"). We use Psalm 104:24 liturgically every morning in the first blessing before the *Sh'ma* (see Volume 1, *The Sh'ma and Its Blessings*, p. 46). The accent on creation as highly thought through and patterned recollects the first creation story (Gen. 1:1–2:4a) more than the second (Gen. 2:4b–3:24), which depicts creation in a more haphazard fashion (on the two stories, see above, "He made it").

[8] *"All evildoers flourish"* Do good things happen to bad people? Not according to the very first psalm (Psalm 1), where they are simply driven like chaff, but here it is acknowledged that the wicked may prosper, at least temporarily. Still, even Psalm 1 concludes, "They [the evildoers] will not survive judgment." These evildoers *(po'alei aven)* are mentioned regularly in the Bible, twenty-four times in all, sixteen of them in the Psalms.

[10] *"Your enemies will perish"* A reference to the Canaanite myth of Baal, who defeats the rebellious Sea: "Now your enemy, O Baal, now your enemy will you smite; now will you cut off your adversaries" (James B. Pritchard, *Ancient Near Eastern Texts Relating to the Old Testament* [Princeton: Princeton Univ. Press, 1969], p. 131, slightly modified). Many biblical texts recognize this myth but alter it to apply to Israel's God, not Baal (see above, "Psalm 29" and "Great water"; also Gen. 1:21; Isa. 51:9–10; Job 26:12–13). The psalmist identifies this mythic enemy as the "evildoers" of verse 8.

[13] *"Lebanese cedar"* Known for their strength and used in constructing the Temple (see above, "Cedar trees of Lebanon"), so a subtle segue into the following verse, on being "planted in God's house."

[16] *"To be able to say* [l'hagid]" A return to the theme of verse 3, "to announce ... by morning," suggesting, quite remarkably, that human beings exist primarily to praise God's perfection.

———◆———

DORFF (THEOLOGY)

independent national life that it represented. The Conservative, Reconstructionist, and Reform movements do not hope to restore the Temple cult of animal sacrifice, and they view the State of Israel as the proper restoration of Jewish national life. Therefore, many synagogues in those movements now use instruments in Sabbath worship to celebrate the Third Jewish Commonwealth that is Israel.

Other halakhic issues arise, however—specifically, the prohibitions against fixing or carrying anything on Shabbat, which rabbis address in various ways.

———◆———

ELLENSON (MODERN LITURGIES)

long before Kabbalah had even been invented). Sometimes (as in Hamburg), Psalm 93 was omitted to shorten the service, but Psalm 92, which is labeled even in the Bible as "A musical psalm for the Sabbath day," seemed an obvious choice for inclusion. Geiger put Psalms 92 and 93 in both his prayer books: the traditional one of 1854 and his more radical 1870 version. But he showed his Reform sensibilities in both cases by including also a silent prayer.

America's Isaac Mayer Wise used both Psalms 92 and 93, but Einhorn used nothing beyond his German version of *Mah Tovu*. Unsurprisingly, the proto-Conservative Benjamin Szold and Marcus Jastrow included both psalms, as Wise had. From the very beginning, the *Union Prayer Book* provided options of psalms (like Psalm 23) for the various Sabbaths in the month, but it gave pride of place to Psalm 92, which appeared in both in Hebrew and in English on the opening page.

◆

FRANKEL (A WOMAN'S VOICE)

traditional cultures, including Jewish culture, old age was also venerated as a time of harvest and reflection. The old were prized for their wisdom and, in many cases, turned to for leadership and judgment. The capstone of Psalm 92 is, therefore, the promise of a creative "old age ... being invigorated, and fresh."

In our own time, Jewish women have sought to celebrate their arrival at old age with new ceremonies, like the one called Simchat Chokhmah, literally, "The Joy of Wisdom," and often entitled "Ceremony of the Wise Woman" or "Crone Ritual." Such rituals are used to mark the transition to this next stage of their lives and to affirm its significance.

One such ceremony, written by Muriel Filman, expresses the hope that "with elderhood, I hope I have achieved the wisdom of accepting whatever life offers and to try to make it better for myself and friends and family. I want to be aware of what I can change and what I cannot." The ceremony concludes with a prayer: "Blessed *Shechinah*, with reverence I give thanks to You for bringing me to this age in good health, good humor, and an appreciation of the beauty and mystery of your universe" ("Ceremony of the Wise Woman," Woman's Institute for Continuing Jewish Education, San Diego, January 9, 1988, in Irene Fine, *Midlife: A Rite of Passage and The Wise Woman: A Celebration* [San Diego: Woman's Institute for Continuing Jewish Education, 1988], pp. 23–24).

◆

arouses rabbinic curiosity and inspires attempts at "gap-filling."

Baruch Halevi Epstein therefore pointed to the midrashic anthology *Yalkut Shimoni,* which claims that the seven mentions of God's Name ("Y-H-V-H") (verses 2, 5, 6, 9, 10, 14, and 16) correspond to the seven blessings that typify the Shabbat *Amidah* (as opposed to the daily *Amidah,* which has nineteen); each one ends with "Blessed are You, Y-H-V-H." Moreover, looking more closely at its content, we see that the psalm praises God from the perspective of someone looking with satisfaction at the final triumph of justice and righteousness. The psalmist calls attention to God's "creations … the work of [God's] hands" (v. 5), the scattering of evildoers (vv. 10, 12), a horn raised high (v. 11), and the righteous, who are in full flower (vv. 13–16). Such a holistic sense of completion and the triumph of righteousness is reminiscent of the messianic era, of which Shabbat itself is a hint (See Volume 7, *Shabbat at Home,* Gray, *"Yom Zeh L'Yisrael,"* p. 124; Gray, *"Havdalah,"* p. 173).

Classical rabbinic interpretation linked this psalm to Adam. According to Midrash T'hillim 92:6, when Adam was expelled from Eden toward the end of the sixth day of the week (Friday evening), he spent Shabbat at Mt. Moriah, where the Temple that would atone for sin was eventually to be built. Shabbat protected him from the dangers he faced outside of the peaceful, paradisiacal Garden, and he recited this psalm in grateful acknowledgment. Genesis Rabbah 22:13 has Adam reciting this psalm much later. Adam encounters Cain after Cain has killed Abel and asks him how his judgment by God went. Cain says that he has repented and his life has been spared. Struck by the power of repentance, Adam repents himself, reciting this psalm as part of his return to God. (For attribution to Moses, see below, "It is good to praise [*l'hodot*] Adonai.")

[2] *"It is good to praise* [l'hodot] *Adonai"* Midrash T'hillim 90:3 attributes this psalm to Moses, who recited it in honor of the tribe of Judah. The allusion to Judah is in verse 2, which is reminiscent of Leah's exclamation upon giving birth to him (Gen. 29:35): "This time I will give praise [*odeh*], God"—from the Hebrew root *y.d.h,* the same as *l'hodot.* (For attribution to Adam, see above, "Psalm 92.")

[5] *"Your creations make me happy"* A student of the famous mystical rabbi R. Shimon b. Yochai went away and made a lot of money. When he returned, the other students were upset that they had not done likewise. R. Shimon took them to a high spot overlooking a valley and called out, "Valley, valley! Fill up with gold!" The valley filled up, and R. Shimon said to the students: "Take all you want. But be aware that what you take is subtracted from your reward in the world-to-come." The students responded by reciting, "Your creations make me happy." Having been assured that God was mindful of their sacrifice in this world, they felt no need to take the gold (Midrash T'hillim 92:8).

[13] *"The righteous bloom like a date tree"* Israel can be compared to a date tree (Midrash T'hillim 92:11). Both are organic wholes consisting of various parts—some

sacred, some not, but all of them equally necessary. A date tree's branches and fibers are used to make a *lulav* and *sukkah* on Sukkot. But its trunk is good for firewood. So too, some Jews are scholars *(b'nei Torah)*, like the parts of the date tree that that are useful for Sukkot. Others are ordinary folk who perform acts of lovingkindness *(g'milut chasadim)*, like the trunk of the date palm, from which firewood is derived.

KIMELMAN (KABBALAH)

the bride of God and the day when God is most recognized as king.

In sum, the six psalms that precede *L'khah Dodi* serve as the wedding processional, *L'khah Dodi* as an epithalamion, and Psalm 92 as the prothalamion. The whole service can also be understood in terms of a diagram:

[Diagram 4]

KABBALAT SHABBAT

I. THE WAY TO SHABBAT
Friday—Psalm 29
Thursday—Psalm 99
Wednesday—Psalm 98
Tuesday—Psalm 97
Monday—Psalm 96
Sunday—Psalm 95

II. THE BRIDGE
L'khah Dodi
Refrain—10 times:
Sabbath as bride
Israel and God as grooms
Stanzas 1, 2, and 9:
Sabbath as sacred time
Stanzas 3–8:
Jerusalem as sacred space

III. THE DESTINATION
Shabbat—Psalms 92–93

J. HOFFMAN (TRANSLATION)

"harps"), either a general description (as translated here) or specific instrumentation, along the lines of "[a musical composition for] ten-stringed harp, ordinary (?) harp, lute, and voice."

[4] *"Melodious lutes"* As immediately above, we don't know exactly what kind of instruments were involved. We may have two kinds of stringed harp-like instruments, one which we translate here as "harp" and the other for which we have to resort to

"lute." "Lyre" would be another choice, equally poor. Another possibility is "voice accompanied by lute." Most translations list some combination of "instruments of ten strings," "harp," "lute," and "lyre."

[5] *"Your creations make me happy"* More literally, "You make me happy with your creations," but we have inverted the word order to maintain the chiasmic affect. (On "chiasm," see above, "Calling them a misguided people," p. 64). In Hebrew, we have "happy … creations / works … celebrate," creating reverse parallel structure. In English, we have "creations … happy / celebrate … works."

[6] *"Deep"* Translated literally from the Hebrew. The application of this directional metaphor to "thought" is common to modern English and both ancient and modern Hebrew, as well as other languages. The expression seems to join a class of other universal directional metaphors, including, for example, the link between "up" and "hot" (as in, "the temperature is rising"). *JPS* prefers "subtle" here.

[8] *"Sprout"* Following *JPS.*

[8] *"Weeds"* Or "grass." The idea is "abundant wild plants." In ancient Israel, grass was such a plant. In modern America, "grass" is what we plant on purpose, while "weeds" grow wild, so we prefer "weeds."

[10] *"Surely"* Following *JPS.* The Hebrew is literally "behold," but that word seems archaic. We would be content to omit the word completely in our translation, but its repetition in the Hebrew adds to the poetry in a way to want to capture.

[11] *"Raise my horn"* This may be a general metaphor for power, or more specifically, sexual power. (See J. Hoffman, Volume 2, *The Amidah,* p. 144.)

[11] *"Like a wild ox"* *JPS*'s "like that of a wild ox" may be the point. As for "wild ox" (*r'em* in Hebrew; *k'rem* in Hebrew means "like a wild ox"), most modern readers don't distinguish between one kind of ox and another, but we prefer to keep the adjective "wild" in the hope that it helps convey accurately the sense of the original. Interestingly, the Septuagint translates *r'em* (here and elsewhere) as *monokeros,* that is, single-horned, or "unicorn," so their version asks that God "raise my horn like a unicorn."

[11] *"Fresh"* As in *NRSV.* Other possibilities include "refreshing" and "invigorating," but the word recurs below, where we will need "fresh." The Hebrew word (*ra'anan*) is frequently tied to trees, so this may actually be a kind of oil ("tree oil"?).

[12] *"Those who lie in wait for me"* Hebrew, *shurai,* which *JPS* translates here as "watchful foes." The word appears to come from the root *sh.r,* which (in addition to several other meanings) means "to watch." So we, following tradition, assume that it might mean people who watch, waiting to pounce. This would explain why it's a good thing that the eye of the hero see them. *Shurai* may have been chosen to form a word play with the previous line, since the same Hebrew letters with almost the same sounds

can spell the word that means "bull" (*shur*—the ending -*ai* means "my"), which would parallel "(wild) ox," immediately above. That possibility is buttressed by the choice of *m're'im* for "to do evil," which sounds remarkably like *k'r'em* "wild ox"; the words are closer in Hebrew than their transliterations would suggest for two reasons: (1) both the *k* and the *m* are prefixes; (2) vowels are less important in Hebrew than consonants. In short, this line contains both a near synonym and a near homonym for "wild ox," immediately above.

[12] *"To do evil"* "With an ax" would preserve the word play on the Hebrew "ox" in Hebrew (see immediately above) but seems too silly to include.

[12] *"Be heard by my ears"* Literally, "will my ears hear." We choose the passive to help maintain good grammar in English while still capturing the chiasmic structure of the Hebrew (on "chiasm," see "Calling them a misguided people," p. 64).

[14] *"Blossom"* The word for "blossom" in Hebrew (*yafrichu*) is from the same root as "bloom" (*bif'ro'ach*) in verse 8, above. We therefore choose similar words in English, too.

[15] *"Produce fruit"* We follow standard translations, but we don't really know what the Hebrew word means.

[15] *"Invigorated"* From the Hebrew word for "fat," which had positive connotations biblically, being the opposite of "scrawny." (For greater detail, see Volume 6, *Tachanun and Concluding Prayers*, p. 108.)

[15] *"Fresh"* Hebrew, *ra'anan* (see above, "fresh").

◆ ◆ ◆

B. PSALM 93: A PSALM TO INTRODUCE SACRED TIME

¹ Adonai is king, majestically robed, robed is Adonai, girded in strength. The world was made firm, unshakable. ² Ever since, your throne has been firm. You have always existed. ³ The oceans sound, Adonai, the oceans sound their thunder, the oceans sound their crushing waves. ⁴ More powerful than the thunder of mighty water are the seabreakers, as Adonai is powerful on high. ⁵ Your decrees endure forever. Holiness befits your house, Adonai, to the end of days.

יְיָ מָלָךְ גֵּאוּת לָבֵשׁ לָבֵשׁ יְיָ עֹז ¹
הִתְאַזָּר אַף־תִּכּוֹן תֵּבֵל בַּל־תִּמּוֹט:
נָכוֹן כִּסְאֲךָ מֵאָז מֵעוֹלָם אָתָּה: ³ נָשְׂאוּ ²
נְהָרוֹת יְיָ נָשְׂאוּ נְהָרוֹת קוֹלָם יִשְׂאוּ
נְהָרוֹת דָּכְיָם: ⁴ מִקֹּלוֹת מַיִם רַבִּים
אַדִּירִים מִשְׁבְּרֵי־יָם אַדִּיר בַּמָּרוֹם יְיָ:
עֵדֹתֶיךָ נֶאֶמְנוּ מְאֹד לְבֵיתְךָ נָאֲוָה־ ⁵
קֹדֶשׁ יְיָ לְאֹרֶךְ יָמִים:

[Mourners' Kaddish is said, separating Psalms 92 and 93 from the Mishnah passage that follows. For complete text of the Mourners' Kaddish, see Volume 5, Birkhot Hashachar (Morning Blessings), p. 197.]

149

BRETTLER (BIBLE)

[1] *"Adonai is king"* The implication here is probably that Adonai has [already] become king, since the whole psalm narrates God's assumption to the throne after defeating the powers of Chaos, represented in verses 3–4 as the Ocean. Again, an Israelite transformation of the Canaanite myth about Baal's kingship (see above, "Psalm 29," "Great water," and "Your enemies will perish").

[4] *"More powerful ... Adonai is powerful"* God successfully vanquishes the rebellious oceans. Quite atypically for biblical poetry, the Hebrew of verses 3, 4, and 5 have three (rather than two) parallel linear sections. *(p. 152)*

FRANKEL (A WOMAN'S VOICE)

[1] *"The world was made firm, unshakable"* This short psalm focuses on God's steadfastness, symbolized by the earth's firmness—*af tikon tevel*—and the image of God's eternal throne, established at the beginning of time and lasting for eternity. In contrast, the ocean is forever restless, thunderously breaking upon the shore.

To the immigrant generation, the restless ocean represented something else: freedom and peril. Their lives were literally in God's hands as they journeyed to the *goldene medinah* of America. The following excerpt is from a Yiddish *t'khinah* written by *(p. 152)*

GRAY (OUR TALMUDIC HERITAGE)

[1] *"Adonai is king, majestically robed"* Psalm 93 was the psalm the Levites recited every Friday in the Temple (M. Tamid 7:4). R.H. 31a explains its choice: "Adonai is king" refers to the fact that God completed creation on Friday and began reigning over it then.

[2] *"Ever since, your throne has been firm"* Midrash T'hillim 93:3 uses this verse as the proof text for the legend that God's throne of glory *(kisei hakavod)* existed before the creation of *(p. 153)*

B. PSALM 93: A PSALM TO INTRODUCE SACRED TIME

[1] Adonai is king, majestically robed, robed is Adonai, girded in strength. The world was made firm, unshakable. [2] Ever since, your throne has been firm. You have always existed. [3] The oceans sound, Adonai, the oceans sound their thunder, the oceans sound their crushing waves. [4] More powerful than the thunder of mighty water are the seabreakers, as

KIMELMAN (KABBALAH)

"Adonai is king, majestically robed" Psalm 93 was appended to Psalm 92 because it begins with "Adonai is king, majestically robed." This confirms Shabbat as the day of divine sovereignty par excellence. The Shabbat *Amidah* (for *Musaf*) confirms: "Those who celebrate Shabbat will rejoice in your kingship" (*yism'chu b'malkhut'kha shomrei shabbat*).

Adding Psalm 93 to the Sabbath psalm (92) is like adding "Blessed is the name of your glorious kingship *(p. 153)*

L. HOFFMAN (HISTORY)

PSALM 92 IS FOLLOWED BY PSALM 93. THE LITURGICAL COMBINATION OF THE TWO PSALMS WAS IN PLACE AS EARLY AS THE FIFTH CENTURY IN ERETZ YISRAEL.

◆

[1] *"Strength"* Or *"glory."* *Oz* is another word that seems to refer at times to godly matters and at other times to military matters (see "Victory," p. 73).

[2] *"Ever since"* JPS: "Of old," the standard translation going all the way back to the Geneva and *King James* Bibles of the sixteenth and seventeenth centuries. But we think this line refers to the time after the world was made firm. That is, first the world was made firm and unshakable, and ever since that time, God's throne has been firm.

[2] *"Existed"* The point is "you have always been there," but that phrase seems too colloquial to us.

[3] *"Oceans sound their thunder"* Basically following JPS. Literally, the Hebrew reads, "rivers lift up their voices." But immediately below, God will be compared to the sounds here, and our version sets the stage nicely for what follows, conveying the sense of the Hebrew, though perhaps using slightly different metaphors.

¹ יְיָ מָלָךְ גֵּאוּת לָבֵשׁ לָבֵשׁ יְיָ עֹז הִתְאַזָּר אַף־תִּכּוֹן תֵּבֵל בַּל־תִּמּוֹט: ²נָכוֹן כִּסְאֲךָ מֵאָז מֵעוֹלָם אָתָּה: ³נָשְׂאוּ נְהָרוֹת יְיָ נָשְׂאוּ נְהָרוֹת קוֹלָם יִשְׂאוּ נְהָרוֹת דׇּכְיָם: ⁴מִקֹּלוֹת מַיִם רַבִּים אַדִּירִים מִשְׁבְּרֵי־יָם אַדִּיר

J. HOFFMAN (TRANSLATION)

[1] *"Adonai is king"* The Hebrew, *Adonai malakh*, literally means "Adonai *was* king," but it was probably a common expression for "Adonai *is* king." We translate the phrase here as we have elsewhere, but also note the likelihood that this psalm may describe the process by which Adonai actually *became* king. If so, a better translation here would be "Adonai became king" (see Brettler).

[1] *"Majestically robed"* More literally, "robed in majesty."

[3] *"Crushing waves"* Others, "roaring" or "pounding." The word, which appears only here (and which is therefore technically called a *hapax legomenon*, from the Greek for "once said"), seems to come from the root "to crush."

[4] *"More powerful than the thunder of mighty water"* The imagery here seems to be that the seabreakers are (p. 153)

Adonai is powerful on high. [5] Your decrees endure forever. Holiness befits your house, Adonai, to the end of days.

בַּמָּרוֹם יְיָ: ⁵עֵדֹתֶיךָ נֶאֶמְנוּ מְאֹד לְבֵיתְךָ נָאֲוָה־קֹדֶשׁ יְיָ לְאֹרֶךְ יָמִים:

[Mourners' Kaddish is said, separating Psalms 92 and 93 from the Mishnah passage that follows. For complete text of the Mourners' Kaddish, see Volume 5, Birkhot Hashachar (Morning Blessings), p. 197.]

BRETTLER (BIBLE)

[5] *"Your decrees endure.... Holiness befits your house"* This defeat of these enemies in the distant past has theological implications for the present.

———◆———

FRANKEL (A WOMAN'S VOICE)

a Jewish woman before embarking on such a transatlantic journey:

> Where does God's spirit move? Where does man sense Him?... Man is often more aware of Him when traversing the great ocean, as is written in the psalm beginning with the words [The Lord reigns ... above the noise of the mighty waters (Psalm 93:4)], which is the tumult of the world; more powerful than the waves of the great sea [is the Lord, majestic on high]; there (on the ocean) one notices how strong and mighty divinity is ... As You have done man many kindnesses, so do I beg of You to have my trip succeed. May the ocean be calm and the ship reach its destination. May it not be struck below the waterline nor run aground. Let not the sailors sleep during their night watch so that ships will not collide; protect us from all misfortunes that might happen at sea, for Your supremacy is over all ... Bring me to a safe landing, uninjured, with nothing to prevent my disembarking. May I find all those (to whom I go) healthy and happy.
>
> As You silence the ocean in the midst of the storm, so may You silence all the enemies of Israel who stew and fret about us. Pour out Your spirit over all Your creatures that they may acknowledge Your oneness. May they be filled with divine knowledge so that the holy words of the prophet Isaiah be fulfilled: The land will be full of the recognition of God, as the waters covering the sea (Isa. 11:9). May it be speedily and in our time. *Omayn.* (Norman Tarnor, ed., *A Book of Jewish Women's Prayers* [Northvale, N.J.: Jason Aronson, 1995], pp. 117–119])

———◆———

GRAY (OUR TALMUDIC HERITAGE)

the world. (So too, goes the legend, did the Messiah, Torah, Israel, Temple, and repentance.)

———◆———

KIMELMAN (KABBALAH)

for ever" *(Barukh shem)* to the *Sh'ma* (see Volume 1, *The Sh'ma and Its Blessings*, p. 87). The two additions make explicit that the Sabbath Psalm and the *Sh'ma* are expressions of divine sovereignty.

———◆———

J. HOFFMAN (TRANSLATION)

more powerful even than the mighty oceans just described. Similarly, Adonai is powerful on high. However, we may have a scribal error. The word for "powerful" here *(adirim)* is plural, because it matches the following plural "seabreakers" *(mish'b'rei yam)*. At the end of a word (as in *adirim*), a *mem* like this indicates the plural. But at the beginning of a word, a *mem* means "than" (like "higher than" or "more than"). If the *mem* is moved from the end of "powerful" *(adirim)* to the beginning of "seabreakers" (changing *mish'b'rei yam* to *mimish'b'rei yam*), we have not "powerful [plural] seabreakers," but "more powerful [singular] *than* the seabreakers." This would give us the poetic "More than the thunder of mighty water, more powerful than the seabreakers, Adonai is powerful on high." In that reading, we would see a progression from the mighty water, to the seabreakers that are even more powerful, to God, who is more powerful yet.

[5] *"Endure forever"* Literally, "are very enduring."

———◆ ◆ ◆———

3 | *From Medieval Babylonia*

Emphasizing Shabbat Light

A. *BAMEH MADLIKIN* ("WITH WHAT MAY WE LIGHT...")

I. MISHNAH SHABBAT 2:1—LAWS OF WICKS

[1] What may we use for the Sabbath light, and what may we not use? [2] We may not use wick of cedar-fiber, uncarded flax, raw silk, wick of bast, wick of the desert, or seaweed, [3] nor pitch, wax, castor oil, burnt oil, grease from the fat tail, or tallow. [4] Nachum of Media says we may use melted tallow. [5] But the sages say that whether or not it is melted, we may not use it.

II. MISHNAH SHABBAT 2:6— RESPONSIBILITIES OF WOMEN

[6] There are three transgressions on account of which women die during childbirth: for not being careful about the laws of menstruation, of *challah*, and of lighting the Sabbath candle.

[1] כַּ מֶּה מַדְלִיקִין וּבַמָּה אֵין מַדְלִיקִין. [2] אֵין מַדְלִיקִין לֹא בְלֶכֶשׁ וְלֹא בְחֹסֶן וְלֹא בְכַלָךְ, וְלֹא בִּפְתִילַת הָאִידָן וְלֹא בִּפְתִילַת הַמִּדְבָּר וְלֹא בִּירוֹקָה שֶׁעַל פְּנֵי הַמָּיִם; [3] וְלֹא בְזֶפֶת וְלֹא בְשַׁעֲוָה וְלֹא בְשֶׁמֶן קִיק, וְלֹא בְשֶׁמֶן שְׂרֵפָה וְלֹא בְאַלְיָה וְלֹא בְחֵלֶב. [4] נַחוּם הַמָּדִי אוֹמֵר: מַדְלִיקִין בְּחֵלֶב מְבֻשָּׁל. [5] וַחֲכָמִים אוֹמְרִים: אֶחָד מְבֻשָּׁל וְאֶחָד שֶׁאֵינוֹ מְבֻשָּׁל אֵין מַדְלִיקִין בּוֹ.

[6] עַ ל שָׁלשׁ עֲבֵרוֹת נָשִׁים מֵתוֹת בִּשְׁעַת לֵדָתָן: עַל שֶׁאֵינָן זְהִירוֹת בְּנִדָּה, בְּחַלָּה, וּבְהַדְלָקַת הַנֵּר.

III. MISHNAH SHABBAT 2:7— SHABBAT PREPARATION

[7]There are three things a man is required to say in his home on Sabbath eve as darkness falls: "Have you taken care of the tithe?" "Have you taken care of the *eruv*?" and "Light the candle." [8]If there is some question as to whether or not darkness has fallen, do not take care of the tithe in the case of that which certainly must be tithed, do not dip utensils, and do not light the candles. But take care of the tithe over that which may have to be tithed, take care of the *eruv*, and store away hot food.

IV. BERAKHOT 64A: TORAH BRINGS PEACE

[9]Rabbi Elazar said that Rabbi Chanina said: Scholars increase peace in the world, as it is said, "All of your children are disciples of Adonai; great is the peace among your children." Do not read this word as "children" but rather as "builders." [10]Let there be great peace for those who love your Torah; let them know no obstacle. [11]May there be peace within your walls, tranquility in your palaces. [12]For the sake of my fellows and friends, I hope that you find peace. [13]For the sake of the house of Adonai our God, I ask that you know goodness. [14]May Adonai give strength to his people. May Adonai bless his people with peace.

שֶׁלֹשָׁה דְבָרִים צָרִיךְ אָדָם לוֹמַר[7] בְּתוֹךְ בֵּיתוֹ עֶרֶב שַׁבָּת עִם חֲשֵׁכָה: עִשַּׂרְתֶּם, עֵרַבְתֶּם, הַדְלִיקוּ אֶת הַנֵּר. [8]סָפֵק חֲשֵׁכָה, סָפֵק אֵינָהּ חֲשֵׁכָה, אֵין מְעַשְּׂרִין אֶת הַוַּדַּאי, וְאֵין מַטְבִּילִין אֶת הַכֵּלִים, וְאֵין מַדְלִיקִין אֶת הַנֵּרוֹת; אֲבָל מְעַשְּׂרִין אֶת הַדְּמַאי, וּמְעָרְבִין, וְטוֹמְנִין אֶת הַחַמִּין.

אָמַר רַבִּי אֶלְעָזָר אָמַר רַבִּי חֲנִינָא:[9] תַּלְמִידֵי חֲכָמִים מַרְבִּים שָׁלוֹם בָּעוֹלָם, שֶׁנֶּאֱמַר: וְכָל בָּנַיִךְ לִמּוּדֵי יְיָ, וְרַב שְׁלוֹם בָּנָיִךְ. אַל תִּקְרָא בָּנָיִךְ, אֶלָּא בּוֹנָיִךְ. [10]שָׁלוֹם רָב לְאֹהֲבֵי תוֹרָתֶךָ, וְאֵין לָמוֹ מִכְשׁוֹל. [11]יְהִי שָׁלוֹם בְּחֵילֵךְ שַׁלְוָה בְּאַרְמְנוֹתָיִךְ. [12]לְמַעַן אַחַי וְרֵעָי, אֲדַבְּרָה נָּא שָׁלוֹם בָּךְ. [13]לְמַעַן בֵּית יְיָ אֱלֹהֵינוּ, אֲבַקְשָׁה טוֹב לָךְ. [14]יְיָ עֹז לְעַמּוֹ יִתֵּן, יְיָ יְבָרֵךְ אֶת עַמּוֹ בַשָּׁלוֹם.

[Kaddish D'rabbanan concludes liturgical study and separates Kabbalat Shabbat from the Ma'ariv service that follows. For complete text of Kaddish D'rabbanan, see Volume 5, Birkhot Hashachar (Morning Blessings), p. 187.]

BRETTLER (BIBLE)

[1] *"What may we use for the Sabbath light"* Lighting Sabbath lamps played no special role in biblical Israel, though we might surmise from Exodus 35:3, "You shall kindle no fire throughout your settlements on the Sabbath day," that it was necessary to kindle lamps before Shabbat. However, nothing is found in the Bible comparable to the detail here.

[6] *"Three transgressions"* The idea that women die during childbirth for particular sins has no biblical precedent. But biblically, all three offenses named are capital crimes. As private infractions, however, they are punishable by God through *karet,* which probably means *(p. 160)*

DORFF (THEOLOGY)

[6] *"Three transgressions on account of which women die during childbirth"* This is clearly not true medically; used to modern medical explanations, we find this not only wrong but offensive. The Mishnah represents an ancient attempt to explain *(p. 161)*

ELLENSON (MODERN LITURGIES)

[1] *"What may we use for the Sabbath light"* No non-Orthodox prayer book contains this Mishnaic reading. As a prayer, it is plainly too legalistic for them; and for those whose worshipers willingly kindle light even on Shabbat, its rulings are irrelevant as well. *(p. 161)*

FRANKEL (A WOMAN'S VOICE)

[6] *"Three transgressions on account of which women die during childbirth"* The original source for what has become known as "women's commandments": *challah* (separating and burning a piece of dough in the oven to commemorate ancient Temple sacrifice), *nidah* (observing the laws of family purity by abstaining from sexual relations with one's husband during menstruation and ending this period through immersion in the *mikveh*), and *hadlakat ner* (lighting candles on Sabbath *(p. 161)*

I. MISHNAH SHABBAT 2:1—LAWS OF WICKS

[1] What may we use for the Sabbath light, and what may we not use? [2] We may not use wick of cedar-fiber, uncarded flax, raw silk, wick of bast, wick of the desert, or seaweed, [3] nor pitch, wax, castor oil, burnt oil, grease from the fat tail, or tallow. [4] Nachum of Media says we may use melted tallow. [5] But the sages say that whether or not it is melted, we may not use it.

GRAY (OUR TALMUDIC HERITAGE)

[1] *"What may we use for the Sabbath light"* The Talmud says clearly, "Lighting the Shabbat light is mandatory" (Shabbat 25b), and Rashi explains, "Where there is no [Shabbat] light, there is no peace." Chapter 2 of Mishnah Shabbat consists of seven *mishnayot* (pronounced mish-nah-YOHT)—recited Friday evening as part of *Kabbalat Shabbat* because they detail *mitzvot* that must be taken care of before the onset of Shabbat (*Tur,* O. Ch. 270). All deal in some way specifically with Shabbat *(p. 162)*

KUSHNER & POLEN (CHASIDISM)

[1] *"What may we use for the Sabbath light"* Mystics have long been fascinated by the spectrum of the light surrounding a burning wick. In one well-known passage, the *Zohar* explains the mystery of the colors of a burning flame:

> But come and see: Whoever desires to penetrate the wisdom of holy unification should contemplate the flame ascending from a glowing ember or a burning candle. The flame ascends only when grasped by coarse substance.

(p. 166)

בַּמֶּה מַדְלִיקִין וּבַמֶּה אֵין מַדְלִיקִין. ²אֵין מַדְלִיקִין לֹא בְלֶכֶשׁ וְלֹא בְחֹסֶן וְלֹא בְכַלָּךְ, וְלֹא בִפְתִילַת הָאִידָן וְלֹא בִפְתִילַת הַמִּדְבָּר וְלֹא בִירוֹקָה שֶׁעַל פְּנֵי הַמָּיִם; ³וְלֹא בְזֶפֶת וְלֹא בְשַׁעֲוָה וְלֹא בְשֶׁמֶן קִיק, וְלֹא בְשֶׁמֶן שְׂרֵפָה וְלֹא בְאַלְיָה וְלֹא בְחֵלֶב. ⁴נַחוּם הַמָּדִי אוֹמֵר: מַדְלִיקִין בְּחֵלֶב מְבֻשָּׁל. ⁵וַחֲכָמִים אוֹמְרִים: אֶחָד מְבֻשָּׁל וְאֶחָד שֶׁאֵינוֹ מְבֻשָּׁל אֵין מַדְלִיקִין בּוֹ.

LANDES (HALAKHAH)

[1] *"What may we use for the Sabbath light [1]"* The ritualized study of Mishnah is common in a rabbinically literate culture. The best-known example is the Shabbat afternoon recitation of *Pirkei Avot* from Passover to Shavuot (or until Rosh Hashanah).

Our Mishnah presupposes two opposing verses: (1) "You shall not kindle a fire in all your habitations on the Shabbat day" (Exodus 35:3) and (2) "You shall call the Sabbath 'joy' *(oneg)*, Adonai's holy day 'honored'" *(p. 167)*

L. HOFFMAN (HISTORY)

THE THIRD AND LAST COMPONENT IN THE KABBALAT SHABBAT LITURGY IS MISHNAH SHABBAT, CHAPTER 2, A TREATISE ON THE REGULATIONS PERTINENT TO KINDLING SHABBAT LIGHTS. OF THE FIRST FIVE PARAGRAPHS, WHICH DETAIL SUCH THINGS AS THE NATURE OF THE WICKS AND OILS THAT MAY BE USED, WE REPRODUCE HERE JUST THE FIRST, TO PROVIDE THE FLAVOR OF THE HALAKHAH THAT IS INVOLVED. WE CONTINUE WITH MISHNAH 2:6, WHICH UTILIZES THE DISCUSSION OF KINDLING SHABBAT LIGHTS FOR A BRIEF ALLUSION TO THREE RESPONSIBILITIES OF WOMEN (SEE ZIERLER, "SHEDDING FEMINIST LIGHT ON THE SABBATH (p. 174)

J. HOFFMAN (TRANSLATION)

[1] *"What may we use"* Literally, "with what do we light..." But as this is an instruction manual of sorts, and clearly not poetry, clarity of expression is more important than the nuances of each phrase.

[2] *"Wick of cedar-fiber"* These are all technical terms. We follow Neusner's translation of them. Some of these Mishnaic terms are explained in the Gemara, but we do not fully understand the Gemara any more than we fully understand the Mishnah. (For traditional explanations, see Landes.)

[3] *"Burnt oil"* That is, oil from a *t'rumah* offering, which is supposed to be burned and destroyed *(p. 174)*

II. MISHNAH SHABBAT 2:6—
RESPONSIBILITIES OF WOMEN

[6] There are three transgressions on account of which women die during childbirth: for not being careful about the laws of menstruation, of *challah*, and of lighting the Sabbath candle.

III. MISHNAH SHABBAT 2:7—
SHABBAT PREPARATION

[7] There are three things a man is required to say in his home on Sabbath eve as darkness falls: "Have you taken care of the tithe?" "Have you taken care of the *eruv*?" and "Light the candle." [8] If there is some question as to whether or not darkness has fallen, do not take care of the tithe in the case of that which certainly must be tithed, do not dip utensils, and do not light the candles. But take care of the tithe over that which may have to be tithed, take care of the *eruv,* and store away hot food.

עַל שָׁלֹשׁ עֲבֵרוֹת נָשִׁים מֵתוֹת בִּשְׁעַת לֵדָתָן: עַל שֶׁאֵינָן זְהִירוֹת בְּנִדָּה, בְּחַלָּה, וּבְהַדְלָקַת הַנֵּר. [6]

שְׁלֹשָׁה דְבָרִים צָרִיךְ אָדָם לוֹמַר בְּתוֹךְ בֵּיתוֹ עֶרֶב שַׁבָּת עִם חֲשֵׁכָה: עִשַּׂרְתֶּם, עֵרַבְתֶּם, הַדְלִיקוּ אֶת הַנֵּר. [8] סָפֵק חֲשֵׁכָה, סָפֵק אֵינָהּ חֲשֵׁכָה, אֵין מְעַשְּׂרִין אֶת הַוַּדַּאי, וְאֵין מַטְבִּילִין אֶת הַכֵּלִים, וְאֵין מַדְלִיקִין אֶת הַנֵּרוֹת: אֲבָל מְעַשְּׂרִין אֶת הַדְּמַאי, וּמְעָרְבִין, וְטוֹמְנִין אֶת הַחַמִּין. [7]

IV. BERAKHOT 64A: TORAH BRINGS PEACE

[9] Rabbi Elazar said that Rabbi Chanina said: Scholars increase peace in the world, as it is said, "All of your children are disciples of Adonai; great is the peace among your children." Do not read this word as "children" but rather as "builders." [10] Let there be great peace for those who love your Torah; let them know no obstacle. [11] May there be peace within your walls, tranquility in your palaces. [12] For the sake of my fellows and friends, I hope that you find peace. [13] For the sake of the house of Adonai our God, I ask that you know goodness. [14] May Adonai give strength to his people. May Adonai bless his people with peace.

אָ֫מַר רַבִּי אֶלְעָזָר אָמַר רַבִּי חֲנִינָא: [9]
תַּלְמִידֵי חֲכָמִים מַרְבִּים שָׁלוֹם
בָּעוֹלָם, שֶׁנֶּאֱמַר: וְכָל בָּנַיִךְ לִמּוּדֵי יְיָ,
וְרַב שְׁלוֹם בָּנָיִךְ. אַל תִּקְרָא בָּנָיִךְ,
אֶלָּא בּוֹנָיִךְ. [10] שָׁלוֹם רָב לְאֹהֲבֵי תוֹרָתֶךָ,
וְאֵין לָמוֹ מִכְשׁוֹל. [11] יְהִי שָׁלוֹם בְּחֵילֵךְ
שַׁלְוָה בְּאַרְמְנוֹתָיִךְ. [12] לְמַעַן אַחַי וְרֵעָי,
אֲדַבְּרָה נָא שָׁלוֹם בָּךְ. [13] לְמַעַן בֵּית יְיָ
אֱלֹהֵינוּ, אֲבַקְשָׁה טוֹב לָךְ. [14] יְיָ עֹז
לְעַמּוֹ יִתֵּן, יְיָ יְבָרֵךְ אֶת עַמּוֹ בַשָּׁלוֹם.

[Kaddish D'rabbanan concludes liturgical study and separates Kabbalat Shabbat from the Ma'ariv service that follows. For complete text of Kaddish D'rabbanan, see Volume 5, Birkhot Hashachar (Morning Blessings), p. 187.]

BRETTLER (BIBLE)

death at a time determined by God, or extirpation of the family line.

[6] *"Menstruation"* Observing menstrual purity is mentioned with other capital offenses in Leviticus 18:19, although Leviticus 15:24 is much more lenient.

[6] *"Challah"* See Numbers 15:19–21: "As the first yield of your baking, you shall set aside a loaf *(challah)* as a gift … to Adonai … throughout the ages." Intentional neglect of this obligation was viewed as a capital crime (v. 30). In later Hebrew, this gift was called *challah,* after a type of bread mentioned regularly in the Bible. Applying the word *challah* to specially prepared Shabbat bread is a later innovation.

[6] *"Lighting the Sabbath candle"* Kindling lights after Shabbat began would have been a capital offense, according to Exodus 35:2–3.

[7] *"Three things"* No special pre-Shabbat preparations are listed in the Bible.

[7] *"The tithe"* Mandated in various places, most clearly in Deuteronomy 14:22 ff.: "You shall set aside every year a tenth part of all the yield of your sowing that is brought from the field…." It was important enough that the narrative of Genesis 28:22 attributes it to Jacob.

[9] *"Scholars* [talmidei chakhamim]*"* A special class during the rabbinic period who took over functions of various biblical groups, including "sages" (who were, however, mostly concerned with secular wisdom), "priests" (who were concerned with preserving torah traditions—see Jer. 18:18; Ez. 7:26), and prophets (who provided oracles or interpretations for new situations).

[9] *"Your children* [banayikh]*"* The proof text is Isaiah 54:13. The second occurrence of *banayikh* is being playfully misread as *bonayikh,* "your builders." However, in the Great Isaiah Scroll (from the Dead Sea Scrolls discovered at Qumran) it appears quite similarly, suggesting that the midrash is actually preserving an earlier reading, which had been lost. We do not know how common it is for the midrash to preserve ancient biblical variants.

[10] *"Those who love your Torah* [ohavei toratekha]*"* Psalm 119:165: In the Bible, *torah* means teaching in general, not our Torah in particular. But here, it is being read as an allusion to "scholars" (*talmidei chakhamim* of v. 1), where study of Torah is intended.

[11] *"Peace"* The last four verses (Pss. 122:7–9, 29:11) extend this notion of *shalom,* both peace and personal well-being, to Israel as a whole, while concluding with a verse used earlier in the *Kabbalat Shabbat* service as part of the kingship psalms (Ps. 29:11).

———◆———

DORFF (THEOLOGY)

why all too many women did, in fact, die in childbirth.

[7] *"Light the candle"* Fire may not be kindled on the Sabbath (Exod. 35:3). Therefore, to avoid desecration of the Sabbath, Jewish law requires that the Sabbath candles be lit a minimum of eighteen minutes before sunset. (See comment by A. Stanley Dreyfus, in Ellenson, *"Kabbalat Shabbat".*)

Candles form an emotionally powerful separation between the work week and the onset of the Sabbath. They symbolize, on one hand, the use of fire and other forms of energy to change the world during the week and, on the other, the warmth and light of the Sabbath. The candles also symbolize the spiritual fulfillment that the Sabbath brings, for, in the words of the biblical Book of Proverbs, God's "commandment is a lamp, God's teaching is a light" (v. 6:23) and "The life-breath [soul] of a person is the lamp of Adonai, revealing all his inmost parts" (v. 20:27).

◆

ELLENSON (MODERN LITURGIES)

The 1985 and 1998 editions of *Sim Shalom* and *Va'ani T'fillati* (all Conservative) provide other readings for study.

[9] *"Rabbi Elazar said"* The only non-Orthodox prayer books in which this passage is found are the Conservative *Sim Shalom* and *Va'ani T'fillati,* where it forms a fitting conclusion to study, as it did in the traditional Siddur. Prayer books that include no alternative study passage here omit this ending as well.

◆

FRANKEL (A WOMAN'S VOICE)

and festivals). But these *mitzvot* appear in negative terms, as if all that is at stake is punishment for not doing them.

The warning of death during childbirth has been associated with the acrostic formed by the initials of the *mitzvot: CH[allah], N[idah] H[adlakat ner],* that is, ChaNaH, the Hebrew for "Hannah," the biblical character associated in later centuries with women's prayer and difficulties with childbearing.

Yet men, too, are halakhically obligated to observe these three commandments. Male bakers are required to separate *challah* and burn it; husbands are to avoid touching their wives during menstrual periods; and men are to light candles when no woman is at home to light them. Only over many centuries did this triad of commandments become associated exclusively with women.

It is likely that the original Mishnaic formulation arose to explain and rationalize the frequent death of women in childbirth. But what may have begun as superstition eventually led to a narrowing of women's aspirations for their own spiritual practice and enfranchisement in Jewish communal life (see Zierler, "Shedding Feminist Light on the Sabbath Candles," pp. 27–31).

"The Three Gates" *(Shloyshe She'orim),* written sometime in the early eighteenth century by Sarah bas Tovim of Satanov, is one of the most beloved *t'khinah* we have. In the first "gate" (section), which is devoted to the three traditional "women's commandments," the author reaffirms the ancient notion that women will experience easy childbirth by observing these *mitzvot*—however, Sarah bas Tovim reformulates the Mishnah's curse into a blessing: "If you keep these three *mitzves* faithfully, 'you will give birth quickly,' that is, your lying-in will be quick and without pain" (Tracy Klirs, ed., *The Merit of Our Mothers: A Bilingual Anthology of Jewish Women's Prayers,* trans. Tracy Klirs, Ida Selavan, Gella Fishman [Cincinnati: Hebrew Union College, 1992], p. 16). In her discussion of *challah,* she explicitly identifies herself with the High Priest, the Temple, and the people of ancient Israel:

> May my *challah* be accepted as the sacrifice on the altar was accepted. May my *mitzvah* be accepted just as if I had performed it properly. In ancient times, the High Priest came and caused the sins to be forgiven; so also may my sins be forgiven with this. May I be like a newborn child. May I be able to honor my dear Sabbaths and holidays. May God grant that I and my husband and my children be able to nourish ourselves. Thus may my *mitzvah* of *challah* be accepted: that my children may be fed by the dear God, be blessed, with great mercy and great compassion. May this *mitzvah* of *challah* be accounted as if I had given the tithe. As I perform my *mitzvah* of *challah* with might and main, so may God, be blessed, guard me from anguish and pain (Chava Weissler, *Voices of the Matriarchs: Listening to the Prayers of Early Modern Jewish Women* [Boston: Beacon Press, 1998], p. 33).

GRAY (OUR TALMUDIC HERITAGE)

light; the seventh expands slightly to stipulate not just Shabbat light but two other things (tithes and *eruv,* discussed below) that a householder must be sure the household took care of at home before the onset of Shabbat.

Though the Talmud demands kindling Shabbat light, it does not mandate the recitation of *Bameh Madlikin* on Friday night. The practice occurs first in *Seder Rav Amram Gaon* (ca. 860 C.E.), possibly a polemic against the Karaites and their literal reading of Exodus 35:3, which precluded not only the lighting of lights on Shabbat but even the presence in the home of lights lit beforehand.

Custom varies as to where *Bameh Madlikin* should be recited. Seder Rav Amram (2:11) places it at the very end, not just of *Kabbalat Shabbat* but of *Ma'ariv,* which follows. The *Tur* (O. Ch. 270) also alludes to an Ashkenazi practice of reciting it then. But David Abudarham (Spain, fourteenth century) commends places where it is recited earlier ("between the afternoon service [*Minchah*] and the evening service [*Arvit* = *Ma'ariv*]"), because if the recitation prompts someone to realize that one of the necessary preparatory *mitzvot* has not been done, there would still be time before Shabbat to fix the situation. Jacob Emden (Altona, Germany, 1697–1776) agrees, identifying this early recital as Sefardi. He also mentions the Ashkenazi custom of reciting it late, explaining that for these Ashkenazim, the recitation is simply Torah study that gives latecomers to the service time to finish their prayers after the service ends, so that the entire congregation can leave for their homes together.

[2] *"We may not use wick of ..."* A listing of items from which wicks may not be made, and flammable substances that may not be used in place of oil. Forbidden items are those that produce weak and sputtering flames, which might tempt a user to tilt the lamp so as to cause the flames to burn brighter and steadier. Causing the light to burn brighter would violate the prohibition against lighting a fire on Shabbat (Maimonides, Shabbat 5:8, based on Exod. 35:3).

[6] *"Three transgressions on account of which women die during childbirth"* Women who are not punctilious about the laws of menstrual purity *(nidah)*, separating *challah* from dough while they are baking bread, or kindling Shabbat light *(ner)* are said to be especially vulnerable during childbirth, even to the point of dying. The Talmud makes this point pithily: "Rava said: 'When the ox is thrown down, sharpen the knife'" (Shabbat 32a)—meaning when a woman is in a vulnerable state (like giving birth), the "knife" is sharpened to punish her for her sins and omissions. R. Natan adds also (Tosefta Shab. 2:10) that women may die during childbirth because of their unfulfilled vows.

The Palestinian Talmud (the Yerushalmi—Shab. 2:6, 5b) explains this stunningly harsh mishnah as the consequence of Eve's disobedience to God and its effect on Adam. Because Eve caused the death of Adam, the "blood of the world," women ever after are responsible for the *mitzvah* of *nidah*. (As proof of "blood," Abudarham cites Genesis 9:6, part of God's final charge to Noah, "Whoever sheds the blood of man [*adam*], by man shall his blood be shed.") Similarly, continues the Talmud, because Eve caused the death of Adam, who, having been created from the earth (Gen. 2:7), was "the pure dough of the world," women are responsible for *challah*. Finally, because Adam was the "light of the world" women are responsible for the Shabbat light (The Palestinian Talmud's proof text for "light" is Proverbs 20:27, "The lifebreath of man is the lamp of Adonai").

A similar teaching appears in the Babylonian Talmud (Shab. 31b–32a), but there, the context is a lengthy sequence of traditions (32a–34a) about dire consequences (including death) for both men and women who fail to perform various *mitzvot*. This broader portrait suggests that all these traditions—those about women as well as men—should be read as strongly worded affirmations of the importance of performing *mitzvot* rather than as statements of cause and effect.

Maimonides ("Shabbat" 5:3) seems to read the mishnah this way. In his view,

"Women are more obligated in this [the Shabbat light] than men because they are found in the house and do the housework." He does not even mention the possibility of death. But he adds, "The man must admonish and check them [the women of his household]." By subjecting women's performance of the *mitzvah* to male oversight he presumably lessens the possibility of their dying, but from a feminist perspective, his diminution of women's autonomy is a troubling addition to an already troubling text.

Maimonides' interpretation is quoted in later codes. The *Tur* (O. Ch. 263:3) also resurrects the Yerushalmi's reference to Eve's sin. The *Shulchan Arukh* (O. Ch. 263:3) adopts Maimonides' language and eliminates the *Tur's* reference to Eve (although some commentators raise it again).

Moses Isserles ("R'ma," Poland, 1530–1575, *Darkhei Moshe* to *Tur,* O. Ch. 263:3) cites the ruling of the Maharil (Jacob Moellin, Germany, fifteenth century) that a woman who forgets to kindle Shabbat lights should forever after add a light to whatever number she has previously lit; she should also fast and recite a confession (*viduii,* pronounced vee-DOO-ee), though presumably only once. R'ma himself is skeptical about forever adding a light but notes that women of his time are, in fact, accustomed to doing it. Was this custom a consequence of the old notion that carelessness with Shabbat lights causes death? Perhaps, but the custom may have had another source: having so few *mitzvot* that they are halakhically obligated to do, women were likely to have applied that much more stringency themselves about the ones they did have.

[7] *"Three things a man is required to say"* Abudarham explains the gravity of these three things by the fact that without them, there will be no *shalom bayit* ("peace in the home"), which is critical to a Shabbat atmosphere. Food prepared without required tithing cannot be eaten on Shabbat; without an *eruv,* the family will be unable to carry items outside; if lights are not lit, eating Shabbat meals will be unpleasant.

[7] *"As darkness falls"* If the head of household mentions these things to the family too early in the day on Friday, they might put off doing them until it is too late (Rashi, Shab. 34a). They should be mentioned at the point when they can still be done in time (before Shabbat arrives) but are unlikely to be put off.

[7] *"The tithe … the* eruv *… the candle"* A person must mention these things gently, so that family members addressed are more inclined to listen (Shab. 34a). A severe tone and a raised voice inspire fear (Abudarham). The head of household *asks* about the tithing and the *eruv,* but *directs* that the light be lit, because there is no way of knowing if the first two have already been done, but the lack of Shabbat light is obvious (Rashi, Shab 34a).

[8] *"Question as to whether or not darkness has fallen* [safek chashekhah, safek einah chashekhah]*"* When the sun begins to set and only one star is visible, it is still considered "day." When three stars appear, it is certainly "night." The doubtful period referred to here is an intermediate period when two medium stars can be seen—called also *bein hash'mashot,* "twilight" (Obadiah of Bertinoro, Italy, ca. 1450–1510).

⁸ *"Do not ... tithe ... dip utensils ... light the candles"* During this twilight period we may not tithe food that we know for certain has not been tithed, since we are thereby "fixing" something during a period of time that, out of stringency, we treat as if it were already Shabbat. Similarly, we do not immerse utensils then (it would be a case of "fixing a utensil" for use), and we certainly do not light candles—an even more serious Shabbat violation than tithing or utensil immersion.

⁸ *"But take care of the tithe ... eruv ... and store away hot food"* The ban against tithing food that has certainly not been tithed does not apply to food about which we are in doubt as to whether it has been tithed: we are entitled to assume that most people tithe and that we are probably not "fixing" anything. As to the *eruv,* the Talmud (Shab. 34a) asks a logical question: Doesn't the Mishnah contradict itself? Initially it said that a person must ask his household about the *eruv* shortly before it gets dark (as if it should already have been done), and now it says that even at twilight an *eruv* may still be prepared. The answer is that we are dealing with two distinct types of *eruv.* The *eruv tehumin* ("*eruv* of the borders," which extends the 2,000 *amah* limit on Shabbat for walking in each direction) is a rabbinic institution based on a biblical verse (Ex. 16:29, "a person should not go out of his place on the seventh day") and is thus considered a matter of Torah law *(d'oraita).* Consequently it may not be prepared during twilight. The *eruv chatzerot* ("*eruv* of the courtyards," allowing people to carry items within their shared space) is simply a rabbinic stringency with no biblical basis. According to the rabbinic principle that "doubtful matters as to rabbinic law are to be resolved in the direction of leniency," the *eruv chatzerot* may be prepared during twilight if it was not done earlier.

⁹ *"Rabbi Elazar said ... "* This short *sugya* (talmudic unit of discourse) concludes tractate Berakhot of the Babylonian Talmud (64a). Interestingly, a portion of verse 1 (up to "great is the peace among your children") also concludes tractates Y'vamot (122b), Nazir (66b), and K'ritot (28b). It is also the conclusion to chapter 4 of tractate Tamid (32b), which is the end of the portion of Tamid that has *gemara* (a talmudic discussion; chapters 5–7 just repeat the Mishnah). The same words conclude Yerushalmi Berakhot (9:8, 14d). This *sugya* was apparently common as the conclusion to fixed literary units of learning. The link between Torah scholars, universal Torah study, and the peace these bring to the Jewish people make this teaching a fit one with which to conclude a talmudic tractate, and it is unsurprising that the teaching was deployed multiple times in that role.

The decision to conclude *Bameh Madlikin* with this *sugya* was already made by the time of *Seder Rav Amram* (ca. 860 C.E.). Abudarham hints that the reason for adding it is to raise the subject of peace, so that after the reader's *Kaddish,* which concludes the service immediately afterward, "the people will depart for their homes in peace." Alternatively, the redactor(s) of *Seder Rav Amram* may have known the practice of using at least the first teaching in the *sugya* as the conclusion to fixed literary units of learning (such as talmudic tractates) and so appended it to the end of the recitation of the

Mishnah here—another fixed literary unit of learning.

"All of your children are disciples of Adonai; great is the peace among your children" (Isaiah 54:13). But even if we grant that "Great is the peace among your children," how is this an adequate proof text for the notion that "Scholars increase peace in the world"? Moses Margaliot (Russia, eighteenth century) explains that the verse as a whole says "your children" twice. This redundancy opens the way to the midrashic interpretation that the second "your children" *(banayikh)* should be read differently—in this case, as "your builders" *(bonayikh),* that is to say, "Torah scholars are the builders of the peace."

◆

KUSHNER & POLEN (CHASIDISM)

> Come and see! In a flame ascending are two lights: one, a white light, radiant; the other, a light tinged with black or blue. The white light is above, ascending unswervingly, while beneath it is the blue or black light, a throne for the white, which rests upon it, each embracing the other, becoming one (*Zohar* I:50b–51a; *The Zohar*: Pritzker Edition, trans. Daniel C. Matt [Stanford: Stanford University Press, 2004], 283–3).

Rabbi Isaiah Horowitz (cited in *Siddur Sha'ar Hashamayim*) teaches that each lamp has its own deep mysteries. There are three colors of light corresponding to the *sefirot* of *Malkhut*, the presence of God; *Tiferet*, harmony; and *Binah*, intuition. (The *sefirot* receive many translations, corresponding to the many ways they are manifest in the universe. That is why the translations here differ somewhat from those used elsewhere in this book.) The dark blue flame closest to the wick represents *Malkhut*. The white of the flame represents *Tiferet*. And the barely visible, ethereal, colorless, and pure light represents *Binah*. This in turn evokes Shabbat, herself a fusion of the feminine *Malkhut* and the masculine *Tiferet*. And literally over this union there hovers the supernal mother, *Binah* (see Kimelman, "Go forth my love [2]]").

The Mishnah passage is all about which wicks can be used. The reason the Mishnah is so concerned is that you need a wick that draws the oil. The wick symbolizes our corporeal being; the oil, the wisdom that flows from above.

[3] *"Oil"* In his commentary on the prayer book *Olat R'iyah*, Rav Abraham Isaac Kook (1865–1935), the first Ashkenazi chief rabbi of Palestine and a legendary spokesman for tolerance and sacred living, notes that at the end of Mishnah 2 (not included here), "Rabbi Tarfon says one should use only olive oil" for the Sabbath lamp. Kook suggests that the reason is that we are, in effect, lighting the lamp of wisdom. The light of awareness flows into and through our souls, and we are sanctified. And each of the different oils (and wicks) referred to in the Mishnah represents different modes of enlightenment. Indeed, there are many different kinds of wisdom, all of which have the capacity to raise our consciousness and ethical standards. But, since on the Sabbath we should seek only the purest and clearest form of wisdom, we must use only the purest "olive oil."

[9] *"Scholars increase peace in the world"* Rabbi Abraham Isaac Kook *(Olat R'iyah)* is puzzled by this awkward construction: How can you "increase" peace? Either you have it or you don't. Kook points out that most people have the mistaken idea that universal peace can only come from universal agreement. They think that peace is the absence of argument, controversy, and contention. For this reason, when they see scholars passionately debating and arguing, each bringing different perspectives, they think that this can only lead away from peace. But, in truth, Rav Kook reminds us that real, genuine, and lasting peace can come only from the multiplication of arguments: that all sides and viewpoints are accorded a place at the table, even viewpoints that seem to be in opposition. Only then does peace (with truth and justice) emerge. In this way, each new conflict literally increases the size of the peace. In the words of the rabbinic dictum, *Elu v'elu div'rei Elohim chayim* ("These and these [both this and that] are the words of the living God"). Now we understand that even obvious contradictions ultimately build the house of reason and enlarge the domain of peace.

◆———

LANDES (HALAKHAH)

(m'khubad)" (Isaiah 58:13). The Rabbis understood the first verse to mean that even though no light may be kindled or transferred on Shabbat, a fire already burning could remain lit until it went out naturally. The second verse, however, implies the need for Sabbath "joy" and "honor," for which a well-lit house seems mandatory. The Talmud (Shab. 25b) applies this understanding to the rabbinic distinction between two levels of commandment: *mitzvah* and *chiyuv* (or *chovah*): A *mitzvah* is a positive act commanded by the Torah but for which there exists some personal discretion regarding whether to do it or not. A *chiyuv* (pronounced khee-YOOV, or *chovah*, pronounced khoh-VAH) is a *mitzvah* that is absolutely obligatory. (It is, for example, obligatory [a *chiyuv*] to eat matzah on the first day of Passover; but although it is a *mitzvah*, it is not a *chiyuv* to eat it every other day of Passover, and one may choose to eat it then or not.) In either case, lighting our homes on Shabbat is more than simply "permitted." Rashi declares it a *chovah*, for "it manifests Shabbat honor, no important meal being possible without light like the day." Tosafot adds, "It is obligatory to eat in a place with light because of the need for Shabbat "joy" (delight/joy). Halakhah therefore codifies Shabbat lights as a *chovah* the worth of which exceeds even that of the Shabbat meal itself and of *Kiddush* (*Sh. A. O. Ch. 263:2*).

A problem arises, however, with the prohibition of adding fuel to the lights, a natural inclination if they threaten to go out early on Friday night, but a clear case of *m'lakhah*, forbidden Shabbat labor. To avoid that temptation, the Rabbis applied yet another halakhic category: *muktzeh*, literally "cut off," a legal term for items that cannot be moved on Shabbat because they are "cut off" from any positive use. *Muktzeh* includes (1) items whose use would violate the Sabbath (like matches); (2) items that are repulsive (like garbage); and (3) items that have no use at all on Shabbat (like stones and dirt). To avoid the inclination to add to the light, the Rabbis declared the entire apparatus (wicks, oil, candles, holder or candlesticks, and certainly matches or lighters) as *muktzeh*.

Bameh Madlikin is therefore a practical yet philosophical meditation on how to balance the two principles: to provide Shabbat joy and honor, on one hand, but to avoid Shabbat labor, on the other.

[1] *"What may we use for the Sabbath light [2]"* According to the *Tur* (Jacob ben Asher, 1270–1340, Toledo, Spain),

> It is customary to say *Bameh Madlikin,* for it contains the law of kindling Sabbath lights and the three things that a person should say within his home Sabbath eve as it becomes dark. It is customary in Ashkenaz not to say it when a Yom Tov falls on Sabbath eve [Friday] because [then] one cannot say, "Have you separated the tithe? Have you prepared the *eruv*?" [Two activities that are forbidden on Yom Tov.] Then [after saying *Bameh Madlikin*] one says *Kaddish* and [everyone] departs for home in peace.

It is important to note that the *Tur* places *Bameh Madlikin* after laws regarding the Shabbat *Kiddush* recited in synagogue as part of the *Ma'ariv* service, but before the laws of the Shabbat meal and *Kiddush* at home. *Bameh Madlikin* must, therefore, have been said at the conclusion of *Ma'ariv*, just before going home from services—not (as we have it here) as part of *Kabbalat Shabbat* at all.

But *Bameh Madlikin* includes the three things that must be said upon coming home Friday evening (see below)—things that should have been done before Shabbat starts. Joseph Caro (1488–1575, Turkey, Greece, Safed) therefore recommends the Sefardi custom of saying *Bameh Madlikin* before the end of *Ma'ariv*, so that the three things will have been brought to mind in a timely fashion: "After *Ma'ariv* ends, what practical advantage is there to mention what must get done before Shabbat, for now [it being dark and Shabbat having commenced], there is nothing one can do about it" (*Bet Yosef*, O. Ch., 170).

The *Bayit Chadash* (Joel Sirkes, 1561–1640, Poland, commentary on the *Tur*, known also as the *BaCH*) agrees with Caro, pointing out that *Bameh Madlikin* also discusses proper oils and wicks, another reason for it to be recited earlier. Nonetheless, he justifies the Ashkenazi custom of reciting it only as *Ma'ariv* ends to answer a halakhic problem. Halakhah permits saying *Ma'ariv* before sunset so as to arrive home for Shabbat while it is still day. But *Kiddush* at home must wait until dark. *Bameh Madlikin* is a "filler," delaying the home *Kiddush* somewhat.

Thus, we have two customs regarding *Bameh Madlikin*: either (1) following Caro, to place it early, at the end of *Kabbalat Shabbat*, but before the community accepts Shabbat via the *Ma'ariv Bar'khu*, or (2) following the *Bayit Chadash*, to say it at the very end of *Ma'ariv*, as a filler before it becomes dark. The Magen Avraham (Avraham Gombiner, 1637–1683, Poland, commentary on the *Shulchan Arukh*) defends the second custom because (1) in "our countries" we no longer use the wicks and oil mentioned in the Mishnah, so that studying the laws connected to them is merely academic; and (2) putting it at the end of *Ma'ariv* extends the service so that stragglers can finish their *Ma'ariv* prayers while the congregation is reciting *Bameh Madlikin*.

The Gra (Elijah of Vilna, 1720–1797) prefers saying it earlier than both opinions. He says it before *Kabbalat Shabbat* begins, so as to make the reminder of the "three things that one must say in one's home" immediately relevant. Nonetheless, the nearly universal custom is to say *Bameh Madlikin* where we have it here—at the end of *Kabbalat Shabbat*, and immediately before the *Bar'khu* of *Ma'ariv*. The *Arukh Hashulchan* (Yechiel Michal Epstein, Lithuania, late nineteenth and early twentieth centuries) offers a further consideration: (1) Current custom places *Kabbalat Shabbat* very close to Shabbat, or even after nightfall; (2) it has become customary to accept Shabbat not with the *Bar'khu* that begins *Ma'ariv*, but with Psalm 92 ("*mizmor shir l'yom hashabbat,*" or even *L'khah Dodi*, both of which precede *Bameh Madlikin*). Either way, then (according to Caro or the BaCH), *Bameh Madlikin* will be recited after Shabbat begins. Indeed, he is not surprised that many prefer a passage entitled *Ki gavna*, a substitution from the *Zohar* that elucidates the mystical unity theme of Shabbat (*T'rumah* 135a/b).

Why, then, do we still say *Bameh Madlikin* if it no longer has the practical impact that it did when Shabbat began only at *Ma'ariv*? I believe that the ritual recitation of *Bameh Madlikin* allows for a symbolic "virtual" lighting that demarcates the time between the preparation for Shabbat (the *Kabbalat Shabbat* service) and the actual commencement of Shabbat (*Bar'khu* of *Ma'ariv*). By going over the details of the halakhic requirements for candlelighting and re-evoking what is to have taken place at home during the last frantic moments before Shabbat, the candle is symbolically "lit" in the minds of all present. *Bameh Madlikin* thus works as education for the future and as an imaginative narrative for the present.

We have seen that *Bameh Madlikin* is not recited on a Friday that is a holiday. That is because a Yom Tov possesses the quality of *k'dushat hayom* ("sanctity of the day"), which forbids two forms of work that *Bameh Madlikin* commands—establishing an *eruv* and tithing. (The third reminder, kindling light, is permitted on Yom Tov as long as it involves the transfer of fire from an already lit source. Kindling a new fire [e.g., striking a match] or extinguishing a fire [putting out a match], however, are forbidden.)

Halakhic authorities extended the times when *Bameh Madlikin* is not said (following the R'ma [Moses Isserles, 1530–1572, Cracow] and Mishnah Berurah of R. Israel Meir Hacohen Kagan [Poland, early twentieth century]):

- Friday that introduces both Shabbat and Yom Tov: since *Bameh Madlikin* doesn't address Yom Tov, reciting it then would slight the holiday.
- Friday evening that introduces *Shabbat Chol Hamo'ed*; one purpose of *Bameh Madlikin* is to extend the period of prayer for latecomers, but on *Chol Hamo'ed*, people work less, if at all, and can be expected to come to synagogue on time.
- Friday during Chanukah; certain wicks and oils that are prohibited for Shabbat are permitted on Chanukah, and we don't wish to confuse people.

[2] *"Seaweed* [biroka she'al p'nei hamayim]" The problem is wicks that do not fully absorb fluid, so that the flame burns, as it were, around the wick. This creates an irregular flame, thereby minimizing Shabbat joy and honor but, more importantly, tempting the user to adjust it.

[3] *"Burnt oil"* The oil of *t'rumah*, which is a gift given to the priest (*kohen*) in the Land of Israel in fulfillment of the verse, "You shall give him [the *kohen*] the first fruit of your new grain, wine and oil" (Deut. 18:4). The oil of *t'rumah* must be ritually pure to be eaten. If it is impure, it must be burned up. Since it must be burned anyway, someone who owns such oil might decide to use it for Shabbat lamps. But burning it is a *mitzvah*; fearing that the owner might hasten its burning on Shabbat, we prohibit its use for Shabbat lights (Gra).

[3] *"Grease from the fat tail* [alyah] *or tallow* [chelev]" The general problem here is oils that do not draw well into the wick, thereby necessitating extra oil to be added to create a more even flame. The flame may also sputter or even go out, destroying Shabbat peace to the point where a householder even leaves home (Maimonides' *Commentary, ad. loc.*). These particular items tend also to dry out, in which case they burn more as a torch than as a flame. Torch fire is considered unpleasant for Shabbat (*Tiferet Yisra'el*, Israel Lipschitz, 1782–1860, Poland).

[4] *"Melted tallow"* At issue is the use of tallow that is melted by the addition of permitted oil. The halakhic consensus is positive (Maimonides, *Hilkhot Shabbat* 5:2).

The next several *mishnayot* are not reproduced here, but their summary can be given. Ill-smelling oils like resins produce a good even light, but they are forbidden because they run counter to Shabbat joy. Very attractive oil like persimmon is forbidden lest we be tempted to reach out and put some on our hands, and inadvertently extinguish the light prematurely. All other fruit oils are permitted. Rabbi Tarfon permitted only costly olive oil, but he was known to be wealthy; as an elitist policy that favored the rich, his view was rejected (*Tanchuma: B'ha'alotcha*).

Tree products cannot be employed as wicks because they sputter *(Tiferet Yisra'el)*. Although flax is described biblically as a form of tree (Joshua 2:6), it differs botanically, so it may be used as a wick (Obadiah Bertinoro, 1450–ca. 1516, Italy).

Wicks made of twisted cloth torn from a garment are problematic because finished items made from natural elements are subject to contracting *tum'ah* ("ritual impurity"—on this concept, see below, "Menstruation"). However, once torn, they are no longer "finished," so they may be used as wicks. But the Rabbis debate what must be done to make them acceptable. Rabbi Eliezer requires singeing the cloth. Rabbi Akiba maintains that just twisting it is sufficient. We follow Akiba, but in practice we singe new wicks anyway because the production of carbon facilitates lighting.

The prohibition against extinguishing flames on Shabbat is extended to encompass the act of reducing the fuel source. Thus, the Mishnah forbids the case of a suspended hollowed-out egg that feeds an oil lamp by dripping oil from a perforation in the bottom (in our time, consider a pottery bowl with an aperture on the bottom). We fear that seeing the eggshell (or pottery) as separate from the oil lamp, we might remove some oil from it. If the entire apparatus is welded together, it is permitted, since it would be obvious that removing oil is forbidden. Similarly, attaching the wick of the lamp to a separate oil dish is prohibited, for fear of someone removing oil from what looks like a separate entity.

In certain cases of fear, however, it is not just permitted but required to extinguish a Shabbat flame. These cases include (1) fear of Zoroastrians, who held fire sacred and forbade its use on their holidays; (2) fear of robbers prone to violence; and (3) fear of severe depression (Maimonides' interpretation of "evil spirit"), where relief comes only by sitting in the dark, or where it is necessary to let the patient who is at risk sleep peacefully. The halakhic principles at stake are these: (1) saving a life takes precedence over Shabbat prohibitions (*pik'uach nefesh docheh et hashabbat*); (2) the danger need only be potential (a *safek*—that is, "probable," but not altogether certain); and (3) the judgment of the beholder is determinative. Indeed later Halakhah praises anyone alert enough to extinguish a necessary light immediately. The act of risking a life by taking time to inquire as to the permissibility of quenching the light is considered "bloodshed" (*Sh. A.*, O. Ch. 328:2).

There are also instances, however, where extinguishing the flame is tempting but punishable: for instance, to spare a lamp that, if used to the very end, might crack; or to keep the wick or oil from being used up. A minority position by Rabbi Yosi holds punishable only the act of extinguishing a flame to save the wick, because carbon (a coal product) is necessarily created around the wick. His reasoning is instructive. In antiquity, Temple lights were extinguished specifically to create coal. Our act of extinguishing for the same end would thereby be a *m'lakhah shetz'richah l'gufa*, "a [prohibited] act of work that is necessary for its own sake." By contrast, quenching a light to spare a lamp from cracking or to save on fuel separates the *m'lakhah* (the act of work) from its definitional purpose, and would be a *m'lakhah she'einah tz'richah l'gufa*, "a [prohibited] act of work that is *not* necessary for its own sake." The template of what should be considered "acts of work" on Shabbat comes from the activities associated with the Temple, so Rabbi Yose excludes a *m'lakhah she'einah tz'richah l'gufa*. We follow the majority opinion, not Rabbi Yose's.

[6] *"Three transgressions"* According to physician Robert Mendelsohn (Chicago, mid-twentieth century), the three major risk factors of late pregnancy and labor are sexually transmitted diseases, poor nutrition, and stress. These, says Mendelsohn, correspond to the laws associated with *nidah* ("menstruation"), *challah* ("separating dough"), and *hadlakat nerot* ("candle lighting"). On *nidah* and *challah*, see below.

Halakhically speaking, the inclusion of candle lighting (*hadlakat nerot*) in this list of sins demonstrates its importance, since the other two inclusions are rooted in laws that derive from Torah (*d'ora'ita*) as opposed to the Rabbis (*d'rabbanan*). Kindling Shabbat light is derived from Isaiah 58:13—the same verse that gives us the rabbinic concepts of Shabbat *kavod* ("honor") and *oneg* ("joy") (see above, "What may we use for the Sabbath light [1]").

[6] *"Women"* This Mishnah is formative in requiring Shabbat lights and in associating their lighting with women (Tosafot to Shabbat 25b). *Nidah* (menstruation) is obviously associated with women, but why the other two? Bertinoro explains that they are home-based *mitzvot*. Indeed, I would argue that they are formative in creating the Jewish home.

[6] *"Menstruation"* Nidah (from the root *n.d.d*, "separated") refers to the sexual separation between husband and wife from the onset of menstruation (Lev. 15:19) until immersion in the *mikveh* (pronounced mik-VEH, but popularly MIK-v'h = "ritual bath"). Punishment for such sexual contact is *karet*, meaning the spiritual severance from one's people and heritage (Maimonides to Lev. 15:31). In practice, the separation is usually about twelve days a month.

The laws of *nidah* are tied to the conceptual dichotomy *tum'ah/tohorah*, which are conveniently translated "unclean/clean" or "impure/pure" but which are better understood as "alienated/potentially integrated." Thus people who have had what Halakhah considers contact with death (preparing a body for burial, for instance, but also just sleeping under the same roof as a corpse) are in a condition of *tum'ah*, alienated from permission to participate in Temple ritual. After *mikveh*, they are in the opposite condition of *tohorah*, potentially integrated into it. *Mikveh* acts as a transformational agent.

Similarly, at the onset of menstruation a woman is "alienated" physically from her husband until *mikveh* potentially integrates her again with him. This reunion is described as a monthly wedding (Nid. 31b).

Writer Sheryl Robbin observes that (1) during *tum'ah* , husband and wife necessarily interact on many human levels without the "quick fix" of sex; (2) *mikveh* is based on trust between husband and wife: he trusts her judgment on when she should go, and her assurance that she has done so; and (3) *mikveh* is an experience in which a woman is aided by other women.

But *mikveh* is not limited to women. Conversion (male and female) requires *mikveh*, and many men go to *mikveh* the day before Yom Kippur and (for some) every *Erev Shabbat* (but without a blessing). Scribes go every time they are about to write the name of God. Religiously observant Orthodox Israeli soldiers go before patrolling the Temple Mount.

Tohorat hamishpachah (the usual term for the laws of *nidah*) should be translated as "family integration," involving the spiritual, emotional, and sexual well-being of the husband and wife.

[6] *"Challah"* The *mitzvah* of giving the *kohen* a portion of the about to-be-baked dough (Num. 15:20) is a subset of the laws of *t'rumah* (see above, "Burnt oil"). *Challah* is taken from dough of the five species grown in Eretz Yisrael (wheat, rye, barley, oat, spelt). In the process, a blessing is recited, and then approximately an ounce of dough is taken. As the *challah* is separated, one declares: *Harei zeh challah* ("This is challah"). Since today we do not give gifts to the priests, the *challah* is burned in the

oven (at a time separate from when the cake or bread is being baked).

⁷ *"Have you taken care of the tithe"* All agricultural foods must be tithed; otherwise, they are considered *tevel* and are forbidden to be eaten. But tithing cannot be done once Shabbat begins.

The laws of tithing are relevant only to produce grown in Eretz Yisrael, where it still occurs. Originally, the tithes were collected for the *kohen*, the Levite, and the poor. Today, tithing is intended only to commemorate original practice, so all the money is given to *tzedakah* ("charity").

⁷ *"Have you taken care of the* eruv*"* Carrying from house to house is forbidden on Shabbat. An *eruv* creates the legal fiction of constituting many households into one. A contemporary example would be a gated community or a condominium building. If all parties agree that food in one of the houses is available to everyone, the disparate households count as one, and carrying from among them is permitted.

⁸ *"If there is some question"* One medium star in the sky signals that it is still day; three medium stars indicate that Shabbat is fully present; with two stars, however, we are half way, in a twilight period. In that period full *m'lakhah* (work) is forbidden. Kindling fire is obviously included, but so is (1) tithing what is known to be still untithed and (2) immersing vessels in a *mikveh* to rid them of *tum'ah* (ritual impurity), because these are acts of "fixing" what is unusable. We may, however, "fix" (on Shabbat) things already said to be in their proper state, so "doubtfully tithed" products can be retithed then.

The *eruv* presents a different consideration. It is permitted because, to begin with, it began as an especially strict rabbinic ruling

⁸ *"Store away hot food"* On Shabbat, one may not create heat. Wrapping hot food in such a way as not to increase heat might technically be allowed, therefore, but it is prohibited lest it lead inadvertently to wrapping in a way that does increase heat. This additional cautionary prohibition is not extended to the twilight period.

⁹ *"Rabbi Elazar said"* From Berakhot 64a. It connects Torah study (in this case, of *Bameh Madlikin*) with the achievement of peace. Parents and children studying together create a spiritual structure of *shalom* ("peace") in the sense of *sh'lemut* ("fullness"). Peace arrives only with this larger fullness.

◆

L. HOFFMAN (HISTORY)

CANDLES," PP. 27–31). MISHNAH 2:7 TURNS TO GENERAL PREPARATION FOR SHABBAT: THE ERUV, TITHING, AND KINDLING SHABBAT LIGHTS. THE MISHNAH IS FOLLOWED WITH A BRIEF TALMUDIC PASSAGE THAT CELEBRATES THE STUDY OF TORAH AS THE ULTIMATE WAY TO MESSIANIC PEACE. AS USUAL, STUDY IS CONCLUDED WITH KADDISH D'RABBANAN, THE FORM OF THE KADDISH THAT PRAYS FOR ALL WHO STUDY TORAH.

[1] *"What may we use for the Sabbath light"* Inserted into the liturgy as a polemic against Karaites who denied the oral law and interpreted the Torah literally to mean that homes had to be darkened from Friday sundown on. The Rabbis cited Isaiah 58:13 ("You shall call the Sabbath 'joy' [*oneg*]") to demonstrate their conviction that light was necessary because Shabbat joy (which requires light) was divinely mandated. Judah Hadassi, a prominent twelfth-century Karaite, countered by identifying "joy" (*oneg*) here as "delight in prayer and contemplation of Torah" only, for which no light is necessary. In keeping with the Karaite emphasis on mourning for Jerusalem (see above, "May God comfort you with the rest of Zion and Jerusalem's mourners"), he urged people to spend Shabbat "fasting and not rejoicing thereby, and mourning over the destruction of his [God's] glory and the desolation of his Temple and city." The Geonim prevailed, and to this day *oneg Shabbat* is central to Judaism.

J. HOFFMAN (TRANSLATION)

after the priest uses it. Neusner calls this: "oil [given to a priest as heave offering which had become unclean and must therefore be] burned."

[6] *"The laws of"* Literally, just "not being careful about menstruation," but we add a few words here to make the intent clear.

[6] *"Sabbath"* Again, we add a word to make the intent clear.

[8] *"Certainly must be tithed"* Hebrew, *vada'i:* a technical term (see Landes).

[8] *"Dip utensils"* See Landes.

[8] *"May have to be tithed"* See Landes.

[9] *"Scholars"* Or "wise students." Or perhaps "students of the wise ones."

[9] *"Builders"* The words for "children" and "builders" in Hebrew are identical except for the vowels, making this a much more reasonable midrash in Hebrew than in English. The Hebrew is like a story in English about "lead" (the metal) read as the word "lead" ("make others follow").

[12] *"Hope that you find peace"* Literally, "I ask for/speak good for you." Here and

immediately below, we find poetic first-person verbs ("ask for/speak" here, "request" below) that we cannot translate. So we reword both phrases to preserve the nearly parallel structure.

[14] *"May Adonai"* We translate this phrase elsewhere as, "Adonai will…" Hebrew is often ambiguous in this regard, using the same language both for a hope for the future and for a description of it. In this context, we think the hope-meaning is better.

◆ ◆ ◆

About the Contributors

MARC BRETTLER

Marc Brettler, Ph.D., is Dora Goldberg Professor of Biblical Studies and chair of the Department of Near Eastern and Judaic Studies at Brandeis University. His major areas of research are biblical historical texts, religious metaphors, and gender issues in the Bible. Brettler is author of *God Is King: Understanding an Israelite Metaphor* (Sheffield Academic Press) and *The Creation of History in Ancient Israel* (Routledge) as well as a variety of articles on the Bible. He is also associate editor of the new edition of the *Oxford Annotated Bible*, and coeditor of the *Jewish Study Bible* (Oxford University Press).

ELLIOT N. DORFF

Elliot N. Dorff, Ph.D., is rector and Sol and Anne Dorff Distinguished Professor of Philosophy at the University of Judaism in Los Angeles. His book, *Knowing God: Jewish Journeys to the Unknowable* (Rowman and Littlefield) includes an extensive analysis of the nature of prayer. Ordained a rabbi at the Jewish Theological Seminary of America, Dorff is vice-chair of the Conservative Movement's Committee on Jewish Law and Standards, and he contributed to the Conservative Movement's new Torah commentary, *Etz Hayim*. He has chaired the Jewish Law Association and the Academy of Jewish Philosophy, and he is now president of Jewish Family Service of Los Angeles. He has served on several federal government commissions on issues in bioethics. Winner of the National Jewish Book Award for *To Do the Right and the Good: A Jewish Approach to Modern Social Ethics*, he has written ten books and more than 150 articles on Jewish thought and ethics.

DAVID ELLENSON

David Ellenson, Ph.D., is president of Hebrew Union College–Jewish Institute of Religion. He holds the Gus Waterman Herrman Presidential Chair and is the I. H. and Anna Grancell Professor of Jewish Religious Thought. Ordained a rabbi by Hebrew Union College–Jewish Institute of Religion, he has served as a visiting professor at Hebrew University in Jerusalem, at the Jewish Theological Seminary in New York, and at the University of California at Los Angeles. Ellenson has also taught at the Pardes Institute of Jewish Studies and at the Shalom Hartman Institute, both in Jerusalem. Ellenson has published and lectured extensively on diverse topics in modern Jewish thought, history, and ethics. His most recent book, *After Emancipation*, was published by HUC Press in 2004.

ELLEN FRANKEL

Dr. Ellen Frankel is currently the CEO and editor in chief of The Jewish Publication Society. A scholar of Jewish folklore, Frankel has published eight books, including *The Classic Tales; The Encyclopedia of Jewish Symbols*, co-authored with artist Betsy Teutsch; *The Five Books of Miriam: A Woman's Commentary on the Torah; The Jewish Spirit;* and *The Illustrated Hebrew Bible.* Frankel travels widely as a storyteller and lecturer, speaking at synagogues, summer study institutes, Hillels, Jewish women's groups, Jewish community centers, museums, schools, retirement communities, and nursing homes, and to radio audiences.

ALYSSA GRAY

Alyssa Gray, Ph.D., J.D., is assistant professor of codes and responsa literature at Hebrew Union College–Jewish Institute of Religion in New York. She has also taught at The Jewish Theological Seminary in New York. Her principal research interests are the Babylonian and Palestinian Talmuds, Jewish law and legal theory, and the history of Jewish law, especially the topics of *tzedakah,* Jewish–non-Jewish interactions, and martyrdom. She has completed a book entitled *A Talmud in Exile,* which is forthcoming from Brown Judaic Studies. Her current research focuses on wealth and poverty in classical rabbinic literature.

JOEL M. HOFFMAN

Joel M. Hoffman, Ph.D., teaches advanced Hebrew, translation, and the history of Hebrew at Hebrew Union College–Jewish Institute of Religion in New York; he has also taught at Brandeis University, and lectures widely in North and South America, Europe, and Israel. He is the author of *In the Beginning: A Short History of the Hebrew Language* (NYU Press). Hoffman's research in theoretical linguistics brings him to a new approach to ancient Hebrew, viewing it not merely as a dead language, but as a spoken language of antiquity. In addition to his graduate-level teaching, Hoffman teaches youngsters at various Hebrew schools. He considers teaching his greatest joy.

LAWRENCE A. HOFFMAN

Lawrence A. Hoffman, Ph.D., has served for more than two decades as the Barbara and Stephen Friedman Professor of Liturgy Worship and Ritual at Hebrew Union College–Jewish Institute of Religion in New York, where he was ordained a rabbi. Widely recognized for his liturgical scholarship, Hoffman has combined research in

Jewish ritual, worship, and spirituality with a passion for the spiritual renewal of contemporary Judaism. He has written and edited numerous books, including *The Art of Public Prayer, 2nd Edition: Not for Clergy Only* (SkyLight Paths)—now used nationally by Jews and Christians as a handbook for liturgical planners in church and synagogue, as well as a revision of *What Is a Jew?*, the best-selling classic that remains the most widely read introduction to Judaism ever written in any language. He is also the author of *Israel—A Spiritual Travel Guide: A Companion for the Modern Jewish Pilgrim* and *The Way Into Jewish Prayer* (both Jewish Lights Publishing). Hoffman is currently a developer of Synagogue 2000, a transdenominational project designed to envision and implement the ideal synagogue of the spirit for the twenty-first century.

REUVEN KIMELMAN

Reuven Kimelman, Ph.D., is professor of rabbinic literature at Brandeis University. He has written extensively on the liturgy, ethics, and the history of the Talmudic period with a special focus on Jewish-Christian relations in late antiquity. He is the author of *The Mystical Meaning of L'khah Dodi and Kabbalat Shabbat* (Magnes Press, The Hebrew University). His book *The Rhetoric of Jewish Prayer: A Historical and Literary Commentary on the Prayerbook* is soon to be published by the Littman Library of Jewish Civilization.

SHARON KOREN

Sharon Koren, Ph.D., teaches history and Jewish mysticism at Hebrew Union College–Jewish Institute of Religion in New York City. She completed her doctorate in medieval studies at Yale University. Her principle areas of research are Jewish mysticism and women's spirituality. She is currently completing a book that explores the nexus between bodily purity and women's spirituality in medieval Jewish mysticism. She lives in New York City with her husband and three daughters.

LAWRENCE KUSHNER

Lawrence Kushner is the Emanu-El scholar at congregation Emanu-El in San Francisco, an adjunct faculty member at Hebrew Union College–Jewish Institute of Religion, and a visiting professor of Jewish spirituality at the Graduate Theological Union in Berkeley, California. He served as spiritual leader of Congregation Beth El in Sudbury, Massachusetts, for twenty-eight years and is widely regarded as one of the most creative religious writers in America. Ordained a rabbi by Hebrew Union College–Jewish Institute of Religion, Kushner led his congregants in publishing their own prayer book, *V'taher Libenu (Purify Our Hearts)*, the first gender-neutral liturgy ever written. Through his lectures and many books, including *The Way Into Jewish Mystical Tradition; Invisible Lines of Connection: Sacred Stories of the Ordinary; The Book of Letters: A Mystical Hebrew Alphabet; Honey from the Rock: An Introduction to Jewish Mysticism; God Was in This Place and I, i Did Not Know: Finding Self, Spirituality, and Ultimate Meaning; Eyes Remade for Wonder: A Lawrence Kushner Reader, Jewish Spirituality: A*

Brief Introduction for Christians, and *Filling Words with Light: Hasidic and Mystical Reflections on Jewish Prayer,* all published by Jewish Lights, he has helped shape the Jewish community's present focus on personal and institutional spiritual renewal.

Daniel Landes

Daniel Landes is director and Rosh HaYeshivah of the Pardes Institute of Jewish Studies in Jerusalem and was an adjunct professor of Jewish law at Loyola University Law School in Los Angeles. Ordained a rabbi by Rabbi Isaac Elchanan Theological Seminary, Landes was a founding faculty member of the Simon Wiesenthal Center and the Yeshiva of Los Angeles. He has lectured and written various popular and scholarly articles on the subjects of Jewish thought, social ethics, and spirituality.

Nehemia Polen

Nehemia Polen is professor of Jewish thought and director of the Hasidic Text Institute at Boston's Hebrew College. He is the author of *The Holy Fire: The Teachings of Rabbi Kalonymus Shapira, the Rebbe of the Warsaw Ghetto* (Jason Aronson) as well as many academic and popular articles on Chasidism and Jewish spirituality, and co-author of *Filling Words with Light: Hasidic and Mystical Reflections on Jewish Prayer* (Jewish Lights). He received his Ph.D. from Boston University, where he studied with and served as teaching fellow for Nobel laureate Elie Wiesel. In 1994 he was Daniel Jeremy Silver Fellow at Harvard University, and he has also been a Visiting Scholar at the Hebrew University in Jerusalem. He was ordained a rabbi at the Ner Israel Rabbinical College in Baltimore, Maryland, and served as a congregational rabbi for twenty-three years. In 1998–1999 he was a National Endowment for the Humanities Fellow, working on the writings of Malkah Shapiro (1894–1971), the daughter of a noted Chasidic master, whose Hebrew memoirs focus on the spiritual lives of women in the context of pre-war Chasidism in Poland. This work is documented in his book *The Rebbe's Daughter* (Jewish Publication Society).

Wendy I. Zierler

Wendy I. Zierler is the assistant professor of feminist studies and modern Jewish literature at Hebrew Union College–Jewish Institute of Religion. Prior to joining HUC–JIR she was a research fellow in the English Department of Hong Kong University. She holds PhD and MA degrees in comparative literature from Princeton University, and a BA from Yeshiva University, Stern College. Her book, *And Rachel Stole the Idols: The Emergence of Hebrew Women's Writing,* was recently published by Wayne State University Press. At HUC she teaches courses on American Jewish literature, popular culture and theology, modern Hebrew literature, Holocaust literature, the Jew and the other, in addition to courses dealing with gender and Judaism.

List of Abbreviations

Artscroll	*Siddur Kol Ya'akov*, 1984.
Birnbaum	*Daily Prayer Book: Hasiddur Hashalem*, 1949.
FOP	*Forms of Prayer*, 1997.
Fox	Everett Fox, *The Five Books of Moses* (New York: Schocken Books, 1995).
GOP	*Gates of Prayer*, 1975.
HS	*Ha'avodah Shebalev*, 1982.
KH	*Kol Haneshamah*, 1996.
King James	*King James Bible*, 1611/1769.
JPS	*Jewish Publication Society Bible* (Philadelphia: Jewish Publication Society, 1985).
NRSV	*New Revised Standard Bible*, 1989.
SLC	*Siddur Lev Chadash*, 1995.
SOH	*Service of the Heart*, 1967.
SSS	*Siddur Sim Shalom*, 1985; revised, 1998.
SVT	*Siddur Va'ani T'fillati*, 1998.
UPB	*Union Prayer Book*, 1894–1895.

Glossary

The following glossary defines Hebrew words used regularly throughout this volume and provides the way the words are pronounced. Sometimes two pronunciations are common, in which case the first is the way the word is sounded in proper Hebrew, and the second is the way it is sometimes heard in common speech, under the influence of Yiddish, the folk language of Jews in northern and eastern Europe (it is a combination, mostly, of Hebrew and German). Our goal is to provide the way that many Jews actually use these words, not just the technically correct version.

- The pronunciations are divided into syllables by dashes.

- The accented syllable is written in capital letters.

- "Kh" represents a guttural sound, similar to the German (as in "sprach").

- The most common vowel is "a" as in "father," which appears here as "ah."

- The short "e" (as in "get") is written as either "e" (when it is in the middle of a syllable) or "eh" (when it ends a syllable).

- Similarly, the short "i" (as in "tin") is written as either "i" (when it is in the middle of a syllable) or "ih" (when it ends a syllable).

- A long "o" (as in "Moses") is written as "oe" (as in the word "toe") or "oh" (as in the word "Oh!").

Acharonim (pronounced ah-khah-roe-NEEM or, commonly, akh-ROE-nim): The name given to Jewish legal authorities from roughly the sixteenth century on. The word means, literally, "later ones," as opposed to the "earlier ones," authorities prior to that time who are held in higher regard and are called *Rishonim* (pronounced ree-shoh-NEEM or, commonly, ree-SHOH-nim). Singular: *Acharon* (pronounced ah-khah-RONE) and *Rishon* (pronounced ree-SHONE).

Adam harishon (pronounced ah-DAHM hah-ree-SHOHN): "The first man," that is, the biblical Adam.

Adon Olam (pronounced ah-DOHN oh-LAHM): An early morning prayer of unknown authorship, but dating from medieval times, and possibly originally intended as a nighttime prayer, because it praises God for watching over our souls when we sleep. Nowadays, it is used also as a concluding song for which composers have provided a staggering variety of tunes.

Adonai elohei yisra'el (pronounced ah-doh-NAH'y eh-loh-HAY yis-rah-AYL): Literally, "Adonai God of Israel." A common appellation for God, used in this series to designate the opening words, and hence, the name of a prayer, that is added to *Tachanun* on Mondays and Thursdays.

Akedah (pronounced ah-kay-DAH): Literally, "binding"; the technical term for the Genesis 22 account of the binding of Isaac on the altar; read liturgically as part of the *Birkhot Hashachar*. By extension, a genre of poem, especially for the High Holy Days, pleading for forgiveness on account of the merit of Isaac's near self-sacrifice.

Al chet (pronounced ahl KHEHT): Literally, "For the sin…" See ***Vidui Rabbah***.

Alenu (pronounced ah-LAY-noo): The first word and, therefore, the title of a major prayer compiled in the second or third century as part of the New Year (Rosh Hashanah) service, but from about the fourteenth century on, used also as part of the concluding section of every daily service. *Alenu* means "it is incumbent upon us…" and introduces the prayer's theme: our duty to praise God.

Amah (pronounced ah-MAH): A rabbinic measure, amounting, roughly, to a forearm: the distance from the elbow to the tip of the little finger.

Amidah (pronounced either ah-mee-DAH or, commonly, ah-MEE-dah): One of three commonly used titles for the second of two central units in the worship service, the first being the *Sh'ma* and Its Blessings. It is composed of a series of blessings, many of which are petitionary, except on Sabbaths and holidays, when the petitions are removed out of deference to the holiness of the day. Also called ***T'fillah*** and ***Sh'moneh Esreh***. *Amidah* means "standing," and refers to the fact that the prayer is said standing up.

Amora (pronounced ah-MOE-rah): A title for talmudic authorities and, therefore, those living from roughly the third to the sixth centuries. Plural: *Amoraim* (pronounced ah-moe-rah-EEM or, commonly, ah-moe-RAH-yim). Often used in contrast to a ***Tanna*** (pronounced TAH-nah), the title of authorities in the time of the Mishnah, that is, prior to the third century. Plural: *Tanna'im* (pronounced tah-nah-EEM or, commonly, tah-NAH-yim).

Arvit (pronounced ahr-VEET or, commonly, AHR-veet): From the Hebrew word *erev* (pronounced EH-rev) meaning "evening." One of two titles used for the evening worship service (also called ***Ma'ariv***).

Ashamnu (pronounced ah-SHAHM-noo): Literally, "We have sinned." See *Vidui Zuta*.

Ashkavah (pronounced ahsh-kah-VAH or, commonly, ahsh-KAH-vah): Sometimes spelled *Hashkavah* (pronounced hahsh-kah-VAH or, commonly, hahsh-KAH-vah). A traditional Sefardi prayer for the dead, recited by mourners following the reading of Torah during the regular service. Said also at the graveside and during the evening service of Yom Kippur.

Ashkenazi (pronounced ahsh-k'-nah-ZEE or, commonly, ahsh-k'-NAH-zee): From the Hebrew word *Ashkenaz,* meaning the geographic area of northern and eastern Europe; Ashkenazi is the adjective, describing the liturgical rituals and customs practiced there, as opposed to Sefardi, meaning the liturgical rituals and customs that are derived from *Sefarad,* Spain (see *Sefardi*).

Ashre (pronounced ahsh-RAY or, commonly, AHSH-ray): The first word and, therefore, the title of a prayer said three times each day, composed primarily of Psalm 145. *Ashre* means "happy" and introduces the phrase "Happy are they who dwell in Your [God's] house."

Atarah (pronounced ah-tah-RAH): A stole worn by some Reform service leaders (in place of an actual *tallit* with *tsitsit*) prior to the liturgical renewal of the late twentieth century that featured a recovery of tradition and the reuse of the traditional *tallit*. (See *tallit*.)

Av harachamim (pronounced AHV hah-rah-khah-MEEM or, commonly, ahv hah-RAH-khah-meem): Literally, "Father of mercy," a prayer composed in the wake of the Crusades to commemorate the death of German Jewish martyrs; now part of the weekly Shabbat service (after reading Torah) and one of the main prayers comprising the Memorial Service *(Yizkor)*.

Avodah (pronounced ah-voe-DAH): Literally, "sacrificial service," a reference to the sacrificial cult practiced in the ancient Temple until its destruction by the Romans in the year 70 C.E.; also the title of the third to last blessing in the *Amidah,* a petition for the restoration of the Temple in messianic times. Many liberal liturgies either omit the blessing or reframe it as a petition for divine acceptance of worship in general.

Avot (pronounced ah-VOTE): Literally, "fathers" or "ancestors," and the title of the first blessing in the *Amidah*. The traditional wording of the blessing recollects the covenantal relationship between God and the patriarchs: Abraham, Isaac, and Jacob. Most liberal liturgies also include explicit reference to the matriarchs: Sarah, Rebekah, Rachel, and Leah.

[The] Bach (pronounced BAHKH): An acronym for Rabbi Joel Sirkes (1561–1640, Poland), formed by juxtaposing the two Hebrew initials of his major legal work, *Bayit Chadash* (BaCH).

Bakashot (pronounced bah-kah-SHOTE; singular, *bakashah*, pronounced bah-kah-SHAH): Petitions; technically, the middle thirteen blessings of the daily ***Amidah***.

Baleh busteh (pronounced bah-l' BUS-tah [the U of "BUS" rhymes with the OU of "could"]): A virtually untranslatable Yiddish phrase meaning "good homemaker."

Bar'khu (pronounced bah-r'-KHOO or, commonly, BOH-r'khoo): The first word and, therefore, the title of the formal Call to Prayer with which the section called the *Sh'ma* and Its Blessings begins. *Bar'khu* means "praise," and it introduces the invitation to the assembled congregation to praise God.

Barukh k'vod (pronounced bah-RUKH k'-VOD): The first two words of a response in the third blessing of the *Amidah* taken from Ezekiel 3:12, meaning "the glory of Adonai is blessed from His place."

Barukh she'amar (pronounced bah-ROOKH sheh-ah-MAHR): Literally, "Blessed is the One by whose speech [the world came to be]," the first words and, therefore, the title of the blessing that opens the *P'sukei D'zimrah,* the "warm-up" section to the morning service composed mainly of biblical material (chiefly psalms) that were intended to be sung as praise of God.

Benediction (also called a "blessing"): One of two terms used for the Rabbis' favorite prose formula for composing prayers. The worship service is composed of many different literary genres, but most of it is benedictions. Long benedictions end with a summary line that begins *Barukh atah Adonai...* "Blessed are You, Adonai..." Short blessings have the summary line alone.

Ben Sirah (pronounced behn SIH-rah): Author of a book of wisdom similar in style to Proverbs, probably dating to 180 or 200 B.C.E., and containing, among other things, a moving description of the High Priest in the Jerusalem Temple. Although not included in the Bible, it is known because it became part of Catholic Scripture. The book carries the author's name, but it is called, by Catholics, Ecclesiasticus. A recently discovered Hebrew edition of Ben Sirah contains a prayer that some identify (probably incorrectly) as an early version of the *Amidah* (see ***Amidah***).

Bet hamikdash (pronounced BAYT hah-mik-DASH): The ancient Temple, either the one built by Solomon (the First Temple) or the one constructed after the return from Babylonian exile (the Second Temple) and sacked by Rome in the war of 70.

Bet Yosef (pronounced bayt yoh-SAYF): Commentary to the *Tur* by Joseph Caro, sixteenth century, Land of Israel, and a precursor to his more popular code, the *Shulchan Arukh*.

Beys hamikdesh (pronounced BAYS ha-MIK-d'sh): Yiddish for *bet hamikdash* ("Temple").

Binah (pronounced bee-NAH or, commonly, BEE-nah): Literally, "knowledge" or "understanding," and the title of the fourth blessing in the daily *Amidah*. It is a petition for human knowledge, particularly insight into the human condition, leading to repentance. In kabbalistic circles, it is one of the uppermost *s'firot*, representing a stage of divine thought prior to creation.

Birkat (pronounced beer-KAHT): Literally, "Blessing of..." The titles of many blessings are known as "Blessing of...," for example, "Blessing of Torah" and "Blessing of Jerusalem." Some titles are commonly shortened so that only the qualifying last words are used (such as "Jerusalem" instead of "Blessing of Jerusalem"), and they are listed in the glossary by the last words, e.g., *Y'rushalayim* instead of *Birkat Y'rushalayim* ("Jerusalem" instead of "Blessing of Jerusalem"). Those blessings that are more generally cited with the full title appear under *Birkat*.

Birkat Hashir (pronounced beer-KAHT hah-SHEER): Literally, "Blessing of song," and the title, therefore, of the final blessing to the *P'sukei D'zimrah*, the "warm-up" section to the morning service composed mainly of biblical material (chiefly psalms) that were intended to be sung as praise of God. Technically, a *Birkat Hashir* concludes any *Hallel* (see **Hallel**), in this case, the Daily *Hallel*, which is the central component of the *P'sukei D'zimrah*.

Birkat Hatorah (pronounced beer-KAHT hah-toe-RAH): Literally, "Blessing of Torah," the title for the second blessing in the liturgical section called the *Sh'ma* and Its Blessings; its theme is the revelation of the Torah to Israel on Mount Sinai.

Birkat Kohanim (pronounced beer-KAHT koe-hah-NEEM): Literally, "Blessing of the Priests," but usually referred to as "the priestly benediction," a reference to Numbers 6:24–26. Also the title of the final blessing of the *Amidah*. See also **Kohanim**.

Birkat yayin (pronounced beer-KAHT YAH-yin or, commonly, BEER-kaht YAH-yin): Literally, "blessing over wine," hence, the benediction recited before drinking wine or grape juice and used especially as part of the *Kiddush* (a prayer announcing sacred time).

Birkhot Hashachar (pronounced beer-KHOT hah-SHAH-khar): Literally, "Morning Blessings," the title of the first large section in the morning prayer regimen of Judaism; originally said privately upon arising in the morning, but now customarily recited immediately upon arriving at the synagogue. It is composed primarily of benedictions thanking God for the everyday gifts of health and wholeness, as well as study sections taken from the Bible and rabbinic literature.

Birkhot mitzvah (pronounced beer-KHOT meetz-VAH): Blessings said upon performing a commandment; normally of the form, "Blessed are You, Adonai our God, ruler of the universe, who sanctified us with commandments and commanded us to…."

Birkhot nehenin (pronounced beer-KHOT neh-heh-NEEN): Blessings said upon enjoyment of God's world (e.g., eating food, seeing rainbows, hearing a thunderstorm, seeing a flower); normally of the form, "Blessed are You, Adonai our God, ruler of the universe, who…."

Bo'i khallah, Bo'i khallah (pronounced boh-EE khah-LAH, boh-EE khah-LAH): Literally, "Come O bride, come O bride," the invitation to Shabbat that concludes *L'khah Dodi* in the Friday night evening *(Ma'ariv)* service (see ***L'khah Dodi***).

B'rakhah (pronounced b'-rah-KHAH): The Hebrew word for "benediction" or "blessing." See ***Benediction***. Plural ("benedictions") is *b'rakhot* (pronounced b'-rah-KHOTE).

Challah (pronounced khah-LAH, or, commonly, KHAH-lah): Originally (in Temple times), following Numbers 15:20, a portion of the about to-be-baked dough given to the priest *(kohen)*. It is still removed today, but because we no longer provide gifts for priests, it is burned. Secondarily, nowadays, *challah* is the name given to the twisted egg bread used on Shabbat and holidays.

Chanukah (pronounced khah-noo-KAH, or commonly, KHAH-noo-kah): An eight-day festival beginning on the twenty-fifth day of the Hebrew month of Kislev, corresponding, usually, to some time in December. Chanukah celebrates the miraculous deliverance of the Jews as described in the books known as *Maccabees* (pronounced MA-kah-beez). Although not canonized in the Bible, Maccabees is carried in Catholic Scripture and describes the heroic acts of a priestly family, known also as the Hasmoneans (pronounced has-moe-NEE-'ns), in 167 B.C.E.

Chanuki'ah (pronounced khah-noo-kee-YAH or, commonly, khah-noo-KEE-yah): An eight-branch candelabra for Chanukah candles.

Chasidei Ashkenaz (pronounced khah-see-DAY Ahsh-k'-NAHZ or, commonly, khah-SEE-day AHSH-k'-nahz): Literally, "The pious of Germany," a loosely knit philosophical school of thought from twelfth- to thirteenth-century Germany, which pioneered a mystical understanding of the liturgy and emphasized an ascetic way of life and a negative view of humanity. See ***Kavod***.

Chasidism (pronounced KHAH-sih-dizm): The doctrine generally traced to an eighteenth-century Polish Jewish mystic and spiritual leader known as the Ba'al Shem Tov (called also the BeSHT, an acronym composed of the initials of his name B, SH, and T). Followers are called *Chasidim* (pronounced khah-see-DEEM or khah-SIH-dim; singular, *Chasid,* pronounced khah-SEED or, commonly, KHA-sid) from the Hebrew word *chesed* (pronounced KHEH-sed), meaning "loving-kindness" or "piety."

Chatimah (pronounced khah-tee-MAH): The final summary line of a benediction (see **Benediction**).

Chatzi Kaddish (pronounced khah-TSEE kah-DEESH or, commonly, KHAH-tsee KAH-d'sh): Literally, "Half *Kaddish,*" a short version of the *Kaddish,* a sort of "oral punctuation," in this case, an "oral semicolon," used to indicate a separation between one major rubric of the service and another.

Chazzan (pronounced khah-ZAHN, or, popularly, KHAH-z'n): In antiquity, a synagogue official with many duties; now, a cantor.

Chazzanut (pronounced khah-zah-NOOT): The traditional art of the cantor (or *chazzan*).

Cheshvan (pronounced KHESH-vahn): A Hebrew month corresponding to late October or November.

Chiasm (pronounced KYE-asm): Also, *chiasmus.* A term for a poetic device widely used in psalms, from the Latinized version of the Greek *chiasma,* "crossing," as in the Greek letter *chi,* X. *Chiasm* is an inverted relationship between syntactic elements of parallel phrases.

Chiyuv (pronounced *khee-YOOV*): Halakhically, a *mitzvah* that is absolutely obligatory (as opposed to a *mitzvah* that is not a *chiyuv,* in which case some individual discretion exists as to whether to perform it or not). It is obligatory (a *chiyuv*) to eat *matzah* on the first day of Passover, for instance; but although it is a *mitzvah,* it is not a *chiyuv* to eat it every other day of Passover, and one may choose to do so or not.

Chokhmah (pronounced khokh-MAH or, commonly, KHOKH-mah): Literally, "wisdom," but in kabbalistic circles, one of the uppermost *s'firot,* representing a stage of divine thought prior to creation.

Chovah (pronounced *khoh-VAH*): A *chiyuv* (see **Chiyuv**).

Chuppah (pronounced khoo-PAH or, commonly KHUH-pah): A wedding canopy.

Confession: See **Vidui Rabbah, Vidui Zuta**.

Daily Hallel (pronounced hah-LAYL or, commonly, HAH-layl): English for *Hallel Sheb'khol Yom.* See **Hallel.**

David (pronounced dah-VEED): Literally, "David," a reference to the biblical King David, and the title of the fifteenth blessing of the daily *Amidah,* a petition for the appearance of the messianic ruler said by tradition to be a descendent of King David. Some liberal liturgies omit the blessing or reframe it to refer to a messianic age of perfection, but without the arrival of a human messianic ruler.

Doxology: Technical term for a congregational response to an invitation to praise God; generally a single line of prayer affirming praise of God forever and ever. Examples in the *Sh'ma* and Its Blessings are the responses to the Call to Prayer and to the *Sh'ma* itself. From the Greek word *doxa,* meaning "glory."

D'vekut (pronounced d'vay-KOOT): Literally, "clinging" to God, a mystical term meaning the soul's temporary separation from the body and its loving unification with God.

Ein Keloheinu (pronounced ayn kay-loh-HAY-noo): Literally, "There is none like our God," a concluding prayer of the *Musaf* service.

Ein sof (pronounced ayn SOHF): Literally, "without end," a kabbalistic term for the absolutely unknowable transcendent God, as opposed to the knowable aspects of God, which appear through emanations called *s'firot* (see *S'firah*).

El Adon (pronounced ayl ah-DOHN): An early medieval (or, perhaps, ancient) poem celebrating God as a king enthroned on high; it is arranged as an acrostic, that is, each line begins with a different letter of the alphabet. Nowadays, *El Adon* is a popular Sabbath morning hymn.

Elohai n'tsor (pronounced eh-loh-HA'y n'-TSOR): Literally, "My God, keep [my tongue from evil]"; the first words and, therefore, the title of a silent prayer following every **Amidah,** attributed by the Talmud (Ber. 17a) to a fourth-century Babylonian sage known for his piety.

Eretz Yisrael (pronounced EH-retz yis-rah-AYL): Hebrew for "the Land of Israel."

Gaon (pronounced gah-OHN; plural: *Geonim,* pronounced g'-oh-NEEM): Title for the leading Rabbis in Babylon (present-day Iraq) from about 750 to 1038. From a biblical word meaning "glory," which is equivalent in the title to saying "Your Excellence."

Gematria (pronounced g-MAHT-ree-yah): The system of assigning a numerical value to each Hebrew letter, then matching the total value of a word or phrase to another word or phrase of the same value, thereby applying the meaning implicit in one word or phrase to the other. *Alef,* the first letter, is 1, *bet,* the second letter is 2, *gimel,* the third letter, 3, and so forth until we get to *yod,* which is 10. From then on, letters increase by tens until we reach *kuf,* which is 100. The increments now progress by hundreds until we reach the last letter, *tav,* which is 400.

Genizah (pronounced g'-NEE-zah): A cache of documents, in particular the one discovered at the turn of the twentieth century in an old synagogue in Cairo; the source of our knowledge about how Jews prayed in the Land of Israel and vicinity prior to the twelfth century. From a word meaning "to store or hide away," "to archive."

Gra (pronounced GRAH): Elijah of Vilna, known also as the Vilna Gaon, outstanding halakhic authority of Lithuania (1720–1797).

Graveside Kaddish: See *Kaddish L'it'chad'ta.*

G'ullah (pronounced g'-oo-LAH): Literally, "redemption" or "deliverance," and the title of the seventh blessing of the daily *Amidah,* as well as the third blessing in the *Sh'ma* and Its Blessings; its theme affirms God's redemptive act of delivering the Israelites from Egypt and promises ultimate deliverance from suffering and want at the end of time.

G'vurot (pronounced g'voo-ROTE): Literally, "strength" or "power," and the title of the second blessing in the *Amidah.* It affirms the power of God to bring annual rain and new growth in nature and, by extension, to resurrect the dead. Some liberal liturgies omit the belief in resurrection or replace it with wording that suggests other concepts of eternal life.

Hachnasat orchim (pronounced hahkh-nah-SAHT ohr-KHEEM): Literally, "bringing guests in," hence, the *mitzvah* of welcoming guests for such things as Shabbat dinner.

Hadas (pronounced hah-DAHS): Myrtle sprigs used on Sukkot as one of the four required species ("You shall take the produce of good trees, branches of palm trees, boughs of leafy trees, and willows of the brook" [Lev. 23:40]); preferred in antiquity for the spices that became part of the *Havdalah* ritual.

Hadlakat nerot (pronounced hahd-lah-KAHT nay-ROHT): Literally, "candle lighting," the liturgical act of kindling lights to inaugurate Shabbat and the Festivals.

Haftarah (pronounced hahf-tah-RAH or, commonly, hahf-TOE-rah): The section of Scripture taken from the prophets and read publicly as part of Shabbat and holiday worship services. From a word meaning "to conclude," because it is the "concluding reading," that is, it follows a reading from the Torah (the Five Books of Moses).

Haggadah (pronounced hah-gah-DAH or, commonly, hah-GAH-dah): The liturgical service for the Passover eve Seder meal. From a Hebrew word meaning "to tell," because the Haggadah is a telling of the Passover narrative.

Hakafah (pronounced hah-kah-FAH): Literally, "going around [the room]," a procession in which the Torah is taken from the ark and carried to the *bimah* during the introductory prayers. As the procession winds its way to the *bimah*, people approach the Torah, even kiss it.

Halakhah (pronounced hah-lah-KHAH or, commonly, hah-LAH-khah): The Hebrew word for "Jewish law." Also used as an anglicized adjective, halakhic (pronounced hah-LAH-khic), meaning "legal." From the Hebrew word meaning "to walk" or "to go," denoting the way in which a person should walk through life.

Hallel (pronounced hah-LAYL or, commonly, HAH-layl): A Hebrew word meaning "praise" and, by extension, the name given to sets of psalms that are recited liturgically in praise of God: Psalms 145–150, the Daily *Hallel*, are recited each morning; Psalm 136, the Great *Hallel*, is recited on Shabbat and holidays and is part of the Passover Seder. Psalms 113–118, the best-known *Hallel*, known more fully as the Egyptian *Hallel*, are recited on holidays and get their name from Psalm 114:1, which celebrates the moment "when Israel left Egypt."

Hallel Sheb'khol Yom (pronounced hah-LAYL [or, commonly, HAH-layl] sheh-b'-khol YOHM): The Hebrew term for "The Daily *Hallel*." See **Hallel**.

Halleluyah (pronounced hah-l'-loo-YAH, but sometimes anglicized as hah-l'-LOO-yah): A common word in Psalms, meaning "praise God," and the final word of a congregational response within the third blessing of the *Amidah* (from Ps. 146:10).

Hat'fillah (pronounced hah-t'-fee-LAH): Literally, "the *T'fillah*," another name for the *Amidah*. See **T'fillah**.

Hatov v'hameitiv (pronounced hah-TOHV v'-hah-mei-TEEV): Literally, "the one who is good and does good," that is, the conclusion of a blessing recited on several occasions such as hearing good news; the name, therefore, for the blessings in question, including the final blessing in the *Birkat Hamazon* (Grace after Meals).

Havdalah (pronounced hahv-dah-LAH or, commonly, hahv-DAH-lah): Literally "separation," hence, the name of the prayer that separates Shabbat from the following week, said as an insertion into the Saturday evening *Amidah* and at home later in the evening. The latter instance, which is accompanied by wine, is called *Havdalah al Hakos* (pronounced hahv-dah-LAH ahl hah-KOHS), "*Havdalah* over a cup [of wine]."

Hoda'ah (pronounced hoe-dah-AH): Literally, a combination of the Hebrew words for "gratitude" and "acknowledgment," so translated here as "grateful acknowledgment." The title of the second to last blessing in the *Amidah,* an expression of our grateful acknowledgment to God for the daily wonders that constitute human existence.

Hoeche K'dushah (pronounced HAY-kh' k'DOO-shah): A Yiddish term combining German and Hebrew and meaning, literally, "the High *K'dushah.*" Refers to a way to shorten the time it takes to say the *Amidah* by avoiding the necessity of having the prayer leader repeat it all after it is said silently by the congregation.

Inclusio (pronounced in-CLOO-zee-oh): A rhetorical style common to biblical prayer, whereby the end of a composition reiterates the theme or words with which the composition began.

Kabbalah (pronounced kah-bah-LAH or, commonly, kah-BAH-lah): A general term for Jewish mysticism, but used properly for a specific mystical doctrine that began in western Europe in the eleventh or twelfth centuries; recorded in the *Zohar* (see **Zohar**) in the thirteenth century, and then further elaborated, especially in the Land of Israel (in Safed), in the sixteenth century. From a Hebrew word meaning "to receive" or "to welcome," and secondarily, "tradition," implying the receiving of tradition from one's past.

Kabbalat Shabbat (pronounced kah-bah-LAHT shah-BAHT): Literally, "Welcoming Shabbat." The preamble to the evening synagogue service *(Ma'ariv)* for Friday night, climaxing in the well-known mystical prayer *L'khah Dodi* (see **L'khah Dodi**).

Kaddish (pronounced kah-DEESH or, more commonly, KAH-d'sh): One of several prayers from a Hebrew word meaning "holy," and therefore the name given to a prayer affirming God's holiness. This prayer was composed in the first century but later found its way into the service in several forms, including one known as the Mourner's *Kaddish* and used as a mourning prayer.

Kaddish D'rabbanan (pronounced d'-rah-bah-NAHN): A form of the *Kaddish* (see **Kaddish**) containing a unique paragraph requesting well-being for all who study Torah. It appears liturgically as a conclusion to study passages.

Kaddish L'it'chad'ta (pronounced l'-it-KHAH-d'-tah): Also called *Kaddish L'chad'ta* (pronounced l'-KHAH-d'-tah). Literally, *Kaddish* "of renewal," the only form of *Kaddish* that includes a reference to the resurrection of the dead and the rebuilding of Jerusalem at the end of days. Recited after concluding a tractate of the Talmud or after a funeral (nowadays, some Jews substitute the Mourner's *Kaddish* for it; see **Kaddish Yatom**).

Kaddish Shalem (pronounced shah-LAYM): Literally, "The Complete *Kaddish*," the same words as **Kaddish Yatom** (The Mourners' *Kaddish*), but with an added line asking that our prayers be accepted on high. A sort of "oral punctuation," in this case, an "oral period," marking the completion of the *Amidah*, which (other than the reading of Torah, on specific days only) is the final major rubric in the service. Known also as *Kaddish Titkabal*, from the first word of the added line *Titkabal [tsalot-hon]*, pronounced tit-kah-BAHL [tsa-lot-HOHN], meaning, "[May our prayer] be accepted."

Kaddish Titkabal: See **Kaddish Shalem**.

Kaddish Yatom (pronounced yah-TOHM): That version of the *Kaddish* that is said by mourners specifically to memorialize the deceased.

Kavod (pronounced kah-VOHD): Literally, "glory," but used philosophically and liturgically by the German pietists (see **Chasidei Ashkenaz**) to refer to the manifest aspect of God, as opposed to the unknown and unknowable divine essence.

Kavod Shabbat (pronounced kah-VOHD shah-BAHT): Literally, "honor [due to] Shabbat."

Kavvanah (pronounced kah-vah-NAH): From a word meaning "to direct," and therefore used technically to denote the state of directing one's words and thoughts sincerely to God, as opposed to the rote recitation of prayer.

K'dushah (pronounced k'-doo-SHAH or, commonly, k'-DOO-shah): From the Hebrew word meaning "holy," and therefore one of several prayers from the first or second century occurring in several places and versions, all of which have in common the citing of Isaiah 6:3: *Kadosh, kadosh, kadosh...*, "Holy, holy, holy is the Lord of hosts. The whole earth is full of his glory."

K'dushat Hashem (pronounced k'-doo-SHAHT hah-SHEM): Literally, "sanctification of the name [of God]," and the full name for the prayer that is generally called *K'dushah* (see **K'dushah**). Best known as the third blessing in the *Amidah*, but found also prior to the morning *Sh'ma*. Used also in variant form *kiddush hashem* (pronounced kee-DOOSH hah-SHEM) as a term to describe dying for the sanctification of God's name, that is, martyrdom.

K'dushat hayom (pronounced k'-doo'-SHAHT ha-YOHM): Literally, "the holiness of the day," hence, the technical name of prayers that express the presence of a sacred day (Shabbat or holidays). There are three instances: the *Kiddush* that inaugurates the day either at the dinner table or at the opening evening *(Ma'ariv)* service; the fourth benediction of the Shabbat or holiday *Amidah;* and the final benediction after the *Haftarah* is recited.

Keva (pronounced KEH-vah): A Hebrew word meaning "fixity, stability," and, therefore, the aspect of a service that is fixed and immutable: the words on the page, perhaps, or the time at which the prayer must be said. In the early years, when prayers were delivered orally and improvised on the spot, *keva* meant the fixed order in which the liturgical themes had to be expressed.

Kibbuts G'luyot (pronounced kee-BOOTS g'-loo-YOTE): Literally, "gathering the exiles," and the title of the tenth blessing of the daily *Amidah,* a petition for Jews outside the Land of Israel to return home to their land as a sign that messianic times are imminent. Some liberal liturgies omit the blessing or interpret it more broadly to imply universal messianic liberation, but without the literal belief that Jews outside the Land of Israel are in "exile," or that they need to or want to "return home."

Kiddush (pronounced kee-DOOSH but, commonly, KIH-d'sh): Literally, "sanctification," hence, a form of *k'dushat hayom* (see ***K'dushat hayom***); in this case, the prayer for the eve of Shabbat and holidays, intended to announce the arrival of sacred time, and accompanied by *birkat yayin,* the blessing over wine. See also ***Birkat yayin***.

Kiddusha Rabbah (generally pronounced kih-DOO-shah RAH-bah): Literally, "the Great *Kiddush.*" The name for the *Kiddush* (see ***Kiddush***) recited at noon on Saturdays and holidays and, ironically, consisting essentially of only the blessing over wine.

Kohanim (pronounced koe-hah-NEEM): Literally, "priests," plural of *kohen* (pronounced koe-HAYN), a reference to the priests who offered sacrifices in the ancient Temple until its destruction by Rome in the year 70 C.E. Also the name of modern-day Jews who claim priestly descent and who are customarily given symbolic recognition in various ritual ways—as, for instance, being called first to stand beside the Torah reader and to recite a blessing over the reading. It is also the title of the last blessing in the *Amidah,* which contains the priestly benediction from Numbers 6:24–26. Another more popular name for that blessing is *Shalom* (pronounced shah-LOME), "peace," because the priestly benediction requests peace. See also ***Birkat Kohanim***.

Kohen gadol (pronounced koh-HAYN gah-DOHL): Literally, "high priest"; first, in the Bible, and thereafter in rabbinic times until the destruction of the Second Temple (70 C.E.).

Korbanot (pronounced kohr-bah-NOHT; singular: *korban,* pronounced kohr-BAHN): Literally, "sacrifices," but used liturgically to denote passages from Torah and rabbinic literature that explain how sacrifices are to be offered. These are inserted especially in the *Birkhot Hashachar* and the *Musaf* service.

Koyen godl (Pronounced KOY-n GU-d'l): Yiddish for the Hebrew *kohen gadol,* "high priest."

K'riat Hatorah (pronounced k'ree-AHT hah-toe-RAH): The public reading of the Torah.

K'riat Sh'ma (pronounced k'-ree-YAHT sh'-MAH): Literally, "reciting the *Sh'ma*," and therefore a technical term for the liturgical act of reading the prayer known as the *Sh'ma* (see *Sh'ma*).

L'chayim (generally pronounced l'-KHAH-yim): Literally, "To life," the common Jewish expression used as a sort of "toast" before drinking wine together, as in the *Kiddush*.

Lechem mishneh (pronounced LEH-khem MISH-neh): "Double bread," referring to the double portion of manna that fell on Fridays (to provide also for Saturdays, when Israel could not collect food because it was the Sabbath).

Licht bentschen (pronounced LIKHT behn-ch'n): Literally, "kindling lights," the Yiddish equivalent of *hadlakat nerot* (see *Hadlakat nerot*).

Liturgy: Public worship, from the Greek word *leitourgia,* meaning "public works." Liturgy in ancient Greece was considered a public work, the act of sacrificing or praising the gods, from which benefits would flow to the body politic.

L'khah Dodi (pronounced l'-KHAH doh-DEE): Literally, "Come, friend." A mystic sixteenth-century prayer that climaxes the Friday night service of *Kabbalat Shabbat* (welcoming Shabbat).

L'khu n'ran'nah (pronounced l'-KHOO n'-rah-n'-NAH, but, commonly, l'-KHOO n'-RAH-n'-nah): Literally, "Let us sing to Adonai," the opening words of Psalm 95, and the common title by which the psalm is known liturgically.

Long Confession (in Hebrew, *Vidui Rabbah,* pronounced vee-DOO'y rah-BAH or, commonly, VEE-doo-y RAH-bah): A lengthy litany arranged alphabetically and recited on Yom Kippur. The acrostic is formed by the initial letter of the first word after the opening phrase for each line, *Al chet shechatanu* (pronounced ahl KHEHT she-chah-TAH-noo), meaning "For the sin that we have committed." Referred to also as *Al chet.*

Ma'ariv (pronounced mah-ah-REEV or, commonly, MAH-ah-reev): From the Hebrew word *erev* (pronounced EH-rev), meaning "evening": one of two titles used for the evening worship service (also called *Arvit*).

Machzor Vitry (commonly pronounced MAKH-zohr VEET-ree): Earliest comprehensive compendium of liturgical custom in France (eleventh to twelfth century).

Mah Tovu (pronounced mah TOH-voo): Technically, the prayer to be said upon approaching or entering a synagogue; in practice, the first prayer of *Birkhot Hashachar*.

Maimonides, Moses (known also as Rambam, pronounced RAHM-bahm): Most important Jewish philosopher of all time; also a physician and very significant legal authority. Born in Spain, he moved to Egypt, where he lived most of his life (1135–1204).

Malkhuyot (pronounced mahl-khu-YOHT): Literally, "kingships." The primary blowing of the shofar on Rosh Hashanah is divided into three parts, each of which features the recitation of biblical verses and surrounding prayers on a different theme. *Malkhuyot* refers to the verses on the theme of God's sovereignty, and, by extension, to the first third of the "shofar service" where the verses are found. The other themes are *zikhronot* ("God's remembrance of us") and *shofarot* (the role of the shofar in the Bible). The three units are commonly referred to by an acronym of their first initials: MaZaSH.

Massekhet Sofrim (pronounced mah-SEH-khet sohf-REEM): Literally, "Tractate [dealing with issues relevant to] scribes," an eighth-century compilation (with some later interpolations) dealing with such matters as the writing of Torah scrolls, but also including much detail on the early medieval (and possibly ancient) prayer practice of Jews in the Land of Israel.

Menorah (pronounced m'-noh-RAH, or commonly, m'-NOH-rah): A candelabra, originally the one in the desert Tabernacle of Exodus, with seven branches. The term was once commonly used also for the eight-branch candelabra for Chanukah, but now the term **chanuki'ah** is preferred for that one.

Mid'ora'ita (pronounced mee-d'-oh-RYE-tah): Strictly speaking, commandments derived directly from Torah, which are of a higher order than those rooted only in rabbinic ordinance (called **Mid'rabbanan**), but all are binding.

Mid'rabbanan (pronounced mee-d'-rah-bah-NAHN): Commandments rooted only in rabbinic ordinance. See *Mid'ora'ita*.

Midrash (pronounced meed-RAHSH or, commonly, MID-rahsh): From a Hebrew word meaning "to ferret out the meaning of a text," and therefore a rabbinic interpretation of a biblical word or verse. By extension, a body of rabbinic literature that offers classical interpretations of the Bible.

Mikvah (pronounced mik-VEH, but, popularly, MIK-v'h: A "ritual bath" used (1) in a variety of cases (a menstruant, for example) as a transformational agent from the state of *t'umah* to *tohorah* ("ritual impurity" to "ritual purity"); (2) for purposes of conversion; (3) generalized, through time, for other ends, such as preparing for Shabbat.

Minchah (pronounced meen-KHAH or, more commonly, MIN-khah): Originally the name of a type of sacrifice, then the word for a sacrifice offered during the afternoon, and now the name for the afternoon synagogue service usually scheduled just before nightfall. *Minchah* means "afternoon."

Minhag (pronounced meen-HAHG or, commonly, MIN-hahg): The Hebrew word for custom and, therefore, used liturgically to describe the customary way that different groups of Jews pray. By extension, *minhag* means a "rite," as in *Minhag Ashkenaz,* meaning "the rite of prayer, or the customary way of prayer for Jews in *Ashkenaz"*— that is, northern and eastern Europe.

Minhag hamakom (pronounced min-HAHG hah-mah-KOHM or, commonly, MIN-hahg hah-mah-KOHM): "The usual custom of the community." In cases where liturgical or ritual practice varies, but where the alternative practices are equally permitted, the rule is to follow *minhag hamakom.*

Minim (pronounced mee-NEEM): Literally, "heretics" or "sectarians," and the title of the twelfth blessing of the daily *Amidah,* a petition that heresy be eradicated and heretics punished. Liberal liturgies frequently omit the blessing, considering it an inappropriate malediction, not a benediction at all, or reframe it as a petition against evil in general.

Minyan (pronounced meen-YAHN or, commonly, MIN-y'n): A quorum, the minimum number of people required for certain prayers. *Minyan* comes from the word meaning "to count."

Mi sheberakh (pronounced, commonly, MEE sheh-BAY-rakh): A standard blessing beginning, "May the One who blessed [our ancestors]…," which could be adapted for any number of instances. This set of prayers requesting God's blessing on those who receive an *aliyah* or on their family members is perhaps the best-known addition to the service.

Mishnah (pronounced mish-NAH, but, commonly, MISH-nah): The name of the definitive six-volume statement of Jewish law from the Land of Israel, ca. 200 C.E., that culminates the era called tannaitic (after the title we give the Rabbis to that point; see *Tanna, Tanna'im*). But equally, the name applied to any particular teaching in that statement, for which the plural, *mishnayot* (pronounced mish-nah-YOHT), exists also (more than one such teaching).

Mishneh Torah (pronounced MISH-n' TOH-rah): Code of Jewish law by Moses Maimonides (composed in 1180), called also the *Yad* (pronounced YAHD), a Hebrew word made of the letters that, together, stand for the number fourteen—a reference to the fact that the Code is divided into fourteen books. Unlike other Codes, the *Mishneh*

Torah sums up every aspect of Jewish law, even hypothetical precepts relevant only in messianic times, as well as philosophical introductions on the nature of God and prayer.

Mishpat (pronounced meesh-PAHT): Literally, "justice," and the title of the eleventh blessing of the daily *Amidah;* a petition for just rulership, a condition associated with the messianic age.

Mitzvah (pronounced meetz-VAH or, commonly, MITZ-vah; plural: *mitzvot,* pronounced meetz-VOTE): A Hebrew word used commonly to mean "good deed," but in the more technical sense, denoting any commandment from God and, therefore, by extension, what God wants us to do. Reciting the *Sh'ma* morning and evening, for instance, is a *mitzvah.*

Mitzvah l'ma'alah min haz'man (pronounced meets-VAH l'-mah-ah-LAH meen hahz-MAHN): Literally, "a commandment that transcends time," a theological correction to *mitzvot* (commandments) that seem otherwise to be "commandments dependent on time" (see ***Mitzvat aseh shehaz'man g'ramah***), and which would then exempt women from required observance.

Mitzvat aseh shehaz'man g'ramah (pronounced meets-VAHT ah-SAY sheh-hah-z'-MAHN g'rah-MAH): Literally, a "positive commandment dependent on time," a category of commandments from which women are normally exempt.

M'kadesh (pronounced m'kah-DESH), or, commonly, m'-KAH-desh): Literally, "to sanctify" or "declare sacred," hence the person who recites *Kiddush,* the home evening prayer that inaugurates Shabbat and holidays.

Modeh/ah ani (pronounced moh-DEH ah-NEE [for women, moh-DAH ah-NEE]): Literally, "I gratefully acknowledge [...that You have returned my soul to me]"— therefore, the standard prayer to be said upon awakening.

Modim D'rabbanan (pronounced moe-DEEM d'-rah-bah-NAHN, or commonly, MOE-dim d'-rah-bah-nahn): *Modim* is the first word of the second to last blessing of the *Amidah* and, therefore, a shorthand way of referring to that prayer. *Modim D'rabbanan* is the name given to the form of the prayer that is reserved for congregational recitation during the repetition of the *Amidah* by the prayer leader. Literally, it means "the *Modim* of our Rabbis," and refers to the fact that the prayer is composed of what were once several alternative responses, each of which was the custom of one of the Rabbis of the Talmud.

Motsi (pronounced MOH-tsee): Literally, "brings forth, extracts," from the blessing over bread, "Blessed are You...who brings forth bread from the earth," and used as a shorthand reference to that blessing (as in, "It is time to make the *Motsi*").

Muktzeh (pronounced mook-TZEH, but, popularly, MOOK-tzeh): Literally, "on the sidelines." A legal term for items that cannot be moved on Shabbat because they are "alienated" from any positive use. This includes (a) items whose use would violate the Sabbath, like a cigarette lighter; (b) items which are repulsive, like garbage; (c) items that have no Shabbat use at all, like stones and dirt.

Musaf (pronounced moo-SAHF or, commonly, MOO-sahf): The Hebrew word meaning "extra" or "added," and, therefore, the title of the additional sacrifice that was offered in the Temple on Shabbat and holy days. It is now the name given to an added service of worship appended to the morning service on those days.

Musar (pronounced moo-SAHR, but, popularly, MOO-sahr): Literally, "ethics," but used specifically for a nineteenth- to twentieth-century movement that emerged in Lithuanian *yeshivot* stressing personal ethics, rooted in Halakhah.

M'zuzah (pronounced m'-zoo-ZAH or, commonly, m'-ZOO-zah): The Hebrew word in the Bible meaning "doorpost" and, by extension, the term now used for a small casement that contains the first two sections of the *Sh'ma* (Deut. 6:4–9; 11:13–21) and is affixed to the doorposts of Jewish homes.

Naches (pronounced NAH-kh's): Pride (in another person), as in the *naches* a parent feels for a son or daughter.

N'filat apayim (pronounced n'-fee-LAHT ah-PAH-yim): Literally, "falling on one's face," and, therefore, a technical term for the ***Tachanun***, the section of the daily service that features supplications and is said with head resting on forearm, as if "prostrate" before God.

Nidah (pronounced nee-DAH, or, commonly, NEE-dah): Menstruant.

N'illah (pronounced n'-ee-LAH or, commonly, n'-EE-lah): The concluding service for Yom Kippur.

Nishmat kol cha'i (pronounced neesh-MAHT kohl KHA'i): A blessing mentioned in the Talmud as one of two benedictions in use as the *Birkat Hashir* (pronounced beer-KAHT hah-SHEER), the blessing that ends a psalm collection known as *Hallel*. (See ***Hallel*.**) Nowadays, we use it (1) as part of a longer ***Birkat Hashir***, after the Daily *Hallel*, that constitutes the central section of the ***P'sukei D'zimrah*** for Sabbaths and festivals; and (2) to conclude a similar *Hallel* in the Passover Haggadah.

N'kadesh (pronounced n'kah-DAYSH): The *Amidah* is first recited silently by each worshiper and then repeated aloud by the prayer leader, at which time its third blessing appears in extended form. *N'kadesh* (literally, "Let us sanctify…") is the first Hebrew word of that extended blessing and is thus, by extension, a common way of referring to it.

Notarikon (pronounced noh-TAH-ri-kohn): A system of acrostics, by which each letter of a single word is treated as the initial letter of another word, until a secret meaning is revealed by the set of new words.

N'shamah y'teirah (pronounced n'-shah-MAH y'-tei-RAH): Literally, "extra soul," referring to the talmudic promise that all who keep Shabbat are granted an extra soul for the day.

Odem horishn (pronounced UH-d'm hah-RIH-sh'n): Yiddish for *adam harishon*, "the first man," that is, Adam.

Oneg Shabbat (pronounced OH-neg shah-BAHT): Literally, "joy of Shabbat."

Orach Chayim (pronounced OH-rakh KHA-yim): Abbreviated as O. Ch. Literally, "The Way of Life," one of four sections in the *Tur* and the *Shulchan Arukh*, two of Judaism's major law codes; the section containing the rules of prayer.

Over la'asiyatan (pronounced oh-VEHR lah-ah-see-yah-TAHN): Literally, "before doing them," the principle that a blessing over an act (such as lighting Shabbat candles) precedes the act.

Payy'tan (pronounced pah-y'-TAHN; plural: *payy'tanim*, pronounced pah-y'-tah-NEEM): A poet; the name given particularly to classical and medieval poets whose work is inserted into the standard prayers for special occasions.

Perek (pronounced PEH-rek; plural: *p'rakim*, pronounced p'-rah-KEEM): Literally, a "section" or "chapter" of a written work; used liturgically to mean the sections of the *Sh'ma*. Each of its three biblical sections is a different *perek*.

Piyyut (pronounced pee-YOOT; plural: *piyyutim*, pronounced pee-yoo-TEEM): Literally, "a poem," but used technically to mean liturgical poems composed in classical and medieval times and inserted into the standard prayers on special occasions.

P'sukei D'zimrah (pronounced p'-soo-KAY d'-zeem-RAH or, commonly, p'-SOO-kay d'-ZIM-rah): Literally, "verses of song," and therefore the title of a lengthy set of opening morning prayers that contain psalms and songs and serve as spiritual preparation prior to the official Call to Prayer.

Purim (pronounced poo-REEM or, commonly, PU-rim): A festival falling on the fourteenth day of the Hebrew month of Adar, generally corresponding to late February or early March. It celebrates the miraculous deliverance referred to in the biblical Book of Esther. Literally, *purim* means "lots," as in the phrase "drawing of lots," because the date on which the Jews were to have been killed was chosen by lot.

Rashba (pronounced rahsh-BAH): Halakhic authority Shlomo ben Aderet (1235–1310, Barcelona).

Rashi (pronounced RAH-shee): Solomon ben Isaac (1040–1105), most significant Jewish biblical exegete and founder of French Jewry.

R'fuah (pronounced r'-foo-AH or, commonly, r'-FOO-ah): Literally, "healing," and the title of the eighth blessing of the daily *Amidah,* a petition for healing.

Riboyne shel oylem (pronounced ree-BOY-n' shel OY-l'm): A Yiddish version of a common appellation for God, *Ribono shel olam* (pronounced ree-boh-NOH shel oh-LAHM), meaning, "master of the universe."

Rosh (pronounced ROHSH): The Rosh (1250–1328), otherwise known as Rabbeinu Asher, or Asher ben Yechiel, was a significant halakhic authority, first in Germany and later in Spain. His son, Jacob ben Asher, codified many of his father's views alongside his own in his influential law code, the *Tur.*

Rosh Chodesh (pronounced rohsh KHOH-desh): Literally, "the head of the month," and, therefore, the Hebrew name for the one- or two-day new moon period with which lunar months begin. It is marked as a holiday in Jewish tradition, a period of new beginnings.

Rubric (pronounced ROO-brick): A technical term for any discrete section of liturgy, whether a prayer or a set of prayers. The *Sh'ma* and Its Blessings is one of several large rubrics in the service; within that large rubric, the *Sh'ma* or any one of its accompanying blessings may be called a rubric as well.

Seder (pronounced SEH-der or, commonly, SAY-der): The Hebrew word meaning "order" and, therefore, (1) the name given to the ritualized meal eaten on Passover eve, and (2) an early alternative term for the order of prayers in a prayer book. The word Siddur (see *Siddur*) is now preferred for the latter.

Seder Rav Amram (pronounced SAY-dehr rahv AHM-rahm): First known comprehensive Jewish prayer book, emanating from Rav Amram Gaon (c. 860 C.E.), a leading Jewish scholar and head of Sura, a famed academy in Babylonia (modern-day Iraq).

Sefardi (pronounced s'-fahr-DEE or, commonly, s'-FAHR-dee): From the Hebrew word *Sefarad* (pronounced s'-fah-RAHD), meaning the geographic area of modern-day Spain and Portugal. Sefardi is the adjective, describing the liturgical rituals and customs that are derived from *Sefarad* prior to the expulsion of Jews from there at the end of the fifteenth century, as opposed to Ashkenazi (see **Ashkenazi**), meaning the liturgical rituals and customs common to northern and eastern Europe. Nowadays, Sefardi refers also to the customs of Jews from North Africa and Arab lands, whose ancestors came from Spain.

S'firot (pronounced s'-fee-ROTE; singular: *s'firah*, pronounced s'-fee-RAH): According to the Kabbalah (Jewish mysticism, see **Kabbalah**), the universe came into being by a process of divine emanation, whereby the divine light, as it were, expanded into empty space, eventually becoming physical matter. At various intervals, this light was frozen in time, as if captured by containers, each of which is called a *s'firah*. Literally, *s'firah* means "number," because early theory conceptualized the stages of creation as primordial numbers.

S'firotic (pronounced s'fee-RAH-tik): Relating to one or more *s'firot* or to the system of *s'firot*.

Shabbat (pronounced shah-BAHT): The Hebrew word for "Sabbath," from a word meaning "to rest."

Shabbos (pronounced SHAH-b's): Yiddish for *Shabbat*, "Sabbath."

Shacharit (pronounced shah-khah-REET or, commonly, SHAH-khah-reet): The name given to the morning worship service; from the Hebrew word *shachar* (SHAH-khar), meaning "morning."

Shalom (pronounced shah-LOME): Literally, "peace," and a popular title for the final benediction of the *Amidah,* more properly entitled *Kohanim* (pronounced koe-hah-NEEM), "priests," or, more fully, *Birkat Kohanim* (pronounced beer-KAHT koe-hah-NEEM), "blessing of the priests," "priestly benediction." See also **Birkat Kohanim, Kohanim.**

Shanim (pronounced shah-NEEM): Literally, "years," and the title of the ninth blessing of the daily *Amidah;* a petition for a year of agricultural abundance, such as that associated with messianic days.

Shefa (pronounced SHEH-fah): In kabbalistic worship, the plenitude of blessing that flows vertically through the *s'firot* to the world we inhabit.

Shekhinah (pronounced sh'-khee-NAH or, popularly, sh-KHEE-nah): From the Hebrew root *sh.kh.n*, meaning "to dwell," and, therefore, in talmudic literature, the "indwelling" aspect of God most immediately empathetic to human experience. As the feminine aspect of God, it appears in Kabbalah as the tenth and final *sefirah*, or emanation.

Shirat Hayam (pronounced shee-RAHT hah-YAHM): Literally, "Song of the Sea," the song of praise and gratitude sung by Israel after the splitting of the Red Sea and, since the Middle Ages, a prominent constituent of the *P'sukei D'zimrah,* the "warm-up" section to the morning service composed mainly of biblical material (chiefly psalms) that were intended to be sung as praise of God.

Shi'ur (pronounced shee-OOR): A talmudic lesson, frequently accompanying (or even fully constituting) the *s'udah sh'lishit* (the "third meal" of Shabbat).

Shiva (pronounced, shee-VAH or, commonly, SHIH-vah): Literally, "seven," denoting the seven days of mourning. A *shiva* home is a home where the seven days of mourning are being observed.

Shivah d'n'chemta (pronounced shih-VAH d'-n'-KHEM-tah): "Literally, the seven weeks of comfort." The seven Sabbaths following Tisha B'av, which take us all the way to Rosh Hashanah, call for *Haftarot* that guarantee hope.

Sh'liach tsibbur (pronounced sh'-LEE-ahkh tsee-BOOR): Literally, the "agent of the congregation," and, therefore, the name given to the person who leads the prayer service.

Sh'lom bayit (pronounced shah-LOHM BAH-yit): Literally, "peace of the home."

Sh'ma (pronounced sh'-MAH): The central prayer in the first of the two main units in the worship service, the second being the *Amidah* (see ***Amidah***). The *Sh'ma* comprises three citations from the Bible, and the larger unit in which it is embedded (called the *Sh'ma* and Its Blessings) is composed of a formal Call to Prayer (see ***Bar'khu***) and a series of blessings on the theological themes that, together with the *Sh'ma,* constitute a liturgical creed of faith. *Sh'ma,* meaning "hear," is the first word of the first line of the first biblical citation, "Hear O Israel: Adonai is our God; Adonai is One," which is the paradigmatic statement of Jewish faith, the Jews' absolute commitment to the presence of a single and unique God in time and space.

Sh'mini Atseret (pronounced sh'-MEE-nee ah-TSEH-ret): Literally, "the eighth day of solemn assembly," and the name given to the eighth and final day of the autumn festival of Sukkot.

Sh'moneh Esreh (pronounced sh'-MOE-neh ES-ray): A Hebrew word meaning "eighteen" and, therefore, a name given to the second of the two main units in the worship service that once had eighteen benedictions in it (it now has nineteen), known also as the *Amidah* (see ***Amidah***).

Shofarot (pronounced shoh-fah-ROHT): Shofar verses (see ***Malkhuyot***).

Shomer Shabbat (pronounced shoh-MAYR shah-BAHT—using the Yiddish pronunciation—SHO-mare SHAH-b's, or even SHOI-mare SHAH-b's). Literally, "keeping Shabbat," meaning the observance of Shabbat regulations.

Shomer Yisra'el (pronounced shoh-MAYR yis-rah-AYL or, commonly, SHOH-mayr yis-rah-AYL): Literally, "keeper of Israel," a designation of God and the opening words—hence, the title—of a medieval poem that is found in *Tachanun.*

Short Confession (in Hebrew, *Vidui Zuta,* pronounced vee-DOO'y ZOO-tah or, commonly, VEE-doo-y ZOO-tah): A short confession of sin, arranged alphabetically, so that each sin that is listed begins with a different letter of the Hebrew alphabet. Also referred to by the opening word, *Ashamnu* (pronounced ah-SHAHM-noo), meaning "We have sinned."

Shul (pronounced SHOOL): Yiddish for synagogue.

Shulchan Arukh (pronounced shool-KHAN ah-ROOKH or, commonly, SHOOL-khan AH-rookh): The name given to the best-known code of Jewish law, compiled by Joseph Caro in the Land of Israel and published in 1565. *Shulchan Arukh* means "The Set Table" and refers to the ease with which the various laws are set forth—like a table prepared with food ready for consumption.

Shulchan Arukh D'rav (pronounced shool-KHAHN ah-ROOKH d'-RAHV or, popularly, SHOOL-khan AH-rukh d'-RAHV): Halakhic compendium by Rabbi Shneur Zalman of Liady, eighteenth-century founder of Chabad Chasidism.

Siddur (pronounced see-DOOR or, commonly, SIH-d'r): From the Hebrew word *seder* (see ***Seder***), meaning "order," and therefore, by extension, the name given to the "order of prayers," or prayer book.

S'lichah (pronounced s'lee-KHAH or, commonly, s'LEE-khah): Literally, "pardon" or "forgiveness," and the title of the sixth blessing of the daily *Amidah,* a petition for divine forgiveness of our sins.

S'mikhah (pronounced s'-mee-KHAH or, commonly, s'-MEE-khah): Literally, "the laying on [of hands], a biblical (Lev. 16:21) and early rabbinic reference to the priestly act of laying hands on a sacrifice, but also Moses' act of passing authority on to Joshua by laying his hands on him (Num. 27:23)—from which is derived the further meaning of laying hands on a candidate for ordination.

Tachanun (pronounced TAH-khah-noon): A Hebrew word meaning "supplications" and, by extension, the title of the large unit of prayer that follows the *Amidah,* which is largely supplicatory in character.

Tallit (pronounced tah-LEET; plural: *tallitot,* pronounced tah-lee-TOTE): The prayer shawl equipped with tassels (see *Tsitsit*) on each corner and generally worn during the morning *(Shacharit)* and additional *(Musaf)* synagogue services.

Tallit katan (pronounced tah-LEET kah-TAHN): Literally, "a little *tallit,*" used originally as an undergarment to allow the wearing of *tsitsit* privately, all day long, in cultures where Jews wanted to look the same as everyone else.

Talmud (pronounced tahl-MOOD or, more commonly, TAHL-m'd): The name given to each of two great compendia of Jewish law and lore compiled over several centuries and ever since, the literary core of the rabbinic heritage. The Talmud Yerushalmi (pronounced y'-roo-SHAHL-mee), the "Jerusalem Talmud," is earlier, a product of the Land of Israel generally dated about 400 C.E. The better-known Talmud Bavli (pronounced BAHV-lee), or "Babylonian Talmud," took shape in Babylonia (present-day Iraq) and is traditionally dated about 550 C.E. When people say "the" Talmud without specifying which one they mean, they are referring to the Babylonian version. Talmud means "teaching."

Tanna (pronounced TAH-nah, plural: *Tanna'im,* pronounced tah-nah-EEM, but commonly, tah-NAH-yim): Aramaic for "teacher," referring to rabbinic authorities in the time of the Mishnah, that is prior to the third century. Often used in contrast to *Amora* (see *Amora*).

Tetragrammaton: The technical term for the four-letter name of God that appears in the Bible. Treating it as sacred, Jews stopped pronouncing it centuries ago, so that the actual pronunciation has been lost; instead of reading it according to its letters, it is replaced in speech by the alternative name of God, Adonai.

T'fillah (pronounced t'-fee-LAH or, commonly, t'-FEE-lah): A Hebrew word meaning "prayer" but used technically to mean a specific prayer, namely, the second of the two main units in the worship service. It is known also as the *Amidah* or the *Sh'moneh Esreh* (see *Amidah*). Also the title of the sixteenth blessing of the *Amidah,* a petition for God to accept our prayer.

T'fillin (pronounced t'-FIH-lin or, sometimes, t'-fee-LEEN): Two cube-shaped black boxes containing biblical quotations (Exod. 13:1–10; 13:11–16; Deut. 6:4–9; 11:13–21) and affixed by means of attached leather straps to the forehead and left arm (right arm for left-handed people) during morning prayer.

T'hillah l'David (pronounced t'-hee-LAH l'-dah-VEED): Literally, "a psalm of David," and the first two words of Psalm 145; hence, the rabbinic name for Psalm 145, which eventually became known, more popularly, as *Ashre* (pronounced ahsh-RAY or, commonly, AHSH-ray). See *Ashre*.

Tiferet (pronounced tee-FEH-reht): In Kabbalah, the sixth *sefirah*, or emanation, associated with the masculine principle in the Godhead.

Tikkun leil shavuot (pronounced tee-KOON layl shah-voo-OHT): A liturgy composed mostly of study passages, designed to be read throughout the night of Shavuot.

Tkhines (pronounced t'KHI-nis): Literally, Yiddish for "supplications," but used technically to denote liturgies for women, common mostly in eastern Europe from the seventeenth- to nineteenth-century liturgy.

T'lata d'puranuta (pronounced t'-LAH-tah d'-poo-rah-NOO-tah): "The three readings of retribution." As the Rabbis saw it, God must have allowed, and perhaps even caused, the Temple to fall as punishment for Israel's sins. The three weeks prior to Tisha B'av, therefore, anticipate the fall, culminating in Shabbat *Chazon* (pronounced khah-ZOHN), "The Sabbath of 'the Vision,'" which features Isaiah's premonitory vision of Jerusalem's fall and the expectation of ultimate recovery (Isa. 1:1–27).

T'murah (pronounced t'-moo-RAH): A substitution code by which one letter takes the place of another, revealing new meanings.

Tosefet k'dushah (pronounced toh-SEH-feht k'-doo-SHAH or, commonly, toh-SEH-feht k'-DOO-shah): Literally, "adding holiness," a halakhic concept that extends the commandment to start Shabbat or holidays early and end them later.

Tsadikim (pronounced tsah-dee-KEEM): Literally, "the righteous," and the title of the thirteenth blessing of the daily *Amidah,* a petition that the righteous be rewarded.

T'shuvah (pronounced t'shoo-VAH or, commonly, t'SHOO-vah): Literally, "repentance," and the title of the fifth blessing in the daily *Amidah,* a petition by worshipers that they successfully turn to God in heartfelt repentance.

Tsitsit (pronounced tsee-TSEET): A Hebrew word meaning "tassels" or "fringes" and used to refer to the tassels affixed to the four corners of the *tallit* (the prayer shawl, see *Tallit*) as Numbers 15:38 instructs.

Tur (pronounced TOOR): The shorthand title applied to a fourteenth-century code of Jewish law, compiled by Jacob ben Asher in Spain, and the source for much of our knowledge about medieval liturgical practice. *Tur* means "row" or "column." The full name of the code is *Arba'ah Turim* (pronounced ahr-bah-AH too-REEM), "The Four Rows," with each row (or *Tur*) being a separate section of law on a given broad topic.

Un'taneh Tokef (pronounced oo-n'-TAH-neh TOH-kehf): A *piyyut* (liturgical poem) for the High Holy Days emphasizing the awesome nature of these days when we stand before God for judgment. Widely, but incorrectly, connected with a legend of Jewish martyrdom in Germany, the poem more likely derives from a Byzantine poet, circa sixth century. It is known for its conclusion: "Penitence, prayer, and charity avert a bad decree."

V'hu rachum (pronounced v'HOO rah-KHOOM): Literally, "He [God] is merciful," and, because of its sentiment, a common introductory line to prayers lauding God's gracious beneficence. The best example is a seven-paragraph penitential prayer that makes up the bulk of the version of *Tachanun* (pronounced TAH-khah-noon) that is said Mondays and Thursdays.

Vidui Rabbah (pronounced vee-DOO'y RAH-bah or, commonly, VEE-doo-y RAH-bah): Literally, "long confession." See **Long Confession**.

Vidui Zuta (pronounced vee-DOO-y ZOO-tah or, commonly, VEE-doo-y ZOO-tah): Literally, "short confession." See **Short Confession**.

Yahrzeit (pronounced YOHR-tseit): A Yiddish word meaning the practice of marking the anniversary of a loved one's death by saying *Kaddish*. People speak of "having *yahrzeit*" on a given day, at which time the name of the person being memorialized may be mentioned aloud at services prior to the Mourner's *Kaddish* (see **Kaddish**).

Yichud (pronounced yee-KHOOD): Literally, "unification"; in kabbalistic worship, prayers have esoteric significance, generally the unification of the letters that make up God's name, but standing also for the conjoining of God's masculine and feminine aspects and, deeper still, the coming together of the shattered universe in which we live.

Yigdal (pronounced yig-DAHL): A popular morning hymn that encapsulates the thirteen principles of faith composed by prominent medieval philosopher Moses Maimonides (1135–1204). These thirteen principles were arranged poetically as *Yigdal* in the fourteenth century by Daniel ben Judah Dayan (pronounced dah-YAHN) of Rome.

Yishtabach (pronounced yish-tah-BAKH): The first word and, therefore, the title of the blessing used as the *Birkat Hashir* for weekdays (see **Birkat Hashir**). On Sabbaths and festivals, it is expanded by the addition of *Nishmat kol cha'i* (pronounced neesh-MAHT kohl KHA'i), a blessing mentioned in the Talmud (see **Nishmat kol cha'i**).

Yizkor (pronounced yeez-KOHR or, commonly, YIZ-k'r): The Memorial Service, said on Yom Kippur and the three Festivals (Passover, Shavuot, and Sh'mini Atseret).

Yotser (pronounced yoe-TSAYR or, commonly, YOE-tsayr): The Hebrew word meaning "creator" and, by extension, the title of the first blessing in the *Sh'ma* and Its Blessings, which is on the theme of God's creation of the universe.

Y'rushalayim (pronounced y'roo-shah-LAH-yeem): Literally, "Jerusalem," and the title of the fourteenth blessing of the daily *Amidah;* a petition for the divine building up of Jerusalem, a condition associated with the imminence of the messianic age. Some liberal liturgies interpret it more broadly to include the restoration of modern-day Jerusalem, currently under way.

Zikhronot (pronounced *zikh-roh-NOHT*): "Remembrance(s)" (see *Malkhuyot*).

Z'mirot (pronounced z'mee-ROHT, or commonly, z'-MEE-roht), sometimes referred to in the Yiddish, *z'meer's* (pronounced z'MEE-r's): Literally, "songs," but used technically for table songs during meals of Shabbat. It is also the preferred Sefardi title for the "warm-up" section of the morning liturgy, called *P'sukei D'zimrah* by Ashkenazim. (See *P'sukei D'zimrah.*)

Zohar (pronounced ZOE-hahr): A shorthand title for *Sefer Hazohar* (pronounced SAY-fer hah-ZOE-hahr), literally, "The Book of Splendor," which is the primary compendium of mystical thought in Judaism; written mostly by Moses de Leon in Spain near the end of the thirteenth century and, ever since, the chief source for the study of Kabbalah (see *Kabbalah*).

Notes

Notes

Notes

Notes

Notes

Notes

Notes

Bar/Bat Mitzvah

The Bar/Bat Mitzvah Memory Book
An Album for Treasuring the Spiritual Celebration
By Rabbi Jeffrey K. Salkin and Nina Salkin
A unique album for preserving the spiritual memories of the day, and for recording plans for the Jewish future ahead. Contents include space for creating or recording family history; teachings received from rabbi, cantor, and others; mitzvot and *tzedakot* chosen and carried out, etc.
8 x 10, 48 pp, Deluxe Hardcover, 2-color text, ribbon marker, ISBN 1-58023-111-X **$19.95**

Bar/Bat Mitzvah Basics: A Practical Family Guide to Coming of Age Together
Edited by Helen Leneman. Foreword by Rabbi Jeffrey K. Salkin.
6 x 9, 240 pp, Quality PB, ISBN 1-58023-151-9 **$18.95**

For Kids—Putting God on Your Guest List: How to Claim the Spiritual Meaning of Your Bar or Bat Mitzvah *By Rabbi Jeffrey K. Salkin*
6 x 9, 144 pp, Quality PB, ISBN 1-58023-015-6 **$14.95** *For ages 11–12*

Putting God on the Guest List: How to Reclaim the Spiritual Meaning of Your Child's Bar or Bat Mitzvah *By Rabbi Jeffrey K. Salkin*
6 x 9, 224 pp, Quality PB, ISBN 1-879045-59-1 **$16.95**

Tough Questions Jews Ask: A Young Adult's Guide to Building a Jewish Life
By Rabbi Edward Feinstein 6 x 9, 160 pp, Quality PB, ISBN 1-58023-139-X **$14.95** *For ages 13 & up*
Also Available: **Tough Questions Jews Ask Teacher's Guide**
8½ x 11, 72 pp, PB, ISBN 1-58023-187-X **$8.95**

Bible Study/Midrash

Hineini in Our Lives: Learning How to Respond to Others through 14 Biblical Texts, and Personal Stories *By Norman J. Cohen*
6 x 9, 240 pp, Hardcover, ISBN 1-58023-131-4 **$23.95**

Ancient Secrets: Using the Stories of the Bible to Improve Our Everyday Lives
By Rabbi Levi Meier, Ph.D. 5½ x 8½, 288 pp, Quality PB, ISBN 1-58023-064-4 **$16.95**

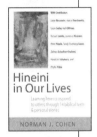

Moses—The Prince, the Prophet: His Life, Legend & Message for Our Lives
By Rabbi Levi Meier, Ph.D.
6 x 9, 224 pp, Quality PB, ISBN 1-58023-069-5 **$16.95**

Self, Struggle & Change: Family Conflict Stories in Genesis and Their Healing Insights for Our Lives *By Norman J. Cohen* 6 x 9, 224 pp, Quality PB, ISBN 1-879045-66-4 **$16.95**

Voices from Genesis: Guiding Us through the Stages of Life *By Norman J. Cohen*
6 x 9, 192 pp, Quality PB, ISBN 1-58023-118-7 **$16.95**

Congregation Resources

Becoming a Congregation of Learners: Learning as a Key to Revitalizing
Congregational Life *By Isa Aron, Ph.D. Foreword by Rabbi Lawrence A. Hoffman.*
6 x 9, 304 pp, Quality PB, ISBN 1-58023-089-X **$19.95**

Finding a Spiritual Home: How a New Generation of Jews Can Transform the
American Synagogue *By Rabbi Sidney Schwarz*
6 x 9, 352 pp, Quality PB, ISBN 1-58023-185-3 **$19.95**

Jewish Pastoral Care: A Practical Handbook from Traditional & Contemporary Sources
Edited by Rabbi Dayle A. Friedman 6 x 9, 464 pp, Hardcover, ISBN 1-58023-078-4 **$35.00**

The Self-Renewing Congregation: Organizational Strategies for Revitalizing
Congregational Life *By Isa Aron, Ph.D. Foreword by Dr. Ron Wolfson.*
6 x 9, 304 pp, Quality PB, ISBN 1-58023-166-7 **$19.95**

Or phone, fax, mail or e-mail to: **JEWISH LIGHTS** Publishing
Sunset Farm Offices, Route 4 • P.O. Box 237 • Woodstock, Vermont 05091
Tel: (802) 457-4000 • Fax: (802) 457-4004 • www.jewishlights.com
Credit card orders: (800) 962-4544 (8:30AM–5:30PM ET Monday–Friday)
Generous discounts on quantity orders. SATISFACTION GUARANTEED. Prices subject to change.

Children's Books

What You Will See Inside a Synagogue
By Rabbi Lawrence A. Hoffman and Dr. Ron Wolfson; Full-color photos by Bill Aron
A colorful, fun-to-read introduction that explains the ways and whys of Jewish worship and religious life. Full-page photos; concise but informative descriptions of the objects used, the clergy and laypeople who have specific roles, and much more.
8½ x 10½, 32 pp, Full-color photos, Hardcover, ISBN 1-59473-012-1 **$17.99** *(A SkyLight Paths book)*

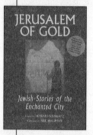

Because Nothing Looks Like God
By Lawrence and Karen Kushner
What is God like? Introduces children to the possibilities of spiritual life. Real-life examples of happiness and sadness invite us to explore, together with our children, the questions we all have about God.
11 x 8½, 32 pp, Full-color illus., Hardcover, ISBN 1-58023-092-X **$16.95** *For ages 4 & up*

Also Available: **Because Nothing Looks Like God Teacher's Guide**
8½ x 11, 22 pp, PB, ISBN 1-58023-140-3 **$6.95** *For ages 5–8*

Board Book Companions to Because Nothing Looks Like God
5 x 5, 24 pp, Full-color illus., SkyLight Paths Board Books, **$7.95** each *For ages 0–4*

What Does God Look Like? ISBN 1-893361-23-3

How Does God Make Things Happen? ISBN 1-893361-24-1

Where Is God? ISBN 1-893361-17-9

The 11th Commandment: Wisdom from Our Children
by The Children of America
"If there were an Eleventh Commandment, what would it be?" Children of many religious denominations across America answer in their own drawings and words.
8 x 10, 48 pp, Full-color illus., Hardcover, ISBN 1-879045-46-X **$16.95** *For all ages*

Jerusalem of Gold: Jewish Stories of the Enchanted City
Retold by Howard Schwartz. Full-color illus. by Neil Waldman.
A beautiful and engaging collection of historical and legendary stories for children. Based on Talmud, midrash, Jewish folklore, and mystical and Hasidic sources.
8 x 10, 64 pp, Full-color illus., Hardcover, ISBN 1-58023-149-7 **$18.95** *For ages 7 & up*

The Book of Miracles: A Young Person's Guide to Jewish Spiritual Awareness
By Lawrence Kushner. All-new illustrations by the author.
6 x 9, 96 pp, 2-color illus., Hardcover, ISBN 1-879045-78-8 **$16.95** *For ages 9–13*

In Our Image: God's First Creatures
By Nancy Sohn Swartz
9 x 12, 32 pp, Full-color illus., Hardcover, ISBN 1-879045-99-0 **$16.95** *For ages 4 & up*

Also Available as a Board Book: **How Did the Animals Help God?**
5 x 5, 24 pp, Board, Full-color illus., ISBN 1-59473-044-X **$7.99** *For ages 0–4 (A SkyLight Paths book)*

From SKYLIGHT PATHS PUBLISHING

Becoming Me: A Story of Creation
By Martin Boroson. Full-color illus. by Christopher Gilvan-Cartwright.
Told in the personal "voice" of the Creator, a story about creation and relationship that is about each one of us.
8 x 10, 32 pp, Full-color illus., Hardcover, ISBN 1-893361-11-X **$16.95** *For ages 4 & up*

Ten Amazing People: And How They Changed the World
By Maura D. Shaw. Foreword by Dr. Robert Coles. Full-color illus. by Stephen Marchesi.
Black Elk • Dorothy Day • Malcolm X • Mahatma Gandhi • Martin Luther King, Jr. • Mother Teresa • Janusz Korczak • Desmond Tutu • Thich Nhat Hanh • Albert Schweitzer.
8½ x 11, 48 pp, Full-color illus., Hardcover, ISBN 1-893361-47-0 **$17.95** *For ages 7 & up*

Where Does God Live? By August Gold and Matthew J. Perlman
Helps young readers develop a personal understanding of God.
10 x 8½, 32 pp, Full-color photo illus., Quality PB, ISBN 1-893361-39-X **$8.99** *For ages 3–6*

Children's Books
by Sandy Eisenberg Sasso

Adam & Eve's First Sunset: God's New Day

Engaging new story explores fear and hope, faith and gratitude in ways that will delight kids and adults—inspiring us to bless each of God's days and nights.

9 x 12, 32 pp, Full-color illus., Hardcover, ISBN 1-58023-177-2 **$17.95** *For ages 4 & up*

But God Remembered

Stories of Women from Creation to the Promised Land

Four different stories of women—Lillith, Serach, Bityah, and the Daughters of Z—teach us important values through their faith and actions.

9 x 12, 32 pp, Full-color illus., Hardcover, ISBN 1-879045-43-5 **$16.95** *For ages 8 & up*

Cain & Abel: Finding the Fruits of Peace

Shows children that we have the power to deal with anger in positive ways. Provides questions for kids and adults to explore together.

9 x 12, 32 pp, Full-color illus., Hardcover, ISBN 1-58023-123-3 **$16.95** *For ages 5 & up*

God in Between

If you wanted to find God, where would you look? This magical, mythical tale teaches that God can be found where we are: within all of us and the relationships between us.

9 x 12, 32 pp, Full-color illus., Hardcover, ISBN 1-879045-86-9 **$16.95** *For ages 4 & up*

God's Paintbrush: Special 10th Anniversary Edition

Wonderfully interactive, invites children of all faiths and backgrounds to encounter God through moments in their own lives. Provides questions adult and child can explore together.

11 x 8½, 32 pp, Full-color illus., Hardcover, ISBN 1-58023-195-0 **$17.95** *For ages 4 & up*

Also Available: **God's Paintbrush Teacher's Guide**
8½ x 11, 32 pp, PB, ISBN 1-879045-57-5 **$8.95**

God's Paintbrush Celebration Kit

A Spiritual Activity Kit for Teachers and Students of All Faiths, All Backgrounds
Additional activity sheets available:
8-Student Activity Sheet Pack (40 sheets/5 sessions), ISBN 1-58023-058-X **$19.95**
Single-Student Activity Sheet Pack (5 sessions), ISBN 1-58023-059-8 **$3.95**

In God's Name

Like an ancient myth in its poetic text and vibrant illustrations, this award-winning modern fable about the search for God's name celebrates the diversity and, at the same time, the unity of all people.

9 x 12, 32 pp, Full-color illus., Hardcover, ISBN 1-879045-26-5 **$16.99** *For ages 4 & up*

Also Available as a Board Book: **What Is God's Name?**
5 x 5, 24 pp, Board, Full-color illus., ISBN 1-893361-10-1 **$7.99** *For ages 0–4 (A SkyLight Paths book)*

Also Available: **In God's Name video and study guide**
Computer animation, original music, and children's voices. 18 min. **$29.99**

Also Available in Spanish: **El nombre de Dios**
9 x 12, 32 pp, Full-color illus., Hardcover, ISBN 1-893361-63-2 **$16.95** *(A SkyLight Paths book)*

Noah's Wife: The Story of Naamah

When God tells Noah to bring the animals of the world onto the ark, God also calls on Naamah, Noah's wife, to save each plant on Earth. Based on an ancient text.

9 x 12, 32 pp, Full-color illus., Hardcover, ISBN 1-58023-134-9 **$16.95** *For ages 4 & up*

Also Available as a Board Book: **Naamah, Noah's Wife**
5 x 5, 24 pp, Full-color illus., Board, ISBN 1-893361-56-X **$7.95** *For ages 0–4 (A SkyLight Paths book)*

For Heaven's Sake: Finding God in Unexpected Places
9 x 12, 32 pp, Full-color illus., Hardcover, ISBN 1-58023-054-7 **$16.95** *For ages 4 & up*

God Said Amen: Finding the Answers to Our Prayers
9 x 12, 32 pp, Full-color illus., Hardcover, ISBN 1-58023-080-6 **$16.95** *For ages 4 & up*

Current Events/History

The Story of the Jews: A 4,000-Year Adventure—A Graphic History Book
Written & illustrated by Stan Mack
Through witty, illustrated narrative, we visit all the major happenings from biblical times to the twenty-first century. Celebrates the major characters and events that have shaped the Jewish people and culture.
6 x 9, 288 pp, illus., Quality PB, ISBN 1-58023-155-1 **$16.95**

The Jewish Prophet: Visionary Words from Moses and Miriam to Henrietta Szold and A. J. Heschel   *By Rabbi Michael J. Shire*
6½ x 8½, 128 pp, 123 full-color illus., Hardcover, ISBN 1-58023-168-3 **$25.00**

Shared Dreams: Martin Luther King, Jr. & the Jewish Community
By Rabbi Marc Schneier. Preface by Martin Luther King III.
6 x 9, 240 pp, Hardcover, ISBN 1-58023-062-8 **$24.95**

"Who Is a Jew?": Conversations, Not Conclusions   *By Meryl Hyman*
6 x 9, 272 pp, Quality PB, ISBN 1-58023-052-0 **$16.95**

Ecology

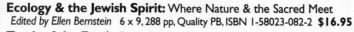
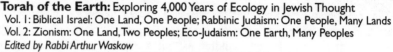

Ecology & the Jewish Spirit: Where Nature & the Sacred Meet
Edited by Ellen Bernstein   6 x 9, 288 pp, Quality PB, ISBN 1-58023-082-2 **$16.95**

Torah of the Earth: Exploring 4,000 Years of Ecology in Jewish Thought
Vol. 1: Biblical Israel: One Land, One People; Rabbinic Judaism: One People, Many Lands
Vol. 2: Zionism: One Land, Two Peoples; Eco-Judaism: One Earth, Many Peoples
Edited by Rabbi Arthur Waskow
Vol. 1: 6 x 9, 272 pp, Quality PB, ISBN 1-58023-086-5 **$19.95**
Vol. 2: 6 x 9, 336 pp, Quality PB, ISBN 1-58023-087-3 **$19.95**

Grief/Healing

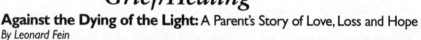

Against the Dying of the Light: A Parent's Story of Love, Loss and Hope
By Leonard Fein
In this unusual exploration of heartbreak and healing, Leonard Fein chronicles the sudden death of his 30-year-old daughter and shares the hard-earned wisdom that emerges in the face of loss and grief.
5½ x 8½, 176 pp, Quality PB, ISBN 1-58023-197-7 **$15.99**

Grief in Our Seasons: A Mourner's Kaddish Companion   *By Rabbi Kerry M. Olitzky*
4½ x 6½, 448 pp, Quality PB, ISBN 1-879045-55-9 **$15.95**

Healing of Soul, Healing of Body: Spiritual Leaders Unfold the Strength & Solace
in Psalms   *Edited by Rabbi Simkha Y. Weintraub, C.S.W.*
6 x 9, 128 pp, 2-color illus. text, Quality PB, ISBN 1-879045-31-1 **$14.95**

Jewish Paths toward Healing and Wholeness: A Personal Guide to Dealing with
Suffering   *By Rabbi Kerry M. Olitzky. Foreword by Debbie Friedman.*
6 x 9, 192 pp, Quality PB, ISBN 1-58023-068-7 **$15.95**

Mourning & Mitzvah, 2nd Edition: A Guided Journal for Walking the Mourner's
Path through Grief to Healing   *By Anne Brener, L.C.S.W.*
7½ x 9, 304 pp, Quality PB, ISBN 1-58023-113-6 **$19.95**

The Perfect Stranger's Guide to Funerals and Grieving Practices
A Guide to Etiquette in Other People's Religious Ceremonies   *Edited by Stuart M. Matlins*
6 x 9, 240 pp, Quality PB, ISBN 1-893361-20-9 **$16.95**   *(A SkyLight Paths book)*

Tears of Sorrow, Seeds of Hope: A Jewish Spiritual Companion for Infertility and
Pregnancy Loss   *By Rabbi Nina Beth Cardin*
6 x 9, 192 pp, Hardcover, ISBN 1-58023-017-2 **$19.95**

A Time to Mourn, A Time to Comfort: A Guide to Jewish Bereavement and
Comfort   *By Dr. Ron Wolfson*   7 x 9, 336 pp, Quality PB, ISBN 1-879045-96-6 **$18.95**

When a Grandparent Dies: A Kid's Own Remembering Workbook for Dealing
with Shiva and the Year Beyond   *By Nechama Liss-Levinson, Ph.D.*
8 x 10, 48 pp, 2-color text, Hardcover, ISBN 1-879045-44-3 **$15.95**   *For ages 7–13*

Abraham Joshua Heschel

The Earth Is the Lord's: The Inner World of the Jew in Eastern Europe
5½ x 8, 128 pp, Quality PB, ISBN 1-879045-42-7 **$14.95**

Israel: An Echo of Eternity *New Introduction by Susannah Heschel*
5½ x 8, 272 pp, Quality PB, ISBN 1-879045-70-2 **$19.95**

A Passion for Truth: Despair and Hope in Hasidism
5½ x 8, 352 pp, Quality PB, ISBN 1-879045-41-9 **$18.99**

Holidays/Holy Days

Reclaiming Judaism as a Spiritual Practice: Holy Days and Shabbat
By Rabbi Goldie Milgram
Provides a framework for understanding the powerful and often unexplained intellectual, emotional, and spiritual tools that are essential for a lively, relevant, and fulfilling Jewish spiritual practice. 7 x 9, 272 pp, Quality PB, ISBN 1-58023-205-1 **$19.99**

7th Heaven: Celebrating Shabbat with Rebbe Nachman of Breslov
By Moshe Mykoff with the Breslov Research Institute
Based on the teachings of Rebbe Nachman of Breslov. Explores the art of consciously observing Shabbat and understanding in-depth many of the day's traditional spiritual practices. 5⅛ x 8¼, 224 pp, Deluxe PB w/flaps, ISBN 1-58023-175-6 **$18.95**

The Women's Passover Companion
Women's Reflections on the Festival of Freedom
Edited by Rabbi Sharon Cohen Anisfeld, Tara Mohr, and Catherine Spector
Groundbreaking. A provocative conversation about women's relationships to Passover as well as the roots and meanings of women's seders.
6 x 9, 352 pp, Hardcover, ISBN 1-58023-128-4 **$24.95**

The Women's Seder Sourcebook
Rituals & Readings for Use at the Passover Seder
Edited by Rabbi Sharon Cohen Anisfeld, Tara Mohr, and Catherine Spector
Gathers the voices of more than one hundred women in readings, personal and creative reflections, commentaries, blessings, and ritual suggestions that can be incorporated into your Passover celebration as supplements to or substitutes for traditional passages of the haggadah.
6 x 9, 384 pp, Hardcover, ISBN 1-58023-136-5 **$24.95**

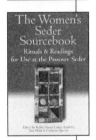

Creating Lively Passover Seders: A Sourcebook of Engaging Tales, Texts & Activities
By David Arnow, Ph.D. 7 x 9, 416 pp, Quality PB, ISBN 1-58023-184-5 **$24.99**

Hanukkah, 2nd Edition: The Family Guide to Spiritual Celebration
By Dr. Ron Wolfson. Edited by Joel Lurie Grishaver.
7 x 9, 240 pp, illus., Quality PB, ISBN 1-58023-122-5 **$18.95**

The Jewish Family Fun Book: Holiday Projects, Everyday Activities, and Travel Ideas
with Jewish Themes *By Danielle Dardashti and Roni Sarig. Illus. by Avi Katz.*
6 x 9, 288 pp, 70+ b/w illus. & diagrams, Quality PB, ISBN 1-58023-171-3 **$18.95**

The Jewish Gardening Cookbook: Growing Plants & Cooking for
Holidays & Festivals *By Michael Brown* 6 x 9, 224 pp, 30+ illus., Quality PB, ISBN 1-58023-116-0 **$16.95**

The Jewish Lights Book of Fun Classroom Activities: Simple and Seasonal
Projects for Teachers and Students *By Danielle Dardashti and Roni Sarig*
6 x 9, 240 pp, Quality PB, ISBN 1–58023–206–X **$19.99**

Passover, 2nd Edition: The Family Guide to Spiritual Celebration
By Dr. Ron Wolfson with Joel Lurie Grishaver 7 x 9, 352 pp, Quality PB, ISBN 1-58023-174-8 **$19.95**

Shabbat, 2nd Edition: The Family Guide to Preparing for and Celebrating the Sabbath
By Dr. Ron Wolfson 7 x 9, 320 pp, illus., Quality PB, ISBN 1-58023-164-0 **$19.95**

Sharing Blessings: Children's Stories for Exploring the Spirit of the Jewish Holidays
By Rahel Musleah and Michael Klayman
8½ x 11, 64 pp, Full-color illus., Hardcover, ISBN 1-879045-71-0 **$18.95** *For ages 6 & up*

Inspiration

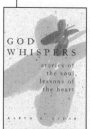

God in All Moments
Mystical & Practical Spiritual Wisdom from Hasidic Masters
Edited and translated by Or N. Rose with Ebn D. Leader
Hasidic teachings on how to be mindful in religious practice and cultivating every-day ethical behavior—*hanhagot*. 5½ x 8½, 192 pp, Quality PB, ISBN 1-58023-186-1 **$16.95**

Our Dance with God: Finding Prayer, Perspective and Meaning in the Stories of Our Lives *By Karyn D. Kedar*
Inspiring spiritual insight to guide you on your life journeys and teach you to live and thrive in two conflicting worlds: the rational/material and the spiritual.
6 x 9, 176 pp, Quality PB, ISBN 1-58023-202-7 **$16.99**

Also Available: **The Dance of the Dolphin** (Hardcover edition of *Our Dance with God*)
6 x 9, 176 pp, Hardcover, ISBN 1-58023-154-3 **$19.95**

The Empty Chair: Finding Hope and Joy—Timeless Wisdom from a Hasidic Master, Rebbe Nachman of Breslov *Adapted by Moshe Mykoff and the Breslov Research Institute*
4 x 6, 128 pp, 2-color text, Deluxe PB w/flaps, ISBN 1-879045-67-2 **$9.95**

The Gentle Weapon: Prayers for Everyday and Not-So-Everyday Moments—Timeless Wisdom from the Teachings of the Hasidic Master, Rebbe Nachman of Breslov
Adapted by Moshe Mykoff and S. C. Mizrahi, together with the Breslov Research Institute
4 x 6, 144 pp, 2-color text, Deluxe PB w/flaps, ISBN 1-58023-022-9 **$9.95**

God Whispers: Stories of the Soul, Lessons of the Heart *By Karyn D. Kedar*
6 x 9, 176 pp, Quality PB, ISBN 1-58023-088-1 **$15.95**

An Orphan in History: One Man's Triumphant Search for His Jewish Roots
By Paul Cowan. Afterword by Rachel Cowan. 6 x 9, 288 pp, Quality PB, ISBN 1-58023-135-7 **$16.95**

Restful Reflections: Nighttime Inspiration to Calm the Soul, Based on Jewish Wisdom
By Rabbi Kerry M. Olitzky & Rabbi Lori Forman 4½ x 6½, 448 pp, Quality PB, ISBN 1-58023-091-1 **$15.95**

Sacred Intentions: Daily Inspiration to Strengthen the Spirit, Based on Jewish Wisdom
By Rabbi Kerry M. Olitzky and Rabbi Lori Forman 4½ x 6½, 448 pp, Quality PB, ISBN 1-58023-061-X **$15.95**

Kabbalah/Mysticism/Enneagram

Seek My Face: A Jewish Mystical Theology
By Dr. Arthur Green
This classic work of contemporary Jewish theology, revised and updated, is a profound, deeply personal statement of the lasting truths of Jewish mysticism and the basic faith claims of Judaism. A tool for anyone seeking the elusive presence of God in the world. 6 x 9, 304 pp, Quality PB, ISBN 1-58023-130-6 **$19.95**

Zohar: Annotated & Explained
Translation and annotation by Dr. Daniel C. Matt. Foreword by Andrew Harvey
Offers insightful yet unobtrusive commentary to the masterpiece of Jewish mysticism that explains references and mystical symbols, shares wisdom of spiritual masters, and clarifies the *Zohar*'s bold claim: We have always been taught that we need God, but in order to manifest in the world, God needs us.
5½ x 8½, 160 pp, Quality PB, ISBN 1-893361-51-9 **$15.99** (A SkyLight Paths book)

Cast in God's Image: Discover Your Personality Type Using the Enneagram and Kabbalah
By Rabbi Howard A. Addison
7 x 9, 176 pp, Quality PB, Layflat binding, 20+ journaling exercises, ISBN 1-58023-124-1 **$16.95**

Ehyeh: A Kabbalah for Tomorrow *By Dr. Arthur Green*
6 x 9, 224 pp, Quality PB, ISBN 1-58023-213-2 **$16.99;** Hardcover, ISBN 1-58023-125-X **$21.99**

The Enneagram and Kabbalah: Reading Your Soul *By Rabbi Howard A. Addison*
6 x 9, 176 pp, Quality PB, ISBN 1-58023-001-6 **$15.95**

Finding Joy: A Practical Spiritual Guide to Happiness *By Dannel I. Schwartz with Mark Hass*
6 x 9, 192 pp, Quality PB, ISBN 1-58023-009-1 **$14.95;** Hardcover, ISBN 1-879045-53-2 **$19.95**

The Gift of Kabbalah: Discovering the Secrets of Heaven, Renewing Your Life on Earth
By Tamar Frankiel, Ph.D.
6 x 9, 256 pp, Quality PB, ISBN 1-58023-141-1 **$16.95;** Hardcover, ISBN 1-58023-108-X **$21.95**

The Way Into Jewish Mystical Tradition *By Lawrence Kushner*
6 x 9, 224 pp, Quality PB, ISBN 1-58023-200-0 **$18.99;** Hardcover, ISBN 1-58023-029-6 **$21.95**

Life Cycle
Marriage / Parenting / Family / Aging

Jewish Fathers: A Legacy of Love
Photographs by Lloyd Wolf. Essays by Paula Wolfson. Foreword by Harold S. Kushner.
Honors the role of contemporary Jewish fathers in America. Each father tells in his own words what it means to be a parent and Jewish, and what he learned from his own father. Insightful photos. 9½ x 7⅞, 144 pp with 100+ duotone photos, Hardcover, ISBN 1-58023-204-3 **$30.00**

The New Jewish Baby Album: Creating and Celebrating the Beginning of a Spiritual Life—A Jewish Lights Companion
By the Editors at Jewish Lights. Foreword by Anita Diamant. Preface by Sandy Eisenberg Sasso.
A spiritual keepsake that will be treasured for generations. More than just a memory book, *shows you how—and why it's important*—to create a Jewish home and a Jewish life. 8 x 10, 64 pp, Deluxe Padded Hardcover, Full-color illus., ISBN 1-58023-138-1 **$19.95**

The Jewish Pregnancy Book: A Resource for the Soul, Body & Mind during Pregnancy, Birth & the First Three Months
By Sandy Falk, M.D., and Rabbi Daniel Judson, with Steven A. Rapp
Includes medical information on fetal development, pre-natal testing and more, from a liberal Jewish perspective; prenatal *Aleph-Bet* yoga; and prayers and rituals for each stage of pregnancy. 7 x 10, 208 pp, Quality PB, b/w illus., ISBN 1-58023-178-0 **$16.95**

Celebrating Your New Jewish Daughter: Creating Jewish Ways to Welcome Baby Girls into the Covenant—New and Traditional Ceremonies
By Debra Nussbaum Cohen 6 x 9, 272 pp, Quality PB, ISBN 1-58023-090-3 **$18.95**

The New Jewish Baby Book: Names, Ceremonies & Customs—A Guide for Today's Families *By Anita Diamant* 6 x 9, 336 pp, Quality PB, ISBN 1-879045-28-1 **$18.95**

Parenting As a Spiritual Journey: Deepening Ordinary and Extraordinary Events into Sacred Occasions *By Rabbi Nancy Fuchs-Kreimer* 6 x 9, 224 pp, Quality PB, ISBN 1-58023-016-4 **$16.95**

Embracing the Covenant: Converts to Judaism Talk About Why & How
Edited and with introductions by Rabbi Allan Berkowitz and Patti Moskovitz
6 x 9, 192 pp, Quality PB, ISBN 1-879045-50-8 **$16.95**

The Guide to Jewish Interfaith Family Life: An InterfaithFamily.com Handbook
Edited by Ronnie Friedland and Edmund Case 6 x 9, 384 pp, Quality PB, ISBN 1-58023-153-5 **$18.95**

Introducing My Faith and My Community
The Jewish Outreach Institute Guide for the Christian in a Jewish Interfaith Relationship
By Rabbi Kerry M. Olitzky 6 x 9, 176 pp, Quality PB, ISBN 1-58023-192-6 **$16.99**

Making a Successful Jewish Interfaith Marriage: The Jewish Outreach Institute Guide to Opportunities, Challenges and Resources
By Rabbi Kerry M. Olitzky with Joan Peterson Littman 6 x 9, 176 pp, Quality PB, ISBN 1-58023-170-5 **$16.95**

How to Be a Perfect Stranger, 3rd Edition: The Essential Religious Etiquette Handbook *Edited by Stuart M. Matlins and Arthur J. Magida*
The indispensable guide to the rituals and celebrations of the major religions and denominations in North America from the perspective of an interested guest of any other faith. 6 x 9, 432 pp, Quality PB, ISBN 1-893361-67-5 **$19.95** *(A SkyLight Paths book)*

The Creative Jewish Wedding Book: A Hands-On Guide to New & Old Traditions, Ceremonies & Celebrations *By Gabrielle Kaplan-Mayer*
Provides the tools to create the most meaningful Jewish traditional or alternative wedding by using ritual elements to express your unique style and spirituality. 9 x 9, 288 pp, b/w photos, Quality PB, ISBN 1-58023-194-2 **$19.99**

Divorce Is a Mitzvah: A Practical Guide to Finding Wholeness and Holiness When Your Marriage Dies *By Rabbi Perry Netter. Afterword by Rabbi Laura Geller.*
6 x 9, 224 pp, Quality PB, ISBN 1-58023-172-1 **$16.95**

A Heart of Wisdom: Making the Jewish Journey from Midlife through the Elder Years
Edited by Susan Berrin. Foreword by Harold Kushner. 6 x 9, 384 pp, Quality PB, ISBN 1-58023-051-2 **$18.95**

So That Your Values Live On: Ethical Wills and How to Prepare Them
Edited by Jack Riemer and Nathaniel Stampfer 6 x 9, 272 pp, Quality PB, ISBN 1-879045-34-6 **$18.95**

Meditation

The Handbook of Jewish Meditation Practices
A Guide for Enriching the Sabbath and Other Days of Your Life
By Rabbi David A. Cooper
Easy-to-learn meditation techniques for use on the Sabbath and every day, to help us return to the roots of traditional Jewish spirituality where Shabbat is a state of mind and soul. 6 x 9, 208 pp, Quality PB, ISBN 1-58023-102-0 **$16.95**

Discovering Jewish Meditation: Instruction & Guidance for Learning an Ancient
Spiritual Practice *By Nan Fink Gefen, Ph.D.* 6 x 9, 208 pp, Quality PB, ISBN 1-58023-067-9 **$16.95**

A Heart of Stillness: A Complete Guide to Learning the Art of Meditation
By Rabbi David A. Cooper 5½ x 8½, 272 pp, Quality PB, ISBN 1-893361-03-9 **$16.95**
(A SkyLight Paths book)

Meditation from the Heart of Judaism: Today's Teachers Share Their
Practices, Techniques, and Faith *Edited by Avram Davis*
6 x 9, 256 pp, Quality PB, ISBN 1-58023-049-0 **$16.95**

Silence, Simplicity & Solitude: A Complete Guide to Spiritual Retreat at Home
By Rabbi David A. Cooper 5½ x 8½, 336 pp, Quality PB, ISBN 1-893361-04-7 **$16.95**
(A SkyLight Paths book)

Three Gates to Meditation Practice: A Personal Journey into Sufism,
Buddhism, and Judaism *By Rabbi David A. Cooper*
5½ x 8½, 240 pp, Quality PB, ISBN 1-893361-22-5 **$16.95** *(A SkyLight Paths book)*

The Way of Flame: A Guide to the Forgotten Mystical Tradition of Jewish Meditation
By Avram Davis 4½ x 8, 176 pp, Quality PB, ISBN 1-58023-060-1 **$15.95**

Ritual/Sacred Practice/Journaling

The Jewish Dream Book: The Key to Opening the Inner Meaning of
Your Dreams *By Vanessa L. Ochs with Elizabeth Ochs; Full-color illus. by Kristina Swarner*
Instructions for how modern people can perform ancient Jewish dream practices and dream interpretations drawn from the Jewish wisdom tradition. For anyone who wants to understand their dreams—and themselves.
8 x 8, 120 pp, Full-color illus., Deluxe PB w/flaps, ISBN 1-58023-132-2 **$16.95**

The Jewish Journaling Book: How to Use Jewish Tradition to Write
Your Life & Explore Your Soul *By Janet Ruth Falon*
Details the history of Jewish journaling throughout biblical and modern times, and teaches specific journaling techniques to help you create and maintain a vital journal, from a Jewish perspective. 8 x 8, 304 pp, Deluxe PB w/flaps, ISBN 1-58023-203-5 **$18.99**

The Rituals & Practices of a Jewish Life: A Handbook for Personal Spiritual
Renewal *Edited by Rabbi Kerry M. Olitzky and Rabbi Daniel Judson*
6 x 9, 272 pp, illus., Quality PB, ISBN 1-58023-169-1 **$18.95**

The Book of Jewish Sacred Practices: CLAL's Guide to Everyday & Holiday
Rituals & Blessings *Edited by Rabbi Irwin Kula and Vanessa L. Ochs, Ph.D.*
6 x 9, 368 pp, Quality PB, ISBN 1-58023-152-7 **$18.95**

Science Fiction/
Mystery & Detective Fiction

Mystery Midrash: An Anthology of Jewish Mystery & Detective Fiction
Edited by Lawrence W. Raphael. Preface by Joel Siegel.
6 x 9, 304 pp, Quality PB, ISBN 1-58023-055-5 **$16.95**

Criminal Kabbalah: An Intriguing Anthology of Jewish Mystery & Detective Fiction
Edited by Lawrence W. Raphael. Foreword by Laurie R. King.
6 x 9, 256 pp, Quality PB, ISBN 1-58023-109-8 **$16.95**

More Wandering Stars: An Anthology of Outstanding Stories of Jewish Fantasy and
Science Fiction *Edited by Jack Dann. Introduction by Isaac Asimov.*
6 x 9, 192 pp, Quality PB, ISBN 1-58023-063-6 **$16.95**

Wandering Stars: An Anthology of Jewish Fantasy & Science Fiction
Edited by Jack Dann. Introduction by Isaac Asimov.
6 x 9, 272 pp, Quality PB, ISBN 1-58023-005-9 **$16.95**

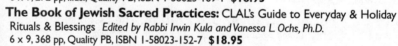

Spirituality

The Alphabet of Paradise: An A–Z of Spirituality for Everyday Life
By Rabbi Howard Cooper
In twenty-six engaging chapters, Cooper spiritually illuminates the subjects of our daily lives—A to Z—examining these sources by using an ancient Jewish mystical method of interpretation that reveals both the literal and more allusive meanings of each. 5 x 7¾, 224 pp, Quality PB, ISBN 1-893361-80-2 **$16.95** *(A SkyLight Paths book)*

Does the Soul Survive?: A Jewish Journey to Belief in Afterlife, Past Lives & Living with Purpose *By Rabbi Elie Kaplan Spitz. Foreword by Brian L Weiss, M.D.*
Spitz relates his own experiences and those shared with him by people he has worked with as a rabbi, and shows us that belief in afterlife and past lives, so often approached with reluctance, is in fact true to Jewish tradition.
6 x 9, 288 pp, Quality PB, ISBN 1-58023-165-9 **$16.95**; Hardcover, ISBN 1-58023-094-6 **$21.95**

First Steps to a New Jewish Spirit: Reb Zalman's Guide to Recapturing the Intimacy & Ecstasy in Your Relationship with God
By Rabbi Zalman M. Schachter-Shalomi with Donald Gropman
An extraordinary spiritual handbook that restores psychic and physical vigor by introducing us to new models and alternative ways of practicing Judaism. Offers meditation and contemplation exercises for enriching the most important aspects of everyday life. 6 x 9, 144 pp, Quality PB, ISBN 1-58023-182-9 **$16.95**

God in Our Relationships: Spirituality between People from the Teachings of Martin Buber *By Rabbi Dennis S. Ross*
On the eightieth anniversary of Buber's classic work, we can discover new answers to critical issues in our lives. Inspiring examples from Ross's own life—as congregational rabbi, father, hospital chaplain, social worker, and husband—illustrate Buber's difficult-to-understand ideas about how we encounter God and each other. 5½ x 8½, 160 pp, Quality PB, ISBN 1-58023-147-0 **$16.95**

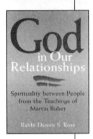

The Jewish Lights Spirituality Handbook: A Guide to Understanding, Exploring & Living a Spiritual Life *Edited by Stuart M. Matlins*
What exactly is "Jewish" about spirituality? How do I make it a part of my life? Fifty of today's foremost spiritual leaders share their ideas and experience with us.
6 x 9, 456 pp, Quality PB, ISBN 1-58023-093-8 **$19.99**; Hardcover, ISBN 1-58023-100-4 **$24.95**

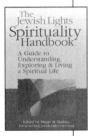

Bringing the Psalms to Life: How to Understand and Use the Book of Psalms
By Dr. Daniel F. Polish
6 x 9, 208 pp, Quality PB, ISBN 1-58023-157-8 **$16.95**; Hardcover, ISBN 1-58023-077-6 **$21.95**

God & the Big Bang: Discovering Harmony between Science & Spirituality
By Dr. Daniel C. Matt 6 x 9, 216 pp, Quality PB, ISBN 1-879045-89-3 **$16.95**

Godwrestling—Round 2: Ancient Wisdom, Future Paths
By Rabbi Arthur Waskow 6 x 9, 352 pp, Quality PB, ISBN 1-879045-72-9 **$18.95**

One God Clapping: The Spiritual Path of a Zen Rabbi *By Rabbi Alan Lew with Sherril Jaffe*
5½ x 8½, 336 pp, Quality PB, ISBN 1-58023-115-2 **$16.95**

The Path of Blessing: Experiencing the Energy and Abundance of the Divine
By Rabbi Marcia Prager 5½ x 8½, 240 pp, Quality PB, ISBN 1-58023-148-9 **$16.95**

Six Jewish Spiritual Paths: A Rationalist Looks at Spirituality *By Rabbi Rifat Sonsino*
6 x 9, 208 pp, Quality PB, ISBN 1-58023-167-5 **$16.95**; Hardcover, ISBN 1-58023-095-4 **$21.95**

Soul Judaism: Dancing with God into a New Era
By Rabbi Wayne Dosick 5½ x 8½, 304 pp, Quality PB, ISBN 1-58023-053-9 **$16.95**

Stepping Stones to Jewish Spiritual Living: Walking the Path Morning, Noon, and Night *By Rabbi James L Mirel and Karen Bonnell Werth*
6 x 9, 240 pp, Quality PB, ISBN 1-58023-074-1 **$16.95**; Hardcover, ISBN 1-58023-003-2 **$21.95**

There Is No Messiah... and You're It: The Stunning Transformation of Judaism's Most Provocative Idea *By Rabbi Robert N. Levine, D.D.*
6 x 9, 192 pp, Hardcover, ISBN 1-58023-173-X **$21.95**

These Are the Words: A Vocabulary of Jewish Spiritual Life *By Dr. Arthur Green*
6 x 9, 304 pp, Quality PB, ISBN 1-58023-107-1 **$18.95**

Spirituality/Lawrence Kushner

The Book of Letters: A Mystical Hebrew Alphabet
Popular Hardcover Edition, 6 x 9, 80 pp, 2-color text, ISBN 1-879045-00-1 **$24.95**
Deluxe Gift Edition with slipcase, 9 x 12, 80 pp, 4-color text, Hardcover, ISBN 1-879045-01-X **$79.95**
Collector's Limited Edition, 9 x 12, 80 pp, gold foil embossed pages, w/limited edition silkscreened print, ISBN 1-879045-04-4 **$349.00**

The Book of Miracles: A Young Person's Guide to Jewish Spiritual Awareness
All-new illustrations by the author
6 x 9, 96 pp, 2-color illus., Hardcover, ISBN 1-879045-78-8 **$16.95** *For ages 9–13*

The Book of Words: Talking Spiritual Life, Living Spiritual Talk
6 x 9, 160 pp, Quality PB, ISBN 1-58023-020-2 **$16.95**

Eyes Remade for Wonder: A Lawrence Kushner Reader
Introduction by Thomas Moore
6 x 9, 240 pp, Quality PB, ISBN 1-58023-042-3 **$18.95**; Hardcover, ISBN 1-58023-014-8 **$23.95**

God Was in This Place & I, i Did Not Know
Finding Self, Spirituality and Ultimate Meaning
6 x 9, 192 pp, Quality PB, ISBN 1-879045-33-8 **$16.95**

Honey from the Rock: An Introduction to Jewish Mysticism
6 x 9, 176 pp, Quality PB, ISBN 1-58023-073-3 **$16.95**

Invisible Lines of Connection: Sacred Stories of the Ordinary
5½ x 8½, 160 pp, Quality PB, ISBN 1-879045-98-2 **$15.95**

Jewish Spirituality—A Brief Introduction for Christians
5½ x 8½, 112 pp, Quality PB Original, ISBN 1-58023-150-0 **$12.95**

The River of Light: Jewish Mystical Awareness
6 x 9, 192 pp, Quality PB, ISBN 1-58023-096-2 **$16.95**

The Way Into Jewish Mystical Tradition
6 x 9, 224 pp, Quality PB, ISBN 1-58023-200-0 **$18.99**; Hardcover, ISBN 1-58023-029-6 **$21.95**

Spirituality/Prayer

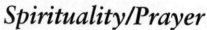

Pray Tell: A Hadassah Guide to Jewish Prayer
By Rabbi Jules Harlow, with contributions from Tamara Cohen, Rochelle Furstenberg, Rabbi Daniel Gordis, Leora Tanenbaum, and many others
A guide to traditional Jewish prayer enriched with insight and wisdom from a broad variety of viewpoints—from Orthodox, Conservative, Reform, and Reconstructionist Judaism to New Age and feminist.
8½ x 11, 400 pp, Quality PB, ISBN 1-58023-163-2 **$29.95**

My People's Prayer Book Series
Traditional Prayers, Modern Commentaries
Edited by Rabbi Lawrence A. Hoffman
Provides diverse and exciting commentary to the traditional liturgy, helping modern men and women find new wisdom in Jewish prayer, and bring liturgy into their lives.

Each book includes Hebrew text, modern translation, and commentaries from all perspectives of the Jewish world.

Vol. 1—The *Sh'ma* and Its Blessings
7 x 10, 168 pp, Hardcover, ISBN 1-879045-79-6 **$23.95**

Vol. 2—The *Amidah*
7 x 10, 240 pp, Hardcover, ISBN 1-879045-80-X **$24.95**

Vol. 3—*P'sukei D'zimrah* (Morning Psalms)
7 x 10, 240 pp, Hardcover, ISBN 1-879045-81-8 **$24.95**

Vol. 4—*Seder K'riat Hatorah* (The Torah Service)
7 x 10, 264 pp, Hardcover, ISBN 1-879045-82-6 **$23.95**

Vol. 5—*Birkhot Hashachar* (Morning Blessings)
7 x 10, 240 pp, Hardcover, ISBN 1-879045-83-4 **$24.95**

Vol. 6—*Tachanun* and Concluding Prayers
7 x 10, 240 pp, Hardcover, ISBN 1-879045-84-2 **$24.95**

Vol. 7—Shabbat at Home
7 x 10, 240 pp, Hardcover, ISBN 1-879045-85-0 **$24.95**

Vol. 8—*Kabbalat Shabbat* (Welcoming Shabbat in the Synagogue)
7 x 10, 240 pp, Hardcover, ISBN 1-58023-121-7 **$24.99**

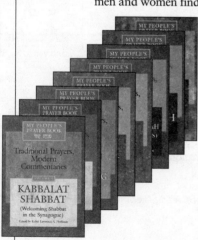

Spirituality/The Way Into... Series

The Way Into... Series offers an accessible and highly usable "guided tour" of the Jewish faith, people, history and beliefs—in total, an introduction to Judaism that will enable you to understand and interact with the sacred texts of the Jewish tradition. Each volume is written by a leading contemporary scholar and teacher, and explores one key aspect of Judaism. *The Way Into...* enables all readers to achieve a real sense of Jewish cultural literacy through guided study.

The Way Into Encountering God in Judaism   *By Neil Gillman*
6 x 9, 240 pp, Quality PB, ISBN 1-58023-199-3 **$18.99**; Hardcover, ISBN 1-58023-025-3 **$21.95**

Also Available: **The Jewish Approach to God: A Brief Introduction for Christians**
By Neil Gillman 5½ x 8½, 192 pp, Quality PB, ISBN 1-58023-190-X **$16.95**

The Way Into Jewish Mystical Tradition   *By Lawrence Kushner*
6 x 9, 224 pp, Quality PB, ISBN 1-58023-200-0 **$18.99**; Hardcover, ISBN 1-58023-029-6 **$21.95**

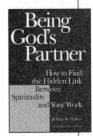

The Way Into Jewish Prayer   *By Lawrence A. Hoffman*
6 x 9, 224 pp, Quality PB, ISBN 1-58023-201-9 **$18.99**; Hardcover, ISBN 1-58023-027-X **$21.95**

The Way Into Torah   *By Norman J. Cohen*
6 x 9, 176 pp, Quality PB, ISBN 1-58023-198-5 **$16.99**; Hardcover, ISBN 1-58023-028-8 **$21.95**

Spirituality in the Workplace

Being God's Partner
How to Find the Hidden Link Between Spirituality and Your Work
By Rabbi Jeffrey K. Salkin. Introduction by Norman Lear.
6 x 9, 192 pp, Quality PB, ISBN 1-879045-65-6 **$17.95**

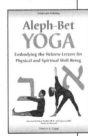

The Business Bible: 10 New Commandments for Bringing Spirituality & Ethical Values into the Workplace   *By Rabbi Wayne Dosick*
5½ x 8½, 208 pp, Quality PB, ISBN 1-58023-101-2 **$14.95**

Spirituality and Wellness

Aleph-Bet Yoga
Embodying the Hebrew Letters for Physical and Spiritual Well-Being
By Steven A. Rapp. Foreword by Tamar Frankiel, Ph.D., and Judy Greenfeld. Preface by Hart Lazer
7 x 10, 128 pp, b/w photos, Quality PB, Layflat binding, ISBN 1-58023-162-4 **$16.95**

Entering the Temple of Dreams
Jewish Prayers, Movements, and Meditations for the End of the Day
By Tamar Frankiel, Ph.D., and Judy Greenfeld
7 x 10, 192 pp, illus., Quality PB, ISBN 1-58023-079-2 **$16.95**

Jewish Paths toward Healing and Wholeness: A Personal Guide to Dealing with Suffering   *By Rabbi Kerry M. Olitzky. Foreword by Debbie Friedman.*
6 x 9, 192 pp, Quality PB, ISBN 1-58023-068-7 **$15.95**

Minding the Temple of the Soul
Balancing Body, Mind, and Spirit through Traditional Jewish Prayer, Movement, and Meditation   *By Tamar Frankiel, Ph.D., and Judy Greenfeld*
7 x 10, 184 pp, illus., Quality PB, ISBN 1-879045-64-8 **$16.95**
Audiotape of the Blessings and Meditations: 60 min. **$9.95**
Videotape of the Movements and Meditations: 46 min. **$20.00**

Spirituality/Women's Interest

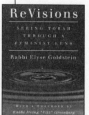

The Quotable Jewish Woman: Wisdom, Inspiration & Humor from the Mind & Heart *Edited and compiled by Elaine Bernstein Partnow*
The definitive collection of ideas, reflections, humor, and wit of over 300 Jewish women.
6 x 9, 496 pp, Hardcover, ISBN 1-58023-193-4 **$29.99**

Lifecycles, Vol. 1: Jewish Women on Life Passages & Personal Milestones
Edited and with introductions by Rabbi Debra Orenstein 6 x 9, 480 pp, Quality PB, ISBN 1-58023-018-0 **$19.95**

Lifecycles, Vol. 2: Jewish Women on Biblical Themes in Contemporary Life
Edited and with introductions by Rabbi Debra Orenstein and Rabbi Jane Rachel Litman
6 x 9, 464 pp, Quality PB, ISBN 1-58023-019-9 **$19.95**

Moonbeams: A Hadassah Rosh Hodesh Guide *Edited by Carol Diament, Ph.D.*
8½ x 11, 240 pp, Quality PB, ISBN 1-58023-099-7 **$20.00**

ReVisions: Seeing Torah through a Feminist Lens *By Rabbi Elyse Goldstein*
5½ x 8½, 224 pp, Quality PB, ISBN 1-58023-117-9 **$16.95**

White Fire: A Portrait of Women Spiritual Leaders in America
By Rabbi Malka Drucker. Photographs by Gay Block.
7 x 10, 320 pp, 30+ b/w photos, Hardcover, ISBN 1-893361-64-0 **$24.95** *(A SkyLight Paths book)*

Women of the Wall: Claiming Sacred Ground at Judaism's Holy Site
Edited by Phyllis Chesler and Rivka Haut 6 x 9, 496 pp, b/w photos, Hardcover, ISBN 1-58023-161-6 **$34.95**

The Women's Haftarah Commentary: New Insights from Women Rabbis on the 54 Weekly Haftarah Portions, the 5 Megillot & Special Shabbatot
Edited by Rabbi Elyse Goldstein 6 x 9, 560 pp, Hardcover, ISBN 1-58023-133-0 **$39.99**

The Women's Torah Commentary: New Insights from Women Rabbis on the 54 Weekly Torah Portions *Edited by Rabbi Elyse Goldstein*
6 x 9, 496 pp, Hardcover, ISBN 1-58023-076-8 **$34.95**

The Year Mom Got Religion: One Woman's Midlife Journey into Judaism
By Lee Meyerhoff Hendler 6 x 9, 208 pp, Quality PB, ISBN 1-58023-070-9 **$15.95**

See Holidays for *The Women's Passover Companion: Women's Reflections on the Festival of Freedom* and *The Women's Seder Sourcebook: Rituals & Readings for Use at the Passover Seder.*

Travel

Israel—A Spiritual Travel Guide: A Companion for the Modern Jewish Pilgrim
By Rabbi Lawrence A. Hoffman 4¾ x 10, 256 pp, Quality PB, illus., ISBN 1-879045-56-7 **$18.95**
Also Available: **The Israel Mission Leader's Guide** ISBN 1-58023-085-7 **$4.95**

12 Steps

100 Blessings Every Day
Daily Twelve Step Recovery Affirmations, Exercises for Personal Growth & Renewal Reflecting Seasons of the Jewish Year
By Rabbi Kerry M. Olitzky. Foreword by Rabbi Neil Gillman.
One-day-at-a-time monthly format. Reflects on the rhythm of the Jewish calendar to bring insight to recovery from addictions.
4½ x 6½, 432 pp, Quality PB, ISBN 1-879045-30-3 **$15.99**

Recovery from Codependence: A Jewish Twelve Steps Guide to Healing Your Soul
By Rabbi Kerry M. Olitzky 6 x 9, 160 pp, Quality PB, ISBN 1-879045-32-X **$13.95**

Renewed Each Day: Daily Twelve Step Recovery Meditations Based on the Bible
By Rabbi Kerry M. Olitzky and Aaron Z.
Vol. 1—Genesis & Exodus: 6 x 9, 224 pp, Quality PB, ISBN 1-879045-12-5 **$14.95**
Vol. 2—Leviticus, Numbers & Deuteronomy: 6 x 9, 280 pp, Quality PB, ISBN 1-879045-13-3 **$14.95**

Twelve Jewish Steps to Recovery: A Personal Guide to Turning from Alcoholism & Other Addictions—Drugs, Food, Gambling, Sex...
By Rabbi Kerry M. Olitzky and Stuart A. Copans, M.D. Preface by Abraham J. Twerski, M.D.
6 x 9, 144 pp, Quality PB, ISBN 1-879045-09-5 **$14.95**

Theology/Philosophy

Aspects of Rabbinic Theology
By Solomon Schechter. New Introduction by Dr. Neil Gillman.
6 x 9, 448 pp, Quality PB, ISBN 1-879045-24-9 **$19.95**

Broken Tablets: Restoring the Ten Commandments and Ourselves
Edited by Rachel S. Mikva. Introduction by Lawrence Kushner. Afterword by Arnold Jacob Wolf.
6 x 9, 192 pp, Quality PB, ISBN 1-58023-158-6 **$16.95**; Hardcover, ISBN 1-58023-066-0 **$21.95**

Creating an Ethical Jewish Life
A Practical Introduction to Classic Teachings on How to Be a Jew
By Dr. Byron L. Sherwin and Seymour J. Cohen
6 x 9, 336 pp, Quality PB, ISBN 1-58023-114-4 **$19.95**

The Death of Death: Resurrection and Immortality in Jewish Thought
By Dr. Neil Gillman 6 x 9, 336 pp, Quality PB, ISBN 1-58023-081-4 **$18.95**

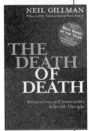

Evolving Halakhah: A Progressive Approach to Traditional Jewish Law
By Rabbi Dr. Moshe Zemer
6 x 9, 480 pp, Quality PB, ISBN 1-58023-127-6 **$29.95**; Hardcover, ISBN 1-58023-002-4 **$40.00**

Hasidic Tales: Annotated & Explained
By Rabbi Rami Shapiro. Foreword by Andrew Harvey, SkyLight Illuminations series editor.
5½ x 8½, 240 pp, Quality PB, ISBN 1-893361-86-1 **$16.95** *(A SkyLight Paths Book)*

A Heart of Many Rooms: Celebrating the Many Voices within Judaism
By Dr. David Hartman 6 x 9, 352 pp, Quality PB, ISBN 1-58023-156-X **$19.95**

The Hebrew Prophets: Selections Annotated & Explained
Translation & Annotation by Rabbi Rami Shapiro. Foreword by Zalman M. Schachter-Shalomi
5½ x 8½, 224 pp, Quality PB, ISBN 1-59473-037-7 **$16.99** *(A SkyLight Paths book)*

Keeping Faith with the Psalms: Deepen Your Relationship with God Using the
Book of Psalms *By Daniel F. Polish* 6 x 9, 272 pp, Hardcover, ISBN 1-58023-179-9 **$24.95**

The Last Trial
On the Legends and Lore of the Command to Abraham to Offer Isaac as a Sacrifice
By Shalom Spiegel. New Introduction by Judah Goldin.
6 x 9, 208 pp, Quality PB, ISBN 1-879045-29-X **$18.95**

A Living Covenant: The Innovative Spirit in Traditional Judaism
By Dr. David Hartman 6 x 9, 368 pp, Quality PB, ISBN 1-58023-011-3 **$18.95**

Love and Terror in the God Encounter
The Theological Legacy of Rabbi Joseph B. Soloveitchik
By Dr. David Hartman
6 x 9, 240 pp, Quality PB, ISBN 1-58023-176-4 **$19.95**; Hardcover, ISBN 1-58023-112-8 **$25.00**

Seeking the Path to Life
Theological Meditations on God and the Nature of People, Love, Life and Death
By Rabbi Ira F. Stone 6 x 9, 160 pp, Quality PB, ISBN 1-879045-47-8 **$14.95**

The Spirit of Renewal: Finding Faith after the Holocaust
By Rabbi Edward Feld 6 x 9, 224 pp, Quality PB, ISBN 1-879045-40-0 **$16.95**

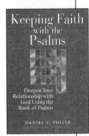

Tormented Master: *The Life and Spiritual Quest of Rabbi Nahman of Bratslav*
By Dr. Arthur Green 6 x 9, 416 pp, Quality PB, ISBN 1-879045-11-7 **$19.99**

Your Word Is Fire: The Hasidic Masters on Contemplative Prayer
Edited and translated by Dr. Arthur Green and Barry W. Holtz
6 x 9, 160 pp, Quality PB, ISBN 1-879045-25-7 **$15.95**

I Am Jewish
Personal Reflections Inspired by the Last Words of Daniel Pearl
Almost 150 Jews—both famous and not—from all walks of life, from all around
the world, write about Identity, Heritage, Covenant / Chosenness and Faith,
Humanity and Ethnicity, and *Tikkun Olam* and Justice.
Edited by Judea and Ruth Pearl
6 x 9, 304 pp, Hardcover, ISBN 1-58023-183-7 **$24.99**

**Download a free copy of the *I Am Jewish Teacher's Guide* at our website:
www.jewishlights.com**

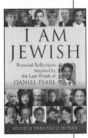

About Jewish Lights

People of all faiths and backgrounds yearn for books that attract, engage, educate, and spiritually inspire.

Our principal goal is to stimulate thought and help all people learn about who the Jewish People are, where they come from, and what the future can be made to hold. While people of our diverse Jewish heritage are the primary audience, our books speak to people in the Christian world as well and will broaden their understanding of Judaism and the roots of their own faith.

We bring to you authors who are at the forefront of spiritual thought and experience. While each has something different to say, they all say it in a voice that you can hear.

Our books are designed to welcome you and then to engage, stimulate, and inspire. We judge our success not only by whether or not our books are beautiful and commercially successful, but by whether or not they make a difference in your life.

For your information and convenience, at the back of this book we have provided a list of other Jewish Lights books you might find interesting and useful. They cover all the categories of your life:

Bar/Bat Mitzvah	Life Cycle
Bible Study / Midrash	Meditation
Children's Books	Parenting
Congregation Resources	Prayer
Current Events / History	Ritual / Sacred Practice
Ecology	Spirituality
Fiction: Mystery, Science Fiction	Theology / Philosophy
Grief / Healing	Travel
Holidays / Holy Days	Twelve Steps
Inspiration	Women's Interest
Kabbalah / Mysticism / Enneagram	

Stuart M. Matlins

Stuart M. Matlins, Publisher

Or phone, fax, mail or e-mail to: **JEWISH LIGHTS Publishing**
Sunset Farm Offices, Route 4 • P.O. Box 237 • Woodstock, Vermont 05091
Tel: (802) 457-4000 • Fax: (802) 457-4004 • www.jewishlights.com
Credit card orders: (800) 962-4544 (8:30AM–5:30PM ET Monday–Friday)
Generous discounts on quantity orders. SATISFACTION GUARANTEED. Prices subject to change.